AVID

READER

PRESS

LIV AND LET DIE

ALAN SHIPNUCK

Avid Reader Press

NEW YORK LONDON TORONTO
SYDNEY NEW DELHI

Avid Reader Press
An Imprint of Simon & Schuster, Inc.
1230 Avenue of the Americas
New York, NY 10020

First Avid Reader Press hardcover edition October 2023

AVID READER PRESS and colophon are trademarks of Simon & Schuster, Inc.

For information about special discounts for bulk purchases, please contact
Simon & Schuster Special Sales at 1-866-506-1949 or
business@simonandschuster.com.

The Simon & Schuster Speakers Bureau can bring authors to your live event. For
more information or to book an event contact the Simon & Schuster Speakers
Bureau at 1-866-248-3049 or visit our website at www.simonspeakers.com.

Manufactured in the United States of America

1 3 5 7 9 10 8 6 4 2

Library of Congress Cataloging-in-Publication Data has been applied for.

ISBN 978-1-6680-2001-2
ISBN 978-1-6680-2003-6 (ebook)

This book is dedicated to my father, David

LIV AND LET DIE

Foreword

IN 1989, WHEN GREG NORMAN WAS THE SECOND MOST charismatic star in golf—Seve, obviously—he founded his own off-season tournament, the Shark Shootout. Ordinarily, it offered low pressure and easy money for the game's top players, but the 1994 Shootout had an edgier vibe. Working in the shadows, Norman had put together the contours of a new global circuit of tournaments that would be a direct competitor to the PGA Tour. Norman was drafting on the game's surging international presence; at that moment, all of the top six and twenty-three of the top fifty players in the Sony Ranking (the precursor to the Official World Golf Ranking) had been born outside the United States. Following a practice round at the Shootout, the Shark gathered his fellow players in a vast wine room within the clubhouse at Sherwood Country Club in Thousand Oaks, California. The space was crowded and the atmosphere tense. "None of us knew what was going on," recalls Peter Jacobsen. "There had been some rumors flying around, but mostly it was an information vacuum. Remember, this was before cell phones and the internet, so most of us were in the dark."

Summoning all of his considerable showmanship, Norman laid out his vision for a worldwide tour underwritten by a five-year, $125 million TV deal from his fellow Australian iconoclast Rupert Murdoch. The eight-tournament schedule would take players from Tokyo to Montreal to Spain to Scotland and points in between. The money was astronomical, with $3 million purses for the forty-man fields. Each winner would claim $600,000; Nick Price, by comparison, had earned $186,000 for taking the 1994 British Open.

When Norman finished speaking, one gent in the room asked how the players could possibly obtain so many releases from the PGA Tour; then, as now, Tour members needed permission to make cameos at competing tournaments, which is akin to asking your spouse for approval to have an affair. It should come as no surprise that the Tour has always been stingy in granting such releases, capping them at a maximum of three per season. Two days before this gathering at Sherwood, PGA Tour commissioner Tim Finchem had sent a strongly worded letter to his members threatening to suspend any player who threw in with the renegade tour. Now Norman assured his colleagues that he was trying to forge a compromise with the Tour, but he also said cryptically that at some point the players might have to pick a side.

The room fell quiet, and then the King stirred. Arnold Palmer was sixty-five, still hale and hearty, with a head of luscious silver hair. The Shark Shootout was one of the few tournaments at which he showed up to charm the galleries.

"Greg, have you ever heard of the Big Three?" Palmer asked. It was a rhetorical question: every professional golfer and golf fan knows that Arnie, Jack Nicklaus, and Gary Player are the Big Three who ushered in the game's commercialized modern era. "How many times do you think we were approached to do our own thing?" Palmer continued. "More than I can count. Do you know why we always said no? Because it would have been bad for the game and bad for the fellas."

A jolt of electricity ran through the room. The most important popularizing figure golf has ever known was offering both a history lesson and a sermon.

"You guys are young and have a lot of golf in front of you," Palmer told the other players in the room. "You can do what you think is best, but I don't want any part of this." He rose from his chair and ambled out of the room.

At that moment, no one, least of all Norman, knew what to say. Then Lanny Wadkins, a gruff old-school player widely admired by his peers for his *cojones*, spoke up: "If it's not good enough for Arnold, it's not good enough for me." He walked out of the room, soon followed by every other player. "That shit was over in the blink of an eye," says Paul Azinger. The Great White Shark was left alone with his pie charts, humiliated and seething. "I was shell-shocked when I got out of that meeting," Norman said. "Are you kidding me? How about having an open discussion about this, guys? How about not slaying the dream and just shutting me down and ostracizing me in front of the other players?"

Says Jacobsen today, "People have asked me a lot lately, 'Why is Greg Norman so angry? Why is he so bitter? Why is he trying to burn the PGA Tour to the ground?' I think a lot of it goes back to that moment, when his reputation got crushed." He chuckles and offers a rueful coda: "Of course, if Greg hadn't choked away the 1996 Masters, I don't think any of us would have ever heard of LIV Golf."

The birth of LIV Golf is often ascribed to the grand ambitions of the crown prince of Saudi Arabia, Mohammed bin Salman, but its creation owes more to MBS's close friend and confidante, His Excellency Yasir Al-Rumayyan. H.E., as he is known to acquaintances, is the governor of the Saudi Public Investment Fund (PIF), which can shape economies and disrupt industries with its $700 billion war chest. He is also the chairman of the board of Aramco, the state-run oil company, making H.E. easily the most powerful person in the world who is not a head of state. It says something about Al-Rumayyan, who holds a degree from the Harvard Business School, that the golfer he would become closest to is dweeby Bryson DeChambeau, a physics major in college. (Just ask him.) "He's a golf nerd. A golf nut," says DeChambeau. "He plays all the time. He hits the ball straight for not having crazy power. He knows how to get the clubface back to the ball. It's kind of fun to watch. He has a good putting game, too. I think he loves everything about the game—the camaraderie, the competition, just getting outside and being in nature."

It was Al-Rumayyan who pushed and prodded his fellow Saudis to become stakeholders in professional golf, beginning in 2019 with a new tournament on the European Tour schedule. "Let's be honest, the key reason the Saudis have become so involved in golf is because of Yasir's enduring love for the game," says Keith Pelley, the CEO of the European Tour. "If he was a volleyball fan, they might be building volleyball arenas and creating a volleyball super league and hosting the volleyball world championships."

During the annual playing of the Saudi International, Al-Rumayyan's yacht, parked just offshore, became a social hub as he hosted golfers for informal gatherings. "It was a relaxed environment that offered privacy, or so we thought," says one player who requested anonymity. "But this was interesting: somehow we started talking about Russia, and just as we were getting going, H.E. nodded at one of his guys, who came over and grabbed both of his cell phones. He set them down next to a speaker and then turned up the music—it was just like in the movies—and then H.E. began speaking very candidly. He nodded toward the phones and said, 'My own people are always listening.' I pulled out my phone to hand it to him, but he waved it off and laughed and said, 'Don't worry, we are not listening to you—we don't care enough!'" Following the playing of the second Saudi International, rumors began being whispered about players attending decadent parties thrown aboard MBS's $470 million, 439-foot yacht, *Serene*, once it reached international waters. (*Serene* features a helicopter hangar that has been converted into a nightclub, replete with stripper poles.) Phones were reputedly not allowed on board.

At the completion of LIV's inaugural tournament in London in June 2022, Al-Rumayyan was called up to the trophy presentation to give a speech. He drew confused whoops from the crowd when he announced a $54 million bonus for any LIV golfer who shoots 54 in competition. (Hey, it's not that outlandish of a thought: Jim Furyk has posted a 58 on the PGA Tour, and in 2019 an Irish golfer named David Carey shot 57 at an Alps Tour Golf event, though it was on a par 68.) His speech was otherwise boilerplate, but his effusiveness, and the bear hugs he received from every player onstage, provided a clue to one of the central mysteries behind LIV: What are the Saudis' motivations? Al-Rumayyan may have bought his way into the chairmanship of the English Premier League football club Newcastle United, and he has been known to have kick-abouts on the field after games, but he'll never connect with his twentysomething players as he did with the more intellectually curious Phil Mickelson during their leisurely pro-am round in London. The Saudi elite can scoop up the most expensive private residence in London, as the late crown prince Sultan bin Abdul-Aziz did with a 62,000-square-foot monstrosity in the shadow of Kensington Palace, but they will never be granted memberships at the old-line, aggressively private golf clubs outside town. Yet during LIV London, Al-Rumayyan strutted around the Centurion Club as if he owned the place, which he kind of did, at least for one week. The status he enjoyed, the reflected glow of hanging out with famous golfers, the connections he made with the London movers and shakers who played in the pro-am and crowded the three-story tower of luxury suites—it's hard to put a price tag on all of that. But for a dude who controls an investment fund that is projected to reach a trillion-dollar valuation by 2025 and an oil company that enjoyed $141 billion in profits in 2022, what's a few billion dollars between golfing buddies?

Norman also spoke at the trophy presentation at LIV London. The stage was high on a hill, and Norman's handsome visage filled a massive screen that loomed over the crowd. As he gesticulated triumphantly, he evoked not Tim Finchem but rather Benito Mussolini. "The evolution of the game of golf has arrived," Norman thundered. "LIV is alive. We did it for all the fans right here today. We did it for you. For twenty-seven years there have been a lot of obstacles put in our path. There have been a lot of dreams squashed. But they couldn't squash us. There is a new energy for the game of golf. This is just the start, trust me. We're going to supercharge the game of golf."

A month later, LIV rolled into Trump National Golf Club Bedminster, with the forty-fifth president of the United States playing host. (While in office, Donald Trump had an instrumental role in keeping MBS in power; more on that later.) In the LIV pro-am, the president played with DeChambeau and Dustin Johnson, whose wife, Paulina, socializes with Kimberly Guilfoyle, Donald Trump, Jr.'s, fiancée. Norman saw them off the first tee, wearing a can-you-believe-this-shit perma-grin. After Trump, Johnson, and DeChambeau hit their opening drives, they were walking off the tee when a voice called out, "One more." It was Al-Rumayyan, wearing a MAKE AMERICA GREAT AGAIN hat. The president, a future Hall of Famer, and a U.S. Open champ stepped aside to let him hit his drive and join the fun. Now, that's juice.

Leading up to LIV Bedminster, I had requested an interview with Trump but he declined, citing through intermediaries his unhappiness with my 2017 *Sports Illustrated* feature that sought to show how his character has been revealed through golf. But during the pro-am, I was walking alone next to the rope line when Trump roared up in his golf cart, a procession of Secret Service officers in hot pursuit. We had met years earlier, at his tournament at Doral, and I have interviewed him by phone, but he reintroduced himself and offered a blast of Trumpian charm, saying "Hey, Alan, you're a great writer with a great reputation." After a little small talk, he added, apropos of nothing, "The PGA screwed me, but I'm going to get them back. Trust me, I'm going to get them back." Then he smashed the gas pedal and was gone, leaving it unclear if he was woofing at the PGA of America, which had stripped him of the 2022 PGA Championship in the wake of the January 6, 2021, Capitol riots, or the PGA Tour, which had taken away his World Golf Championship at Doral. Works either way.

LIV is about many things besides golf, chief among them money, power, and politics. But there is a darker, more elemental force at work: vengeance.

1.

IN THE YEARS BETWEEN THE WORLD WARS, BEING A professional golfer was typically a part-time gig. To make ends meet, almost all of the competitors held down pro shop jobs at country clubs. Many were itinerant workers: In the winter, when the golf courses in the Northeast and Midwest went dormant, the pros would flock south, looking for work and action. The PGA of America, the umbrella organization for the six thousand or so club pros around the country, began organizing tournaments, and by the 1920s, a reliable winter schedule had coalesced.

Byron Nelson won his first tournament in 1935, the year of the second Masters Tournament. Sam Snead broke through in 1936, Ben Hogan in 1938. That legendary triumvirate generated widespread fan interest, and Nelson, whose draft status was 4-H because of a blood disorder, kept golf in the public consciousness during World War II, highlighted by his record eleven-tournament winning streak in 1945. In the boom years that followed, golf thrived as both a leisure activity and a competitive sport. Bing Crosby hosted his first Crosby Clambake at Pebble Beach in 1947, bringing glamour and more money to the circuit. Dwight D. Eisenhower became the first golfing president, putting more focus on the game. Arnold Palmer arrived at the same time as color television, dazzling the folks at home with a game as vibrant as the flowers at Augusta National. He won four Masters titles from 1958 to 1964, becoming an earthy, sexy icon. The King's lone U.S. Open victory came in 1960, though Hogan said afterward, "I played 36 holes today with a kid who should have won this Open by 10 shots." Soon enough, Jack Nicklaus would start piling up major championship victories, lifting the sport to even greater heights with his transcendent brilliance. In 1958, the total prize money available on tour was $1 million; a decade later, it had spiked to $5.6 million.

Yet even as the professional game was exploding, the tournaments were still administered by the PGA of America, a parochial organization with the mission of supporting teaching pros at the grassroots level. The PGA's Tournament Bureau was run by a committee of four players and three PGA executives. The first stirrings of rebellion came in 1966, when Frank Sinatra proposed a tournament in Palm Springs, California, with a $200,000 purse. There was some consternation that an event hosted by Ol' Blue Eyes would steal some sparkle from Bob Hope's tourney, to be played a couple of weeks later, but the tournament committee voted 4–3 to add it to the schedule. Decisions by the Tournament Bureau were subject to review by the PGA's executive committee, made up of sixteen PGA pencil pushers and—get this—only one touring pro. PGA president Max Elbin was a staunch traditionalist who opposed the Sinatra tournament. He rounded up four members of the executive committee for a fishy ad hoc vote and overruled the tournament committee by a 3–1 margin, squashing the event. It was the first veto in the fifty-two-year history of the PGA, and the touring pros were rightfully pissed.

"The problem was that the whole operation was being run part-time by three club pros," said Bob Goalby, the 1968 Masters champ. "They didn't have the time to handle everything we needed, from pensions to course setup, and when they did, they approached it as a club pro would."

Tensions continued to escalate when the tour pros found out that the PGA intended to siphon off $50,000 from the purse at the

Westchester Country Club tournament and put it into the general pension fund for all of its members.

On June 1, 1967, the players began their uprising, producing a seven-point manifesto demanding greater control over the schedule, the disbursement of funds, and the hiring of administrative staff. They also insisted on taking away the PGA's veto power. More than 130 players signed the letter, which included a stunning ultimatum: if the PGA didn't acquiesce to all of their demands by June 15—the day of the first round of the U.S. Open—the players would boycott the PGA Championship, to be played a month later.

Once the rift went public, the touring pros and the PGA's rank-and-file club pros were set in opposition to one another. The hard feelings were so palpable that Kermit Zarley said, "I didn't feel very comfortable for a while going into some pro shops at golf clubs."

Elbin agreed to meet with the players in Cleveland following the U.S. Open. But he ramped up the incendiary rhetoric by co-opting a phrase from the Jim Crow era, labeling the opposition leaders "agitators." He added, "Many of the players are following blindly a trail baited with half-truths, insinuations, and outright lies."

After a tense nine-hour meeting, the PGA gave in on six of the seven demands but retained its veto power, forging an uneasy truce that lasted all of two weeks, when the players rejected the deal.

Most of the 1968 season was played under a cloud of uncertainty, as lawyers for both sides maneuvered behind the scenes. Rumors were rampant that the players were going to split off and create their own tour. Enter Nicklaus. The Bear had been a leader in the player revolt all along, but he began taking the fight public. After he missed the cut at the 1968 PGA Championship, he was asked what he thought of the composition of the field, which included a whopping 112 club pros and only 56 touring pros. "It's absurd and unfortunate," he harrumphed, rankling PGA officials and souring the negotiations.

Following the tournament at Westchester Country Club, a hundred touring pros convened to vote on the future of golf in the United States. The vote was unanimous: the players committed to forming a breakaway league, American Professional Golfers (APG). A thirteen-member APG advisory committee was created, headlined by Nicklaus. The PGA of America made its stance clear: it was us or them. "If a player decides to go with the other group, his PGA card will be lifted immediately," Elbin said. "We will continue to play tournament golf. It will be tough at first, but we will endure." His lieutenant, Leo Fraser, noted that the PGA still represented the club pros, who ministered to young golfers around the country. "We've got six thousand little factories turning out potential stars," he said.

Nicklaus continued to throw haymakers in the press, publishing an extraordinary first-person essay in the September 16, 1968, issue of *Sports Illustrated*. It began, "That verbal attack recently unleashed on me by Leo Fraser, the secretary of the Professional Golfers Association, was, on the whole, inaccurate. Fraser did spell my name correctly—Jack Nicklaus. He even had my age right—28. And he signed his own name properly—Leo Fraser. The rest of his cutting statement, though, was a personal assault."

Lurking in the background was Palmer, who remained the game's biggest star even though he had been supplanted by Nicklaus as its best player. Palmer idolized his father, Deacon, the superintendent and then the head pro at Latrobe [Pennsylvania] Country Club and did not want to publicly battle the PGA of America, an organization putatively dedicated to growing the game. Arnie was also worried about moving product, presaging Michael Jordan's famous explanation about why he was not more politically outspoken: "Republicans buy sneakers, too." Said Goalby of Palmer, "He was selling clubs, so it was hard for him to alienate the club pros. He had to worry if they were going to stop carrying his stuff." Palmer began meeting privately with PGA officials, trying to forge a compromise.

But the PGA refused to make the necessary concessions, and Arnie reluctantly pledged his fealty to his fellow players.

The game's other stakeholders made it clear that they would side with the players. ABC had just signed a two-year deal to televise ten tour events, including the PGA Championship, and its legendary executive Roone Arledge said, "I'm not sure how the present controversy will affect us, but we won't televise a tournament with nobodies in it." On September 24, 1968, the PGA went to court and obtained a temporary restraining order against the APG. It took a while, but the players had finally come to realize that they were the product, not the organizing tour. They made a presentation to the International Golf Sponsors Association, and afterward its outgoing president, Angus Mairs, made it clear that his organization would side with talent over bureaucracy: "We have decided to go with the dancing girls."

When a half-dozen tournament sponsors announced that they would shift their allegiance—and corporate dollars—to APG events, the PGA of America retaliated by saying that it would sue any player who competed in an APG tournament that took place the same week as a PGA event, because that would be a violation of existing rules. (To that point, none of the pros had renounced their PGA memberships.) But in mid-October, the judge rescinded his restraining order, neutering the PGA's legal case. Outmaneuvered and lacking leverage, PGA officials quietly began seeking a truce, a process that accelerated after Elbin's term as president expired in November 1968. Within a few weeks the war was over and the players had won. They got the autonomy they had sought under a new umbrella organization: the PGA Tour. (In a notable concession, the PGA of America retained ownership of the Ryder Cup, a sleepy affair dating to 1927 that would grow into golf's Super Bowl.)

It has become common to call the LIV Golf era the most contentious period in professional golf history. This overlooks the fact that the PGA Tour was born of a rebellion fueled by secret player meet-ings, lawsuits, threats of suspension and boycotts, and very public recriminations. Ever since then, the PGA Tour has tried to sell a polished image of golfing gentlemen, but bitchiness and controversy will always be in the professional game's DNA.

2.

GOLF IS OFTEN THE STORY OF FATHERS AND SONS, BUT
it was Greg Norman's mother, Toini, who altered the game's future.
In 1970, the Normans moved from Townsville, a remote little coastal
town in Queensland, Australia, to the more cosmopolitan Brisbane
so Greg's father, Merv, could take an engineering job. Toini was
the jock in the family and immediately joined a country club. One
day she was walking out the door to go play golf when her fifteen-
year-old son, Greg, bored and friendless in the new town, offered
to caddie for her. It was the first time on a golf course for a strap-
ping lad who played cricket and rugby and excelled at Australian
rules football. After the round, while Toini enjoyed a beverage in the
clubhouse, Greg nabbed her clubs and played a handful of holes by
himself. He instantly fell under the game's spell.

Norman began haunting Virginia Golf Club until after the sun set
and all day on the weekends. He devoured golf instruction books—
Jack Nicklaus's *Golf My Way* became a touchstone—and began taking group lessons for 20 cents apiece. In April 1971, nine months
after first touching a club, Norman claimed his first trophy, team-
ing with his dad to win a four-ball event at the club. Three months
later, he made the Queensland junior team, and in 1973, he won the
Queensland Junior Championship.

Even as Norman bloomed as a golfer, he was living a feckless life.
He liked to surf and spearfish and occasionally "liberated" horses to
ride them bareback on the beach. During one vacation he spent a
few weeks working as a "jackeroo" on a cattle ranch. He found the

classroom stifling and did just enough to skate by. After graduating from high school, he lived for a while with his dog in a tent on the beach, a surf bum forever seeking mischief. "He was very aggressive with the girls," his boyhood friend Glen Cogill told Lauren St. John, Norman's biographer. "Very aggressive guy. He used to get into a few scraps with the blokes over the girls. And he would not back off from anybody. Tough as nails."

Norman had a moment of clarity after nearly drowning while surfing at Noosa Beach the day after a cyclone had blown through: golf would be his ticket to a better life. Shortly thereafter, on a long bus ride to an amateur tournament, he announced, "Before I'm thirty, I'll be a millionaire. I'll be the best golfer in the world, and I'll be married to an American." His baffled mates burst out laughing.

Merv was far less amused. He had hoped that Greg would follow in his footsteps and become an engineer, but his son's lack of interest in academics torpedoed that idea. Greg had been in the air cadets at Aspley State High School in Brisbane and talked often about joining the Royal Australian Air Force, stirring the dreams that Merv had once had for himself. The two even visited a recruiting office. In the ensuing decades, Greg would dine out on the story of sitting in the RAAF office with his dad, pen poised to sign the enlistment papers, only to renounce his old man's wishes in favor of a life in golf. Everyone from his mom to his former manager James Marshall has debunked the tale. "He's given to gross exaggeration," Marshall said. "The story that it was the air force or golf, it's a load of bullshit. Greg no more would have qualified academically to get into the Australian Air Force than fly to the moon. He was no Einstein when he left school." To those close to Norman, there is no question that his lifelong, insatiable need to achieve stems from the simmering disapproval of his stern, taciturn, workaholic father.

In 1973, Greg took a job in the pro shop at the Royal Queensland Golf Club in Brisbane for the princely sum of $38 a week. It allowed him to hit all the balls he wanted under the watchful eye of the head pro, Charlie Earp. Over the next three years Norman toiled in anonymity, building a powerful, repeatable swing one blister at a time and testing his mettle in big-money games against the members. (The most he won in a day was $1,200.) Norman always had a clear idea of where the game would take him. One day on the range, Earp was dismayed that his pupil was sending iron shots to the moon and expressed doubt that such a towering ball flight would work on the European Tour, where aspiring Aussie pros had always cut their teeth.

"I'll be all right," Norman said. "I'm designing my game for America."

In 1976, Norman finally earned a place on the PGA of Australia's developmental circuit. He finished in the top ten in each of his first three events, and at the Queensland Open, the Brisbane *Courier-Mail* reported, he had missed only ten greens in regulation across seventy-two holes and on the eighteenth hole uncorked a drive measured at 394 yards. Still, he was an unknown quantity when he arrived at his first big-time tournament, the West Lakes Classic, which featured most of Australia's top pros. It took all of one round for Norman to make a name for himself as he shot 64 in high winds to set a course record. He kept the pedal down over the next two rounds, becoming national news as he forged a 10-shot lead. After he completed the victory, the dean of Australian golf, Peter Thomson, weighed in with a rare bit of hyperbole: "We have a young golfer in the Nicklaus mold—dare I say better? What incredible heights must be before him now."

Norman claimed his first European Tour title in 1977, at age twenty-two, shooting a course-record 66 in the final round to win the Martini International by three. On a circuit populated by scoundrels and ruffians, he stood out from his peers with his sobering focus. "For the Aussies in the generation before Greg, it was almost a badge of honor to drink ten beers and then shoot sixty-eight the next morning," says Mike Clayton, a fellow Australian pro and contemporary of Norman. "He took it seriously. He wasn't out there to make friends, really. I never, ever went to dinner with him. I don't think anyone did. He would get to the course early, put in long hours, and then disappear."

The disapproval of his father followed Norman like a shadow. "Even when I started climbing the ladder," he said, "[my dad] didn't think I'd be anything. I had a point to prove to him. To everybody."

By 1980, he was emerging as a dominant force, winning the Open de France by 10 strokes and taking the prestigious Australian Open among his four worldwide wins. He had also acquired the nickname "Hollywood" for his increasingly lavish lifestyle; he bought a silver Ferrari to complement the red one he already roared around in. "He had two things that were always bubbling to the surface that needed controlling," said Marshall. "One was that he had a phenomenal ego, even at that age. Secondly, he was ultramaterialistic. Very impressed by money, very impressed by people who had money. Those, to me, were slight danger signs."

Commuting between Australia and Europe, Norman developed an increasingly global perspective on the game, and he developed a kinship with Seve Ballesteros, the hot-blooded Spaniard who was always raging against the machinery of professional golf. In 1981, Ballesteros resigned from the European Tour Players Division in a dispute over appearance fees and in retaliation was left off the Ryder Cup team. (He would later lose his PGA Tour membership and be banned for a year for failing to play the minimum fifteen tournaments.) Norman was one of the few players to ride to Seve's defense, hailing him as "the Arnold Palmer of Europe."

In 1981, Norman married the former Laura Andrassy. Two years earlier, he had been flying to his first U.S. Open when Andrassy, a flight attendant, sashayed down the aisle. Norman had been thunderstruck by her beauty and blurted out to Marshall, "I bet you I'll marry that woman." Before the plane landed, he had persuaded

Andrassy to have dinner with him. That was also the year when he began to prove himself on the world stage, finishing fourth in his Masters debut. The following year, he topped the European Tour's money list. He was twenty-six, married to an American, and clearly one of the best players in the world. One day he totted up all of his holdings and realized that he was, in fact, a millionaire. Everything he had predicted for himself on that long ago bus ride had come true. He picked up the phone and called each of the boyhood friends who had laughed at his vision for his future, to make sure that they knew the score.

It is a measure of Norman's hubris that in 1983, at the age of twenty-eight, he published his autobiography, *My Story*. He took numerous shots at his colleagues, including a passage that set Fleet Street ablaze: "So many talented golfers on the British Tour have not got the drive, have not got the guts or that inner power that is needed to go on and win when victory is in sight. There are too many good-time players on the British Tour who would be better off spending their spare time on the practice fairway." Those were fighting words to many players on tour, and Norman became a pariah. Amid the blowback he announced that he was quitting the European Tour for "personal reasons" and decamped to the PGA Tour. It would hardly be the last time he napalmed the bridges on his way out of town.

Norman won his first Tour event in 1984, the old Kemper Open. The following week, at the U.S. Open at Winged Foot Golf Club, he wound up in a final-round dogfight with Fuzzy Zoeller. Standing in the eighteenth fairway, tied with Zoeller, Norman froze over his ball. "It was as if that final green was a dark room and I was a little boy, afraid to open the door," he later said, admitting that he had "choked" on the shot, a blocked 6-iron that had sent his ball sailing into the grandstands. Yet he willed in a forty-footer to save par, a putt that would have become iconic if he hadn't gotten run over by Zoeller in the Monday playoff, 67–75.

The runner-up finish at Winged Foot kicked off a dozen years of melodrama, during which Norman became both the most maddening and the most thrilling antihero in the game. He won the 1986 Open Championship at Turnberry in Scotland by five shots, one of eleven worldwide victories that season, sending him to the summit of the nascent world ranking. He took the 1987 Australian Open by a record 10 strokes at Royal Melbourne Country Club, maybe the best golf course in the world. He prevailed at the Open Championship again in 1993 with a 64 that is one of the greatest final rounds in golf history and the following year shot a mind-bending 24 under to smash every record at the Players Championship. By 1995, he had three times led the PGA Tour's money list and three times had the lowest scoring average. Along the way he acquired a monumental ego and an abrasive manner, earning a reputation as a caddie killer and having a series of contentious business breakups. Many personal friendships also ended abruptly. "I feel sorry for Greg," Laura said in 1996. "What's happened is really sad. I know Greg would love to have a close male friend, someone to get drunk with and just tell anything. But there's nobody."

Norman's maniacal focus helped him build a sprawling business empire, as he put his name on everything from a line of clothes to a golf course design business to a wine label. In 1991, he bought 12 percent of Cobra Golf for $1.9 million, and when the company was sold five years later, he cashed out for $40 million. At one point in the mid-1990s, he owned a Gulfstream IV, two helicopters, five boats, three Harleys, six SUVs, a Rolls-Royce, a Bentley, a Mercedes, and six or seven Ferraris—he wasn't sure how many. He would later add a 228-foot yacht, which he named *Aussie Rules*. The rough-around-the-edges surfer with no golf pedigree had succeeded beyond his wildest dreams. Yet it is a hard truth that Norman is better known for his crack-ups and implosions than any of his spectacular achievements.

Consider the wrenching fifty-three-week stretch that began with the 1986 Masters. That tournament is synonymous with Jack Nicklaus turning back the clock, but Norman was tied with the Golden Bear standing on the seventy-second fairway, riding the momentum of having made four straight birdies. With the pin on the back shelf of a dangerous green, Nicklaus played the eighteenth hole cautiously, with an iron shot well below the hole and a textbook two-putt. Speaking more generally of the game's greatest winner in his book *Shark Attack!: Greg Norman's Guide to Aggressive Golf*, Norman had the temerity to chide Nicklaus by saying his "overall game management is a shade on the conservative side." Now, with the Masters hanging in the balance, Norman decided against a 5-iron into the heart of the green, potentially giving himself an uphill putt to win but more likely ensuring a two-putt for a sudden-death playoff, and instead tried to stuff a 4-iron next to the flag for a walk-off birdie. He blocked the *Fore!*-iron miles right of the green and took a fatal bogey. "It was the first time all week I let my ego get the best of me," he said. But what a time!

Norman redeemed himself a month later at the British Open, conquering Turnberry in southwest Scotland in weather so nasty that Nicklaus tabbed it "the Survival Open." Tom Watson, who as a five-time winner of the Claret Jug knows a thing or two about Open golf, called Norman's second-round 63 "the greatest round I've ever seen." Norman had already set a PGA Tour record for winnings in a season ($644,000) when he traveled to Inverness for the PGA Championship, looking to put an exclamation point on a wild year. That tournament is remembered for Bob Tway holing out from a greenside bunker on the seventy-second hole to vanquish Norman, but the Shark had put himself in position to get beat by playing the back nine in 40, frittering away a 4-stroke lead. "Norman likes to talk about how fate always conspired against him, but he totally blew that PGA," says his contemporary Mike Clayton. At the next major championship, the 1987 Masters, Larry Mize trumped Norman in a playoff by jarring a seemingly impossible 140-foot bump-and-run from well off the sloping eleventh green. (Again, Norman had tempted fate by missing a twenty-foot birdie putt on the seventy-second hole for the victory, the kind of putt every boy dreams about until he grows up and is actually confronted with it.) Tway and Mize had produced two of golf's all-time thunderbolts, and it had to be Norman who suffered them back to back. When he returned home from Augusta in 1987, he sat on the beach staring at the waves for hours on end.

More anguish awaited. At the 1989 British Open, Norman shot a final-round 64 to force a four-hole aggregate playoff versus Mark Calcavecchia and Wayne Grady. On the final extra hole, Norman drove into a bunker, slashed his ball into another bunker, and then knifed that shot off the Troon clubhouse, out of bounds. He never completed the hole, and his score has forever been recorded as an ignominious X. Another grim denouement came at the 1993 PGA Championship, when Norman lipped-out a five-foot par putt on the second hole of sudden death, three-putting to hand the Wanamaker Trophy to Paul Azinger. That meant Norman had lost a playoff at each of the four major championships, thus becoming the first player to achieve the Grand Slammed. (Norman's playoff record on the PGA, European, and Australasian Tours is 6–12.)

Of course, all of that was just a prelude to the 1996 Masters. In the first three rounds, Norman played as if in a lucid dream, tying the Augusta National record in the first round with a 63 and forging a 6-shot lead over Nick Faldo through fifty-four holes. Peter Dobereiner, the esteemed British golf writer, found Norman in the clubhouse on Saturday evening, grabbed him by the shoulders, and bellowed, "Greg, old boy, there's no way you can fuck this up now!"

Oh, but there was. Norman slowly, agonizingly succumbed to

the crushing pressure and Faldo's relentless excellence. A sickening feeling swirled in the dogwoods by the time Norman finished his 78, 11 shots worse than Faldo. On the final green, the champion wrapped Norman in a manly embrace and whispered, "I don't know what to say. I just want to give you a hug. I feel horrible about what happened. I'm so sorry."

Three months later Norman parted ways with Butch Harmon, the most celebrated swing coach in the game. It's true that Norman's overactive lower body created some minor technical flaws in his swing, but his action seemed to hold up just fine for the first fifty-four or sixty-three or sixty-eight or seventy-one holes of major championships. As Norman wrote in his own book, "So many talented golfers on the British Tour have not got the drive, have not got the guts or that inner power that is needed to go on and win when victory is in sight." The late Bruce Edwards caddied for both Norman and Watson, calling the latter "a true champion." Years ago, Edwards ruminated on the difference between the two competitors and said, "Talent-wise, Norman was probably superior. He was much longer and straighter off the tee and a more consistent putter. But Tom had all the intangibles: guts, grittiness, heart. He had the perfect attitude for competition. If Tom hit a perfect drive that landed in a divot hole in the fairway, he would wink at me and say, 'Hey, Bruce, watch what I do with this!' If the same thing happened to Greg, he would bitch and moan about his rotten luck. Then he'd hit a bad shot and pout about it for the next two holes. That's the fundamental difference between them."

There is a deeper void within Norman, one that can't be measured on money lists or in world ranking points. In the minutes after Norman's most crushing defeat, the sportswriter Rick Reilly encountered him in the Augusta National locker room. Golf is often a story of fathers and sons. Reilly asked Norman how he was holding up. "He said, 'It's okay, it's okay. That hug Faldo gave me on the eighteenth was the greatest hug I ever got in my life,'" recalls Reilly.

" 'It was almost worth the pain for that hug.' And he started talking about how his dad never hugged him."

Norman should have been remembered as a great player, a gracious loser, and a successful brand builder, but his Machiavellian streak has long clouded his legacy. In 1994, the PGA Tour created the Presidents Cup in large part to give Norman (and other non-Europeans) a Ryder Cup–like stage. But he came down with the flu the week of the inaugural event, bowing out of the competition. He finally showed up on the last day to support his team from the sidelines. He asked his captain, David Graham, if he could be mic'd up for the telecast, to which Graham tartly replied, "Not if I have anything to do with it. This isn't going to be the fucking Greg Norman show." Before the next Presidents Cup, Graham, a fellow Australian, was forced out as captain in a player mutiny that he has always blamed in large part on Norman, whom he calls an "egomaniac."

The failed World Tour did far more lasting damage to Norman's reputation. He has always couched the idea as a way of giving back. "It was audacious," he said with typical modesty. "I was ahead of my time, I guess. I could see the way golf was growing on a global front, because I was a global player. . . . The PGA Tour wasn't out there, understanding what global golf was doing. They were focused on growing domestic tournaments. I thought, *Wow, wouldn't it be cool if we could still play our 15 tournaments in America, still be obligated to the PGA Tour, and yet still be able to grow the game of golf on a global basis?*"

That was more than a little disingenuous, because he knew if the top players scooped up all that World Tour cash, they most likely would cut back significantly on their PGA Tour starts, hurting both TV ratings and sponsor interest. (In those days, before the outlandish money of the FedEx Cup, renouncing Tour membership and its fifteen-tournament minimum came with minimal downside for a player.) Norman hurt his cause by acting unilaterally and making no effort to collaborate with the PGA Tour, which quickly ostracized him as a moneygrubbing traitor. The Tour's messaging was amplified by traditionalists in the golf press. *Baltimore Sun* columnist John Steadman wrote, "What Greg Norman, in a self-serving way, has proposed will destroy the American professional golf tour."

"Norman's gall and greed stunned much of golf," wrote Thomas Boswell, a renowned columnist for the *Washington Post*. He called the World Tour a "brazen display of self-interest" and an "ugly idea, both crass and alien to golf."

Other powerful forces were aligned against Norman, who two years earlier had had an acrimonious parting from the industry behemoth International Management Group. Now many of the superagency's biggest clients, including Palmer, happily stood in opposition to the World Tour. Bev Norwood, a longtime IMG executive, summarized the situation thus: "Karma is a bitch, and she fucking hates Greg Norman." Faldo, another IMG client, drove a stake through the heart of the World Tour. In December 1994, three weeks after Norman was shamed in his boardroom debacle at Sherwood Country Club, Faldo was among the top players who gathered at Tryall Golf Club in Jamaica for the Johnnie Walker World Golf Championship. At that point, Norman had presented few specifics about the operations of his would-be tour. One night in Jamaica, an envelope was slipped under the door of each of the players' hotel rooms like a note from the concierge. It contained a document that remained light on details, but Norman beseeched the players to sign it as a kind of pledge of allegiance. When Faldo was asked about the mysterious piece of paper, he snapped, "What world tour? It's not going to happen. There is nothing concrete at all, and the proposals have not been thought out. Nothing makes sense. If Greg had got the support of the leading players before making an announcement, it would have made a bigger impact, but he never spoke to anybody.

The first approach I've had was when something was shoved under my door this week." His words ripped through the golf world.

All these years later, Norman is still holding on to boxes full of legal documents he claims show the Tour's nefarious dealings and collusion to humiliate him. As I reported this book, he promised to let me see them but then reneged. It's easy to imagine Norman, as alone as King Lear, digging through the boxes in the wee hours, searching for a vindication that will never come.

For Norman, a bitter coda to the demise of the World Tour came in 1996 when the PGA Tour announced the formation of the World Golf Championships, a quartet of annual tournaments with small fields, no cuts, and huge purses that would visit all corners of the globe. Norman first heard that his idea had been ripped off and repackaged while he was at the 1996 Presidents Cup. Furious, he cornered PGA Tour commissioner Tim Finchem in the lobby of the player hotel.

"How long have you known about this?" Norman asked Finchem.

"About a month."

"Fuck you."

The antipathy remains mutual. Finchem's predecessor, Deane Beman, said in an interview, "What Norman did with the World Tour amounted to insurrection. The PGA Tour gave him a platform to become an international star and make more money than he ever dreamed of, and he tried to tear it down. Those of us who love the Tour, who helped build it, the players who supported it and benefited from it all these years, we will never forget, and we will never forgive."

In 2005, Norman turned fifty, setting off a very public midlife crisis. It had been brewing for a while. As his playing profile waned, his clothing line went increasingly down-market. In the 1990s, the creation of Sand Hills Golf Club in Mullen, Nebraska, and Bandon

Dunes Golf Resort in Bandon, Oregon, returned golf course design to a more natural and minimalist style, and suddenly Norman's tricked-up target golf courses were no longer in demand. He also began to feel unwelcome in his adopted hometown. He had been the first big-name golfer to colonize Jupiter Island, Florida, building a palatial residence, Tranquility, and creating a macho private club in his own image, Medalist Golf Club. But in 2006, Tiger Woods bought a spread down the road, and the island was not big enough for both of their egos.

The relationship between Norman and Woods had been frosty ever since 1996, when Butch Harmon had been teaching both players but made it clear that the twenty-year-old Tiger was the higher priority. When Woods turned pro that August, Norman was atop the world ranking and therefore, given Tiger's worldview, an existential threat who needed to be treated as such. A member of Norman's inner circle says, "Greg grew up idolizing Jack [Nicklaus], learned how to play golf from Jack's books, and he paid Jack the utmost reverence and respect and looked at him as a mentor. Greg felt he was passing the baton to Tiger, but Tiger didn't reciprocate. Greg was offended by that. Tiger moved next door to Greg, he joined Greg's club, their boats were docked next to each other, but Tiger didn't give Greg the time of day." That is the Woods way, though Johnny Miller once diagnosed the behavior more generally: "Hall of Fame guys are not really talkative with other males, you know."

There is an oft-told story around Jup, usually conveyed with a cackle by Woods loyalists, of the time Tiger and the Shark wound up next to each other at a red light. Norman kept looking over and gesturing, trying to get Woods's attention. Tiger was aware of Norman's presence but didn't deign to make eye contact. When the light turned green, he smashed the gas pedal, leaving the fuming Norman in the dust.

Woods has an elephantine memory. At the 2013 Masters, he took a fishy drop and signed an incorrect scorecard but was spared a disqualification thanks to a benevolent ruling by the chairman of the rules committee, Fred Ridley. Norman indignantly tweeted, "It is all about the player and the integrity of the game. Woods violated the rules as he played. [Being] #1 carries a greater burden. WD for the game." In the wake of Woods's stunning victory at the 2019 Masters, Norman confided, "Very few people know this: when Tiger won the Masters this year, I wrote him a handwritten note and drove down my road, maybe a quarter of a mile, and hand-delivered it to his guard at his gate. I said, 'Hey, this is Greg Norman here. I've got a note for Tiger—can you please hand-deliver it to him?' Well, I never heard a word back from the guy. When I won my first major championship, Jack Nicklaus was the first person to walk down out of the TV tower and congratulate me. I don't know—maybe Tiger just dislikes me." You think?

The messiness that had always surrounded Norman as a player and businessman spilled over into his personal life. In June 2006, he filed for divorce from Laura, ending their twenty-five-year marriage. The division of an estimated $600 million fortune played out in the tabloids, with Norman at one point threatening to sue his ex-to-be for defamation. (Laura raised two kids while her husband traveled the world, but in court documents her role in his career was devalued: "The wife did not teach the husband how to swing a club" and "The wife did not teach the husband how to win" were among the petitioner's claims.) The headlines became more salacious when Norman began dating tennis Hall of Famer Chris Evert, who abruptly ended her own marriage to Andy Mill, a former Olympic skier. The couples had often socialized together, and Mill was one of the few friends Norman had left. (They won the 2002 member-guest tournament at Medalist.) "Greg Norman at one time was my best friend and a year and a half ago I would have taken a bullet for this guy," Mill said. "I didn't realize he was the one that was going to pull the trigger."

Evert was in the gallery for Norman's surprise near miss at the

2008 British Open, wearing a wedding ring the size of a satellite dish, as they had tied the knot a few weeks earlier in a $2 million extravaganza in the Bahamas. A year later the marriage was kaput, as Norman had taken up with an old flame, Kirsten Kutner. *They* wed in 2010, leading to even more unflattering headlines, including this 2022 doozy from RadarOnline: "Twisted Double Life: Golf Kingpin Greg Norman & His Mistress-Turned-Wife Are SERIAL CHEATERS Who Destroyed Four Separate Marriages over Two Decades."

Norman's marital misadventures scandalized Jupiter, which is as cloistered and gossipy as high school. Even Medalist stopped being a refuge. In 2013, the club hired Bobby Weed to renovate the course, which Norman had spent the previous quarter century tweaking. He called the club's decision a "slap in the face" and, in an act of pique, reclaimed a stuffed great white shark that had long hung above the bar. He became a ghost at the club he had founded.

But Norman has always had a knack for staying in the public spotlight. In 2015, despite having no experience as a broadcaster, he wangled a spot in the eighteenth-hole tower as Fox televised its first U.S. Open. He never seemed comfortable during four chaotic days at Chambers Bay. After watching Dustin Johnson three-putt the final hole from twelve feet to hand the championship to Jordan Spieth, Norman was strangely mute—who more than he could empathize with Johnson's anguish in that moment? He was let go a few months later, and folks from the network wasted no time burying him in the press. One anonymous Fox source told Golf.com, "It was tough for the whole staff because he wasn't involved in the shows like a lead analyst should be. Maybe he thought just being Greg Norman was enough."

It was just another public embarrassment for a Hall of Famer who had lost his way. In the wake of the Fox firing, Norman became increasingly desperate for attention, regularly posting shirtless thirst traps on Instagram. He finally went full monty in *ESPN the Magazine*'s "Body Issue" in 2018, at the age of sixty-three. For those who had grown up playing alongside him, his very public failings were not a surprise. "He has always had the personality of an attack dog," says Australian pro Mark Hensby. "He barks and barks and is always coming at you. I guess that served him well as a player, even though it led to a lot of hard feelings. But take away the golf, and all that noise just reveals a raging insecurity. He has this endless need to be talked about, to be revered, to be worshipped. It's sad, mate. You look at Greg, and it just shows you that you can have everything in life and still be unhappy as shit."

As Norman reached his late sixties, it was hard to imagine that he would ever again have a voice in the golf world. For that to happen, the landscape would have to change dramatically.

3.

IN MAY 2018, THOMSON REUTERS WRITER ANDREW Both uncovered a nice little scoop: a British-based company, the World Golf Group, was trying to launch something called the World Golf Series, which would consist of fifteen to twenty annual tournaments played around the world, each offering a $20 million purse. The story reported, "The series sounds eerily similar to the world tour proposed by then-number one Greg Norman more than two decades ago—a plan that went nowhere after the PGA Tour played hardball. It divided and conquered by issuing an 'us or them' ultimatum, threatening to scrap the membership of any player who signed up for the doomed venture." A leading British player agent, Andrew "Chubby" Chandler, outlined one of the fundamental challenges to the concept: "Every player's deal is centered around world ranking points," he said in the article. "This series will never get world ranking points, so it will cost people money in the end." It was a one- or two-day story in the golf world, and then it receded from view. But beneath the surface, powerful forces kept grinding along, threatening tectonic change.

The Reuters article didn't mention by name the propulsive force behind the Series: Andy Gardiner, a successful corporate finance lawyer and obsessive golf fan. Like many folks who consume a lot of professional golf, he had become disenchanted with the product. The European Tour was still using the same business model as when it was founded in 1972. A slew of Hall of Famers had come through in the 1980s, leading to epic Ryder Cups that helped float the European Tour. But Tiger Woods turned professional in 1996, drastically reshaping the finances of the game. Inexorably, the best players from all over the world migrated to the PGA Tour, which offered significantly more money and world ranking points. As the European Tour lost its star power this century, the PGA Tour enjoyed a monopoly on big-time golf, and its bloated, boring product betrayed the lack of competition: an endless slog of unimaginative seventy-two-hole stroke-play events; outdated telecasts with little innovation and an onslaught of commercials; erratic streaming services that made it difficult for even the most dedicated fans to tune in; social media offerings as analogue as a MySpace page.

Gardiner sought out friends and clients in the golf world, and for four years before the Reuters story broke he had been engaging them in discussions about ways to improve, if not entirely rethink, the professional game. "Funny enough, one of the first conversations I ever had was with Rory [McIlroy]," he said. "I was explaining the concept, and at the time he was of the view that actually this is what golf needs. That was some time ago. He's entitled to change his opinion, but had Rory said to me, 'Andy, that's rubbish,' I would've probably stopped. But on we went."

Gardiner looked to Formula One as an inspiration. He had grown up a huge fan and knew the sport's history: in the late 1970s, the circuit had been dogged by inconsistent venues and TV presentations and the uncertainty of which teams/drivers would show up at any given race. The first Concorde Agreement of 1981 had unified F1, establishing best practices for the tracks and compelling every team to compete in every race, which spiked fan interest and allowed for more fruitful TV negotiations. Gardiner's ideas for golf began to take shape; he recalls a three-day fever dream during which he hardly slept, filling yellow legal pads with the framework for a new world tour.

He was so persistent in bending the ear of key stakeholders that his ideas wafted all the way to PGA Tour headquarters in Ponte

Vedra Beach, Florida. As rival leagues came to threaten the Tour's existence, a Watergate-era refrain would be applied to commissioner Jay Monahan: What did he know, and when did he know it? The answer is a stunner: in the summer of 2017. "I was in my office. It was sunny and warm out," he says with a tight smile. "I always think someone's trying to take my lunch. I spend a lot of my time thinking about what do we need to do to improve. And if you were trying to create something new and different, what would that be? So I wasn't necessarily surprised by it at that point in time. But anytime you hear something for the first time it gets your attention, and it got my attention." It was also in 2017 that Gardiner had his first meeting with Keith Pelley, the CEO of the European Tour.

By July 2018, Gardiner had produced a painstakingly detailed, 116-page prospectus crystallizing his thoughts on how to reimagine professional golf. Early the next year he branded his idea as the Premier Golf League (PGL). It sought to create a more global, more consumable, glitzier product, designed to guarantee that the top players would gather much more often. The schedule called for eighteen tournaments per season: a dozen in the United States, one in Australia, one in the Middle East, and two apiece in Europe and Asia, each with a $20 million purse. (The final event would be a $50 million blowout.) To add more urgency to the proceedings, tournaments would be only fifty-four holes. Field size would be capped at forty-eight players, competing concurrently in individual stroke play and as four-man teams. The first two rounds would be a shotgun start, which is a dream for TV and streaming, as all the players are on the course at the same time. (This is good for on-site fans, too, as they can glimpse their favorites without having to suffer through dawn-to-dusk morning *and* afternoon waves.) But to preserve the integrity of the host course's design, the shotgun start would be ditched for the final round. The events conducted in the Middle East, Australia, and Asia would be played at night on courses illuminated by floodlights to reach prime-time audiences in the United States. Every shot from every player would be available to fans through various streaming channels, including a stat-heavy one targeting bettors. Each caddie would be mic'd and wearing a camera on his person, like a cop. Page after page of the prospectus annotated new ways to engage golf fans, with the author's disdain for traditional telecasts distilled into one biting sentence: "For lengthy periods during a typical live broadcast, fans are obliged to listen to anecdote and whimsy whispered by members of a maturing generation, out of touch with younger players and the modern game."

Most significantly, a player would have to commit to playing all eighteen PGL events per season, whereas on the European and PGA Tours they can pick and choose their schedule, leaving less desirable tournaments with few if any stars in the field, which ultimately reduces fan interest. "We are looking to create a better product which happens to pay the best players more," said Gardiner. "If you don't make the product better but just pay the best players more, you're sort of missing the point."

Gardiner believed the team concept to be the big creative breakthrough. (A list of names the team managers could choose from included the Commandos, Reapers, Samurai, and Wolfhounds, which are pretty badass.) "I wanted the team component because of the Ryder Cup," he said. "If you can bring any of the brilliance of the Ryder Cup into a more regular format, then it's got to be a good thing. It's easier for a fan to have allegiance to a team than it is to an individual." Crucially, the team structure would also provide robust revenue streams, as the franchises were to be sold off to bored billionaire types, who would then market and monetize the teams. (The value cited for each team was $500 million.)

Gardiner began collaborating with Jed Moore, a former University of St. Andrews golfer who is the managing director of Performance54, a consulting and marketing firm specializing in golf, and Gary Davidson, P54's executive director. They knew they needed more capital to launch the PGL, so in the summer of 2018, Gardiner began discussions with Colin Neville, who has brokered numerous high-profile sports deals as a partner at the Raine Group, a powerhouse private equity company in New York.

As Gardiner, Moore, and Davidson made their way through the firmament, folks began to wonder more about them. "They were not Google-able," says a person who had dealings with them. "In the background check they came back as ghosts. Nothing they had done in their professional lives suggested they could pull this off. But they were very smart and very passionate."

After extensive talks, Raine agreed to put $500 million into the PGL in exchange for an equity stake that would grow to nearly 50 percent, but only after certain benchmarks were met, including the signing of top players and the securing of a TV deal.

The PGL concept sounded swell, but one thing was missing: golfers. For years Gardiner had been meeting with top players and their agents to recruit them to his league. At the 2019 Masters, he set up shop at a grand estate near Augusta National, receiving players, agents, and a number of the game's power brokers, including Pelley. Just two months earlier, Golf Saudi had launched its first tournament, the Saudi International on the European Tour, and Moore had wooed two key power brokers as investors in the PGL: His Excellency Yasir Al-Rumayyan, the governor of the Public Investment Fund (PIF), and Majed Al-Sorour, the CEO of Golf Saudi. Both made the scene in Augusta. A lot of grand talk and fantastical dollar amounts were tossed around. "You've never seen such a dick-measuring contest," says one agent. Sir Nick Faldo invited Al-Rumayyan to dine with him in the champions' locker room at Augusta National—Golf Saudi would sponsor Faldo's series of junior tournaments the following year—but Jack Nicklaus beat him to it, hosting His Excellency for lunch in one of the game's ultimate inner sanctums.

Despite the high-level schmoozing, Gardiner was finding the PGL to be a tough sell. PGA Tour membership has become increasingly valuable since the advent of the FedEx Cup playoffs in 2007; by 2019, $60 million in bonuses was being doled out to the top thirty players on top of the $430 million for that season's purses. As in the days of Norman's uprising, Tour members had to be granted a release to play in an event on another circuit, and they remained capped at three per season. American pros were dubious that the Tour would grant a single release that would allow them to moonlight on the PGL, a competing tour playing the bulk of its schedule in the United States. Most of the top international players have taken up membership on the PGA Tour; they are allowed to compete in unlimited events on their "home" circuit in Europe, Asia, South Africa, or Australia as long as they play the mandated minimum fifteen events on the PGA Tour. The lords of Ponte Vedra Beach are quite strict on this point. In 2015, Germany's Martin Kaymer, coming off a season in which he had won the Players Championship and the U.S. Open, opted to cash in with more international appearance fees and did not squeeze in fifteen Tour events; he was unceremoniously stripped of his membership for the following year. (He still played a handful of events through sponsor exemptions but was not eligible for the FedEx Cup playoffs.) No one believed that the PGA Tour would allow the PGL to be designated as a home tour.

For many of the game's biggest stars, who were growing ever richer in the warm embrace of the PGA Tour, the PGL was an idea that seemed easy to ignore. Jordan Spieth says he first heard about it in early 2019, when he became one of the four players on the Tour's all-powerful board of directors; a fifth seat for the players would later be added. "My initial reaction was I didn't see how it could be a big threat," he says. "How could they get enough players to go over there? It seemed far-fetched. And without the best players, it seemed like it would be another Challenge Tour"—that is, the minor-league feeder to the European Tour.

In the face of such apathy, the PGL realized that it needed to win more hearts and minds. Gardiner and Neville zeroed in on an iconoclast who was perennially battling the PGA Tour leadership and self-described gambling addict who regularly had millions of dollars flowing into and out of his offshore bank accounts: Phil Mickelson. In January 2020, Gardiner journeyed to King Abdullah Economic City to play with Mickelson in the pro-am at the Saudi International, the event on the European Tour schedule that had debuted the year before. Al-Sorour and Neville were also in the powerhouse pairing. Those amateurs with funky swings were unknown to casual golf fans, but they had billions of dollars at their fingertips and were eager to disrupt an old, proud, tired sport. Mickelson was easily seduced. "It was fascinating to talk with them and ask some questions and see what their plans are," he said following the pro-am. "Where they started, how they started, why, and just their background, which was very interesting. I haven't had the chance to put it all together and think about what I want to say about it publicly, but I do think it was an informative day for me to have the chance to spend time with them."

To Mickelson, Gardiner hammered on one of the key themes in the original prospectus: the era of free agency has arrived for global golf. "As far as we're concerned, we have a situation that is analogous to 1968," he said, referencing the Nicklaus-Palmer uprising that had birthed the modern PGA Tour. He fleshed this out further in his prospectus: "History tends to repeat itself, and the leading players in the world might argue it is time for a new body to help them reach their full commercial potential and to precipitate golf's most natural next evolutionary step. . . . Consider the adverse [public relations] implications an existing tour would face should it seek to act in an anti-competitive manner by seeking to derail a format that is more appealing to fans, players and those who fund the sport, its sponsors and broadcasters. Structural and legal practicalities aside, given that the PGA Tour's principal mission is to promote the common interests of touring golf professionals by protecting the integrity of the game and helping to grow the reach of the game in the U.S. and around the world, it should regard the [PGL] as being compatible with, not contrary to its mission."

Of course, that rated somewhere between wishful thinking and pure puffery. The top players rarely tee up in more than twenty-five tournaments per calendar year. Playing in eighteen PGL events (plus, presumably, the four major championships) would leave them little to no room to play in any PGA or European Tour events. The PGL was basically proposing to raid all of the top players and expecting that every other tour would passively let it happen.

Monahan, the PGA Tour commissioner, wasn't having it. In January 2020, during the same week that Mickelson teed it up with Gardiner in Saudi Arabia, Monahan sent a strongly worded letter to his players affirming the Tour's commitment to "strict enforcement of the Conflicting Event and Media Rights/Release rules." He wrote that if the PGL were to get off the ground "our members will have to decide whether they want to continue to be a member of the PGA Tour or play on a new series." When news of the letter inevitably leaked, GolfChannel.com summed up the Tour's stance nicely in one headline: "Monahan to Players Regarding Premier Golf League: Us or Them."

With its attempt to poach players turning out to be problematic, a more realistic way forward for the PGL was to mount a legal challenge against professional golf's potentially monopolistic practice of restraining where and when its players can compete. In 1994, at the end of a four-year investigation, Federal Trade Commission attorneys determined that the PGA Tour had violated antitrust laws and recommended government action to overturn the rules concerning player releases. It has passed into legend that the newly installed PGA Tour commissioner, Tim Finchem, a lawyer by training and onetime political operative for President Jimmy Carter, mounted a furious behind-the-scenes lobbying effort that persuaded the FTC commissioners to overrule their own staff and vote to end the probe with no action being taken. Gardiner was convinced that the PGA

Tour remained vulnerable to a legal challenge. The PGL prospectus included a detailed analysis of the Sherman Antitrust Act of 1890 and the Foreign Trade Antitrust Improvements Act of 1982. It cited a ruling of the Singapore High Court from 2010 concerning fines that the Asian Tour had levied against four players for failing to get conflicting-event releases. The court deemed that to be an "unreasonable restraint of trade," and the Tour had been obliged to reverse the policy and pay back the fines. That ruling cited as precedent a 1986 case heard by the Federal Court of Australia, *Hughes v Western Australia Cricket Association (Inc)*: "It is well established that the doctrine of restraint of trade may operate in the case of sportspersons who derive income from the sport they played. A whole series of Australian authorities are cited in support of that proposition. It is also relevant that that case itself involved a cricketer and various cricket associations, and it was held that a certain rule, which prevented the cricketer from playing in a cricket match without obtaining consent from certain parties, was void as being a restraint of trade."

In February 2020, the PGL rented a big house near Riviera Country Club in Pacific Palisades, California, and held an informational meeting with players and agents during the week of the Los Angeles Open. Al-Rumayyan and Al-Sorour attended but did not speak, underscoring their role as silent investors; with a commitment of up to $500 million, their money spoke loudly enough. In the wake of that meeting, the PGL made its first formal offers: $200 million to Tiger Woods and $50 million each to Phil Mickelson, Rory McIlroy, Brooks Koepka, Jordan Spieth, Dustin Johnson, Justin Thomas, and Rickie Fowler. Those eight players would be team captains, and four other squads would have cocaptains: Justin Rose ($25 million) and Henrik Stenson ($10 million); Matt Kuchar and Gary Woodland ($10 million apiece); Ernie Els and Jason Day ($10 million apiece); Adam Scott ($15 million) and Hideki Matsuyama ($5 million). The signing bonuses would be paid in equal installments over four years, and the captain(s) would be given 30 percent equity in the teams. With that much money being spent up front, the eighteen PGL events would have purses of "only" $10 million. The term sheets received a mixed reaction. "Of course, some players felt they should be paid more than other guys," says a PGL source. "Absolutely no one had a problem with how much Tiger was being offered—except Phil." Various stakeholders pushed to have the signing bonuses reduced so more money could be put into the purses, making it more attractive for the second wave of recruits.

Much back-and-forth ensued between the PGL and players and their agents. Another big gathering was convened for early in the week of the Players Championship. "We were very, very close to launching this," says a PGL source, "and I say that even knowing how greedy the players are and how slimy the agents can be and that they might come back asking for more, as they always do. It honestly felt like we were days away."

Then the covid pandemic hit, halting the PGL's momentum. But covid also provided a new opening for the PGL because it put the European Tour under intense financial pressure. The circuit's cobbled-together schedule for the latter half of 2020 featured purses as low as $1 million, and the tour was borrowing money to pay its operating costs. The PGL began a full-court press to forge a partnership with the European Tour. Negotiations were fast and furious throughout the spring as Neville began leading the talks. "That changed things," says Pelley. "No one really took the PGL seriously as long as it was just Andy Gardiner. But Raine was a strong merchant bank with a big portfolio and credibility."

In June 2020, the PGL sent out revised offers to players. The schedule featured seventeen tournaments with $20 million purses and then a team-oriented grand finale with $45 million up for grabs. Woods's offer was reduced to $100 million and Mickelson's bumped up to $80 million, including a $50 million "consulting fee." Ten players—Spieth, Koepka, Johnson, Thomas, Scott, Rose, Stenson,

Fowler, Bryson DeChambeau, and Jon Rahm—were offered a $30 million signing bonus, with half paid up front and the remainder paid over four years. Each player would be given 50 percent equity in his team, which he could then split off to attract new recruits. The idea was to have all of the keynote players sign their contract on the same day.

That June, the PGL also formally made its offer to the European Tour: $100 million of equity financing in exchange for 15 percent of European Tour Productions, a quiet moneymaker that employs 1,600 staffers to create the world television feed of tournaments that is sold to distributors around the globe, plus an equity stake in the PGL and a revenue-sharing agreement in exchange for adding eighteen PGL tournaments to a rejiggered global schedule. The top forty-eight players would be compelled to compete in all of the PGL events and could also fill out their schedules with any of the other traditional tournaments still being conducted by the European Tour. The signing bonuses, the $20 million PGL purses, and the promise of team equity—Gardiner was touting a selling price of $500 million—would finally give the European Tour a way to woo back its wayward stars and recruit top Americans.

Pelley now had a potentially viable path forward for his beleaguered tour. But the PGL offer also gave him something the European Tour had never enjoyed: leverage with its richer, protectionist competitor, the PGA Tour. The PGL folks were unbothered. Says Pelley, "If Raine Capital, and before that Andy Gardiner, said it to me once, they said it to me a hundred times: 'The PGA Tour can't do anything to stop us.' Their view was that the PGA Tour was too reliant on what they called an old-fashioned, not-for-profit model and that they had little room to maneuver."

That wasn't exactly true. The time had arrived for Jay Monahan to play his hand.

4.

JAY MONAHAN GREW UP IN BOSTON IN A GOLFING family—his grandfather played in the 1947 U.S. Amateur Championship, and his dad won the 1966 New England Intercollegiate Golf Association Championship—but his hockey career is more revealing of his character. At Trinity College in Hartford, Connecticut, he was an undersized defenseman (while also playing for the golf team). "How you play the game says a lot about your personality. You can't hide in hockey," said Monahan's coach at Trinity, John Dunham. "You either stick your nose in there or you sit on the periphery and wait for something to happen. Jay stuck his nose in there. He loved to go into the corners. He had a feisty streak to him."

And a spontaneous side. The night before his graduation from Trinity—Monahan earned Academic All-America honors as a senior—three fraternity brothers talked him into cycling with them from coast to coast. The next day they dipped their bike tires into the Atlantic Ocean near Kennebunkport, Maine, and then, without any training, Monahan spent the next fifty-five days pedaling to Seattle, covering more than 3,500 miles before the fellas dipped their tires into the Pacific Ocean.

He brought the same tenacity to his work life, as a mad man at an advertising agency and then as an executive at Woolf Associates, a northeastern specialty foods distributor. Monahan crossed over into sports by becoming the director of global sponsorships and branding programs for EMC Sports. In 2002, at the age of thirty-two, he reunited with his first love, golf, taking a job at IMG. Among his primary duties was launching a PGA Tour event outside Boston, sponsored by Deutsche Bank; he earned the title of tournament director. During his three years at IMG, one of his mentors was Mark "Dr. No" Steinberg, Tiger Woods's agent. Steinberg had pushed for Monahan to get the tournament director position because it aligned with his own interests: Woods's eponymous charitable foundation was the host and beneficiary of the Deutsche Bank Championship. (The banking behemoth's CEO at the time was Seth Waugh, who would go on to run the PGA of America, another relationship that would prove useful to both Steinberg and Monahan.) The connection between Monahan and Steinberg would have sweeping ramifications in the years ahead. "They got on well, for sure," says Alastair Johnston, both men's boss at IMG. "Jay is a very easy guy to get along with, if you're allied with him. He and Steinberg built a good working relationship and a good friendship."

After a stint at Fenway Sports Management, Monahan joined the PGA Tour in 2008 as the tournament director of the Players Championship. In the years that followed, he quickly blasted his way up the bureaucracy: executive vice president and chief marketing officer . . . senior vice president for business development . . . deputy commissioner . . . chief operating officer. He became thick as thieves with Tim Finchem, who had presided as commish since 1994. A lawyer by training, Finchem spoke in dense word salads, delighting in obfuscation. His diminutive stature and reserved manner disguised a bloody boardroom warrior. It was in his first year as commissioner that he outmaneuvered, humiliated, and marginalized Greg Norman, stealing the Great White Shark's idea and turning it into the PGA Tour's World Golf Championship franchise. That touched off two decades of relentless growth under Finchem, who had had the good fortune to take the reins of the Tour a couple of years before Woods arrived. He created the FedEx Cup, spearheaded the drive to get golf back into the Olympics, and established feeder tours in Canada, Latin America, and China. As he gained absolute dominion over global golf, it was hard not to think of Hans Gruber's riff in *Die Hard*, name-checking one of Mohammed bin Salman's heroes, Alexander the Great: "When Alexander saw the breadth of his domain, he wept for there were no more worlds to conquer."

Finchem had long been grooming Monahan to be his successor. He recognized a fellow brawler cloaked in an Italian blazer; around Tour headquarters, underlings sometimes whispered about the dark side of Monahan's personality: "Hockey Jay." In the fall of 2015, Finchem and Monahan engaged in an impressive male bonding ritual, a nine-day, sixty-four-mile trek at fourteen thousand feet in the Himalayas. A year later, Finchem announced his retirement— a membership at Augusta National beckoned—and Monahan became commissioner on January 1, 2017. He was to be a caretaker, riding the coattails of young stars including Rory McIlroy, Jordan Spieth, Dustin Johnson, Jason Day, and Justin Thomas while trying to squeeze out a little more magic from the aging Woods and his foil, Phil Mickelson.

For three years, the Tour chugged along under Monahan's steady but unimaginative stewardship. Finchem had always been aloof with the players, giving off the air of a persnickety school principal, but Monahan generated loyalty with the kind of gentle humanity that had eluded his predecessor. Said Finchem, "He's from Boston, and he's Irish. Making a relationship is a slam dunk for him. Makes me jealous."

Bubba Watson invited Monahan to the Pensacola [Florida] Country Club member-guest, and they won in a playoff, with the two-time Masters champ calling his partner "Mr. Clutch" in a celebratory tweet. Tour veteran J. T. Poston says, "Years ago, I ran into Jay at dinner and talked to him for a second and said, 'This is my dad, Ty, and this is my girlfriend, Kelly.' And ever since he's asked about Kelly, who is now my wife. Fast-forward, my dad hadn't seen him in years, and at the [2022] Open this year, we ran into him again at dinner and he's like 'Hey, Ty, how are you doing?' And to me that is wildly impressive that he cares about my family like that. It makes me feel he's in my corner—not just mine but all of the players."

Throughout 2019, the threat of the Premier Golf League gathered like a storm on the horizon. Monahan would not speak about the competition publicly, but behind the scenes he made a move that would have far-reaching consequences, focusing on negotiations for the PGA Tour's new media rights deals. The contracts would expire at the end of 2021 and Monahan would need a war chest to battle any upstart competitors. TV money was the easy answer, so he pushed his media partners hard to get the deal done. The official announcement came on March 9, 2020: a nine-year deal bringing in $700 million annually, a 60 percent increase over the previous contract. NBC and CBS would split the telecasts and ESPN would handle the streaming, meaning that the Tour had locked down three of the most important networks. "Getting the TV deal completed when he did was one of the smartest things Jay has ever done," says Pelley—especially when, two days later, the coronavirus changed everything.

Life as we knew it began shutting down on March 11, 2020, just one day after the PGL secretly met with players and agents during the week of the Players Championship. On that Wednesday, the World Health Organization declared a global pandemic and the NBA suspended its season. All of that happened on the eve of the PGA Tour's flagship event. Monahan was caught flat-footed, and even after a young player named C. T. Pan withdrew from the tournament in protest against the lack of covid precautions, the Tour played the first round on March 12, business as usual. The tournament was finally canceled that night.

Monahan recovered from that early stumble. He endeared himself to his players by refusing to draw a paycheck from his $14.2 million salary as long as no tournaments were being conducted. The Tour is a traveling circus that visits a different state seemingly every week, and amid the early chaos and confusion of the pandemic,

Monahan somehow got the rejiggered schedule up and running again after only a three-month hiatus. He sweet-talked, cajoled, and threatened his players to accept stringent covid-testing protocols, even though their TV viewing habits skew heavily toward Fox News. Through sheer force of will, Monahan kept any sponsors from deserting the Tour. One of his players, Max Homa, hails the commissioner for "monumental leadership," adding "I'm someone who is attracted to leaders with a calm demeanor. He does a really good job with that. He has been in the thick of it for years now, but no matter what gets thrown his way, he is calm and cool and collected and we all feel that confidence he projects."

Covid and the PGL presented Monahan with simultaneous crises. When he caught wind of the PGL's bid to merge with the European Tour, he made an audacious counteroffer to Pelley: the PGA Tour would bring the European Tour under its own banner, underwriting its purses for fifteen years. "Jay and the Tour were focused on a full consolidation," says Pelley. "Only our board knew we were contemplating a merger."

"Jay came in heavy," says Paul McGinley, then a member of the European Tour's board of directors. "He showed us the color of his eyes." A PGL investor adds, "Monahan basically threatened to destroy the European Tour. He promised to take all of their sponsors and said he would pump money into the purses of Tour events played opposite the Euro Tour's flagship events so all the top Europeans stayed in the States. He might as well have parked tanks outside of Keith Pelley's office."

The European Tour brought in outside consultants to examine the PGA Tour and PGL offers and created a task force to game the future. Two top executives were put into opposition with each other, advocating to Pelley and the tour's board of directors, with Guy Kinnings pushing the PGA Tour alliance and Rufus Hack selling the PGL merger. The decision-making process ground on for months.

Pelley did not solicit the input of any top American golfers, but one rang him up out of the blue: "Your boy Phil," he says with a chuckle. "He said, 'Keith, you're a visionary. You gotta go with the PGL. It's going to work. All they have to do is sign one player and the rest will follow, even Tiger.' It was a full pitch."

But after years of talk, the PGL had yet to snag an ironclad commitment from a single player. The European Tour's board of directors began losing faith in the PGL's financial model and ability to lock down top talent. Pelley says he beseeched Raine Capital to sweeten its offer. "If it was four or five hundred million dollars in cash, and not a hundred million in equity we couldn't put into the prize fund, we would have taken the offer," he says. "I know we would have."

A PGL source calls that "absolute fucking bullshit. Between Raine and the Saudis, we had a billion dollars committed—we could have come up with the money with a couple of phone calls. Keith is just trying to cover his ass because the Tour was afraid to reinvent itself." That will go down as one of golf's all-time what-ifs, an unconsummated deal that could have created a European-PGL supertour that would have offered true competition to the PGA Tour. An adviser to Pelley lays blame on both sides, saying "Raine and Gardiner were too stubborn to change their thinking. They were trying to keep costs down because in their model they had to turn a profit quickly to make it work. They refused to accept that the only way to launch this thing was by putting in two or three billion dollars up front and waiting five or seven or ten years for an ROI that might never come. We told them that over and over, but they wouldn't listen. Of course, Raine's job is to make money, so I understand their reluctance. For Keith, he was forced to think small because any changes to the structure of the tour would have required approval in a vote by seventy-five percent of the membership, and that was going to be damn near impossible in any scenario." Indeed, many European Tour journeymen believed that the PGL would doom them to a life of servitude in small-time, starless tournaments. And the European Tour allows all past champions to remain voting members as long as they pay their annual dues, meaning that its ranks are populated by old farts and fuddy-duddies pining for the halcyon days of yesteryear. Neither constituency was likely to embrace wholesale change, perhaps for fear of rousing Seve Ballesteros's ghost.

Despite a half century of competition and bitter Ryder Cup feuds, the European Tour deemed the PGA Tour to be the better partner—or perhaps the safer one. But a full merger was considered highly unappetizing for a proud, scrappy, parochial tour. After having ghosted him for months, Pelley reached out to Monahan in November 2021 and told him to find another way to get a deal done. The PGL offer served as a handy blueprint and Monahan swung into action, knowing that a combined PGL/European Tour would be an existential threat to his business. After a series of emergency meetings and calls with his board members, he came back with a new offer in less than seventy-two hours: $100 million in cash to buy 15 percent of European Tour Productions. "Jay stole our idea, and not for the last time," says the PGL source. Monahan's offer would give the European Tour a needed cash infusion without it having to sell its soul, while allowing the PGA Tour to thwart a formidable competitor for a reasonable price; part of the deal was that the European Tour would be barred from partnering with or supporting any other tour. Thus a new "strategic alliance" was born, with the public announcement coming on November 27, 2021. Because the terms were not made public, the deal seemed modest without an eye-catching number attached, but it still came with a powerful message: The old guard was aligning against any insurgent breakaway tours.

"I wouldn't put it like that," says Monahan. "It came down to: What's best for the game in the long term? Are we better off working together or working apart?"

That show of strength had an unintended and far-reaching consequence: the Saudis lost faith in Gardiner and walked away from their commitment to the PGL. They began hunting for other ways to invest in professional golf.

Outmaneuvered in the boardroom, Gardiner decided to plead his case publicly. In June 2021, the PGL finally launched a website and Twitter handle, and Gardiner did a media blitz. In trying to build support for his vision, he chided the Pelleys and Monahans of the world for running a closed shop. "All we want is a conversation," he said. "We've never been the enemy. I can understand why we've been perceived as such. But we'd love to be friends."

Hoping to send a message of public reassurance to the players and agents he was still wooing, he told the BBC, "Think about the individual's right to work. Thomas Jefferson, the declaration of independence, talked about life, love and the pursuit of happiness and that includes the ability to work as you want to. . . . Competition law exists to ensure there is a level playing field and everybody in these circumstances can compete for the services of the best players in the world. . . . You've got to allow people to live their own lives. That's why I'm confident."

Highfalutin rhetoric is nice, but for professional golfers, money talks. Gardiner belatedly realized that it was time to rethink his business model; what he calls the "reputational costs" of joining a "breakaway league" were proving to be prohibitive in recruiting players. Instead of trying to compete with the PGA Tour, suddenly he proposed to partner with it. In October 2021, he sent a letter to Rory McIlroy, the chairman of the PGA Tour's Player Advisory Council, offering what he described as a "once-in-a-lifetime windfall bonus" to the players. (The PAC has no real authority but builds consensus and makes recommendations to the Tour's board of directors, which sets policy in concert with the commissioner.) The PGL proposed a partnership in which it would commit 75 percent of its equity for its events to become cosanctioned as part of a redesigned PGA Tour schedule. Fifty percent of the equity would be distributed to PGA Tour players, 7.5 percent to Korn Ferry Tour members, 2.5 percent to European Tour players, 5 percent to the PGA Tour's commercial partners, 2.5 percent to PGL directors, and 7.5 percent to a charitable foundation dedicated to growing amateur golf. The proposal optimistically stated that the PGL would generate $10 billion of equity value by 2030, which would mean roughly $20 million to each of the 200 or so PGA Tour members and $3 million to all the Korn Ferry Tour dreamers living on the margins of professional golf. More immediately, the PGL offered to pay a cash advance of $460 million upon the launch of the PGL, equating to $2 million for each PGA Tour player and $300,000 for the two hundred or so Korn Ferry Tour members.

McIlroy was all ears.

"In my role as PAC chairman and now [about to begin a term] on the Policy Board, I have to think of those guys that are down at the bottom, right?" he said in December 2021. "I'm not doing a good job for the players if I don't bring that to the attention of the Tour and be like . . . just sit down and listen to this guy, do something. . . . If someone comes along and says I think I can create this amount of revenue and distribute it amongst every player, you have to listen to that, right? Because again, that's my responsibility to all the players who voted me into this position."

Monahan remained unmoved and stuck to his plan of ignoring the PGL; he steadfastly refused to take a meeting with Gardiner or even publicly acknowledge the PGL's existence. In January 2021, he had already moved to placate his biggest stars by creating the Player Impact Program, a bonus pool that would pay out $40 million to the ten Tour members who most effectively drove fan and sponsor engagement. The results would come by way of a secret algorithm; the whole thing was basically a slush fund for Monahan to buy the loyalty of his most important players. Stymied at every turn, Gardiner became increasingly desperate and publicly appealed to Tour players to tweet their support for an open dialogue between the PGL and Monahan.

Crickets.

The problem with trying to rally professional golfers is that they are rugged individualists whose concerns vary wildly based on where they fall on the money list. Getting a quorum to agree on anything is borderline impossible. And unlike in every other team sport, golfers don't have a union to look after their collective interests. In the late 1990s, Mark Brooks, Danny Edwards, and Larry Rinker tried to unionize their colleagues through the Tour Players Association, but it fizzled when the biggest stars aligned against them (with the notable exception of Greg Norman, who became a dues-paying member). The voice of the establishment, Davis Love III, dismissed the TPA leadership as "divisive" and scoffed, "What are they going to do, overthrow the Tour?" In the end, only 53 of the 447 members on the PGA, Senior, and Ben Hogan tours joined the TPA, and some of them never bothered to pay the $1,000 membership fee.

More than two decades later, McIlroy was a lone voice in publicly calling for the PGL's offer to be taken seriously. But behind the scenes, Mickelson was scheming, as always. He created a group text thread including himself, McIlroy, and the three other players on the Tour's board of directors: James Hahn, Charley Hoffman, and Kevin Kisner.

"Phil had a lot of information on the PGL," says Hahn. "He was advocating for the PGL. He was telling his side of the story, and we were getting a different story from Jay [Monahan]."

The commissioner brought in outside consultants to analyze the PGL offer, and they, too, declared the financial model unsound. Monahan nixed any further discussion of a potential deal. The PGA Tour players—remember, they would have received a $2 million advance and equity potentially worth tens of millions of dollars—were never presented with the full details of the PGL proposal or given an opportunity to hear directly from Gardiner. "If this tour were truly run by the players and if it's a player's tour, then absolutely we should have had all of that information," says Hahn. "We should have had full transparency of what was going on. There was a glaring lack of that, and it created a lot of animosity between the players and the executives who were making the decisions for us."

But Monahan's hardball tactics worked; the PGL was dead in the water. Gardiner, a romantic who wanted to improve the game but was outfoxed by more skilled corporate operatives, would disappear from public view. The PGL's demise offered a stark lesson: however appealing the product may or may not be, the top PGA Tour players would not be seduced into joining a breakaway league with only the promise of future riches. To be lured from their gilded cages, they (and their rapacious agents) would need barrels full of up-front money. Just as the PGL was being vanquished, another would-be world tour began to emerge from the ashes, having curiously copied almost every detail of the PGL's proposed format. The difference was that this other upstart league had seemingly unlimited resources. Who could possibly be so ambitious—or desperate—as to shower billions of dollars on mere golfers?

5.

THE NATION-STATE OF SAUDI ARABIA COALESCED IN 1932, when King Abdulaziz Ibn Saud united the warring tribes of the Arabian Peninsula and rechristened the country in his own name. But modern Saudi Arabia was born in 1938, when native desert scouts and engineers from Standard Oil of California—the behemoth that would become Chevron—struck black gold on a rocky outcropping near the eastern coast, revealing a vast ocean of oil beneath the sand. The official name of the well was Dammam No. 7, but it would come to be known as the "Prosperity Well." That discovery changed geopolitics forever.

Oil would be of increasing strategic importance throughout World War II and necessary to fuel the United States' postwar boom. On Valentine's Day 1945, President Franklin D. Roosevelt held a secret meeting with King Abdulaziz on a U.S. naval destroyer in the Suez Canal. They hit it off famously, with Roosevelt gifting one of his wheelchairs to the king, who had been hobbled by old battle injuries. Thus began the U.S.-Saudi alliance and a crude oil–for–security pact that endures to this day.

The ruling family, the House of Saud, was sitting on the largest oil reserves in the world, but the country had a small, aging population, shared a border with hostile Iraq, and had more than 1,500 miles of coastline to defend. The United States was happy to supply military firepower, but at a steep price: by 1948, the companies that would become Exxon, Texaco, and Mobil, along with Chevron, owned 100 percent of the Arabian American Oil Company (Aramco). In 1950, after King Abdulaziz threatened to nationalize Aramco, a 50/50 split of profits was hammered out. By 1976, the state had taken full ownership of the rechristened Saudi Aramco, which would become the most profitable company in the world.

Over time, the Saudis maneuvered their way into the elite circles of U.S. politics and oil. Prince Bandar bin Sultan, the Saudi ambassador to the United States from 1983 to 2005 and a grandson of King Abdulaziz, played racquetball with Secretary of State Colin Powell, took hunting trips with George H. W. Bush, and once hosted Bush's daughter Dorothy and her children for Thanksgiving dinner, which led Barbara, the first lady, to begin referring to him as "Bandar Bush." Powell would later say that Prince Bandar had been like a shadow member of Bush's cabinet. How did that benefit the American political class? The Saudis helped facilitate all manner of dealmaking, both personal and political. As an authoritarian monarchy with none of the checks and balances of the U.S. Constitution, the House of Saud was free to do dirty work on behalf of its American allies. That's why, when Bush was Ronald Reagan's vice president, Saudi Arabia funneled $32 million to the rebels battling the left-wing government of Nicaragua, helping finance what would come to be known as the Iran-Contra Affair. (As a reward, "President Reagan invoked emergency measures to bypass Congress and 400 Stinger missiles were secretly flown to Saudi Arabia," Craig Unger wrote in *House of Bush, House of Saud: The Secret Relationship Between the World's Two Most Powerful Dynasties.*)

As the Saudi Arabian rulers became unimaginably wealthy oil barons, one of their most favored patrons was the construction magnate Mohammed Bin Laden, whose company, Saudi Binladin Group (SBG), built castles for the royal family and rebuilt the mosques in Medina and Mecca, among the holiest sites in the Islamic world. It is said that Mohammed Bin Laden had fifty children by more than a dozen wives; his most pious son was Osama. SBG would become a business associate of George H. W. Bush by investing in the Car-lyle Group, the monolithic private equity firm based in Washington, DC, that moves billions of dollars around the world in what the writer Michael Lewis dubbed "access capitalism."

In the 1980s, as the global jihadist movement was fermenting, the USSR invaded Afghanistan. Islamists from around the world made pilgrimages to the battlefield in what they considered to be a holy war. Osama Bin Laden fought on the front lines and used his family's construction company to build roads and depots for the insurgents. In battling the Soviets, Bin Laden's zealotry converged with President Reagan's geopolitical interests. In a secret program overseen by Vice President Bush, the U.S. government funneled state-of-the-art weaponry to the jihadists, sending them $700 million worth of hardware in 1987 alone. Much of it went directly to Maktab al-Khidamat, a fighting force cofounded by Osama Bin Laden. It remains mind blowing: the United States armed Bin Laden and helped him form the precursor of al-Qaeda. The Soviet Union's bitter defeat in Afghanistan hastened the end of the Cold War, but there were unforeseen consequences. Among the new radical Islamic leaders who emerged from the ashes was Omar Abdel-Rahman, the "blind sheik," who masterminded the 1993 bombing of the World Trade Center, which presaged the September 11, 2001, attacks. The infrastructure built during wartime subsequently helped facilitate the heroin trade that would fund terrorism for the next three decades. And Osama Bin Laden became a folk hero, commanding a global audience and his own private army.

In 1991, with Bush now president, the United States launched the Persian Gulf War against Saddam Hussein. The U.S. military operated largely out of bases in Saudi Arabia. That "infidels" were allowed to use the holy land to kill Muslims enraged Bin Laden and his fellow jihadists. The United States was once again positioned as the Great Satan, and a decade of Bin Laden–sponsored terror began: the blind sheik's bombing of the World Trade Center; the 1993 ambush and killing of eighteen Army Rangers in Somalia, memorialized in

Black Hawk Down; the 1995 car bombing at a military installation in Riyadh, which left five American soldiers dead; the 1998 bombing of U.S. embassies in Tanzania and Kenya, which killed more than two hundred; and the 2000 assault on the U.S.S. *Cole*, which felled seventeen U.S. Navy sailors. Unless you were directly affected, it was easy to ignore the complicated questions of why the attacks were happening. On September 11, 2001, virtually every American was unsure as to who was attacking. It was viewed as an unprovoked onslaught. In fact, the 9/11 attacks had been two decades in the making. It would take years for the pieces to fall into place, showing how the Saudi Arabian elite had played a key role in the financing of the attacks.

In 2002, Bosnian authorities raided the Sarajevo office of the Benevolence International Foundation, a multinational Islamic charity through which millions of dollars passed annually. Among the computer files recovered were the founding documents of al-Qaeda. The most significant item recovered would come to be known as "the Golden Chain." It listed twenty wealthy Saudi donors to al-Qaeda, including three billionaire bankers, a former government minister, and leading merchants and industrialists. The bringing to light of those links was what prompted more than five hundred 9/11 families to file the civil lawsuit *Thomas Burnett Sr., et al., v. Al Baraka Investment and Development Corporation, et al.*, which sought to hold responsible the individuals, banks, corporations, and charitable fronts that had been implicated in sponsoring al-Qaeda's terrorist activities.

The Saudi Arabian government's position has long been that it was exonerated by *The 9/11 Commission Report*, which devoted only three pages of boilerplate copy to the Saudi question. Sworn affidavits related to *Burnett et al.* paint a much different picture. "I am convinced that there was a direct line between at least some of the terrorists who carried out the September 11th attacks and the government of Saudi Arabia," said since retired senator Bob Graham, a Democrat from Florida, who led a 2002 congressional probe of 9/11, the findings of which would be redacted until 2016. Senator Bob Kerrey, a Democrat from Nebraska and a member of the 9/11 Commission, said in his affidavit that it was "incorrect" for the Saudis to claim they had been exonerated. "Significant questions remain unanswered," he said. "Stated simply, the 9/11 Commission did not have the time, opportunity or resources to pursue all potentially relevant evidence on that important question, and the American public deserves a more comprehensive inquiry into the issue."

The 9/11 lawsuits kept the pressure on both the U.S. and Saudi governments. (*Burnett et al.* was eventually consolidated along with several other lawsuits into the overarching case *In re: Terrorist Attacks on September 11, 2001*.) For more than a dozen years, the fight for justice was hampered by a 1976 law that protected foreign governments from being sued in U.S. courts. Heavy lobbying by 9/11 families finally led Congress to pass in 2016 the Justice Against Sponsors of Terrorism Act, or JASTA. (President Barack Obama's veto was overridden; he maintained that the law would set a troubling precedent, allowing foreigners to sue the U.S. government.) The Saudi Arabian government lobbied vigorously against JASTA, even threatening widespread divestiture from American companies. But the passage of the law finally allowed the lawsuit to proceed and compelled the Obama administration to release what had become known as "28 pages," the redacted material from the 2002 congressional inquiry that the Bush administration had kept hidden from the American public, to say nothing of the *Burnett* lawyers.

What were they hiding? The material in "28 pages" focuses largely on Omar al-Bayoumi and Fahad al-Thumairy, Saudis who allegedly provided material support to the 9/11 hijackers as they settled in the United States ahead of the attacks. The report makes a persuasive case that al-Bayoumi served as an agent of the Saudi intelligence community, while al-Thumairy was described as a diplomat at the Saudi Consulate in Los Angeles. At long last, and despite the stonewalling of the Bush and Obama administrations, a direct link had been traced between the 9/11 terrorists and the Saudi Arabian government. A document later declassified by the FBI stated, "Omar Albayoumi was paid a monthly stipend as a cooptee of the Saudi General Intelligence Presidency." Support for that foreign agent came "via then Ambassador Prince Bandar bin Sultan Alsaud"—aka Bandar Bush.

Despite myriad betrayals and suspicions, the U.S.-Saudi alliance remained intact post-9/11, aided by having another Bush in the White House: George W. After al-Qaeda orchestrated a series of bombings in Riyadh in 2003, targeting Westerners working in the kingdom, the Saudis redoubled their partnership in the War on Terror.

In 2005, the fifth king in modern Saudi Arabia's history, Fahd, died of natural causes. He was succeeded by his brother Abdullah, who at eighty-one had little interest in reform. For the next decade, Saudi Arabia remained largely under the sway of ultraconservative clerics and the *hai'a*, the religious police who patrolled the streets with sticks, beating any citizen who ran afoul of the country's rules and customs, many of which were unwritten. (The official name of the religious police is Orwellian: Commission for Promotion of Virtue and Prevention of Vice.) Saudi Arabia has traditionally been so resistant to change that it didn't outlaw slavery until 1962, under heavy pressure by President John F. Kennedy.

Abdullah died in January 2015, and his brother Salman, then seventy-nine, ascended the throne. He seemed destined to be another caretaker king. Salman named his half brother Muqrin bin Abdulaziz as crown prince and his nephew Mohammad bin Nayef, known as MBN, as deputy crown prince. Salman kept his favorite son, Mohammed bin Salman, known as MBS, out of the immediate line of succession but made him defense minister, the first public position for the stocky twenty-nine-year-old. Six days after his dad became king, MBS claimed the chairmanship of a new entity called the Council of Economic and Development Affairs, which was given broad powers to oversee the national economy. Then MBS took control of Aramco, the engine that drives the country. His most audacious act came eight weeks into his reign as defense minister, when he ordered a bombing campaign against Iran-backed Houthi rebels in neighboring Yemen. That was the most ambitious military campaign in Saudi history and left U.S. diplomats scrambling to learn more about MBS, a virtual unknown just a few months earlier. MBS cited Alexander the Great and Niccolo Machiavelli as the two historical figures who impacted him the most and *Game of Thrones* as his favorite TV show, although he once joked that too many royals were killed off. He was already channeling the cunning and lust for conquest of of the key family on the show, the Lannisters.

Acknowledging that he had been outmaneuvered in his own game of thrones, Muqrin removed himself from the line of succession and MBS became the deputy crown prince, behind his cousin MBN. As a show of strength, MBS celebrated with a lavish spending spree: $470 million on a yacht and $300 million to build Château Louis XIV in Louveciennes, France, which makes Versailles look spartan. (He would later spend $450 million on a Leonardo painting of questionable provenance, *Salvator Mundi*.) In July 2015, according to the biography *Blood and Oil*, MBS dropped $50 million to rent an opulent resort in the Maldives for a monthlong getaway with a couple dozen buddies. The rapper Pitbull and a celebrated Dutch DJ, Afrojack, were paid to perform. Some 150 "models" were flown in from Brazil and Russia; upon arrival they were taken directly to a medical clinic to be tested for sexually transmitted diseases. After rumors of the debauchery were leaked, MBS cut the vacation short after only one week.

As his father increasingly retreated from public life, MBS continued to consolidate his power. He seized on the Public Investment Fund as a way for the kingdom to become a bigger player in the global financial ecosystem, and soon the PIF had made a $3.5 billion investment in Uber; the governor of the PIF, His Excellency Yasir Al-Rumayyan, took a seat on Uber's board. In early 2016, when MBS floated the idea of making Aramco a publicly traded company, power brokers flocked to Saudi Arabia to kiss his ring and try to get in on the gold rush, including former U.S. Treasury secretary Larry Summers and former House majority leader Eric Cantor, both working with investment banks, and former UK prime minister Tony Blair, who was whoring himself out to JPMorgan Chase.

In April 2016, MBS further burnished his reputation as a sweeping agent of change when he announced Vision 2030, a trillion-dollar initiative designed to remake the Saudi economy, to say nothing of its society. Vision 2030 was a belated nod to the inevitability that someday the oil would run out, so the goal became to turn Saudi Arabia into a diversified banking, commercial, and tourist destination. To attract investment—and talent—MBS knew he would have to reform Saudi Arabia's image. He banished the religious police from the streets and displayed an openness to finally granting women the right to drive. He was uniquely suited to be the ruler who would take on the hard-core religious clerics. His older brothers went overseas to fancy colleges, but MBS stayed home so as not to dilute his Saudi identity, ultimately earning a law degree from King Saud University. At the palace, he often engaged scholars and religious leaders in deep debate. He came to champion the more moderate vision of Islam that had been ascendant in Saudi Arabia before 1979, when a dissident preacher and his armed followers had taken control of the Grand Mosque of Mecca, calling for the overthrow of the House of Saud and turning the holiest site in Islam into a killing field. That act of rebellion had radicalized the royal family and the religious leaders who supported them, sending Saudi Arabia backward into a deep conservatism. Speaking of the years before the mosque seizure, MBS said of Saudi society, "We were living a normal life like the rest of the Gulf countries, women were driving cars, there were movie theaters in Saudi Arabia." After assuming power, he declared himself *wali al-amr*, the head of the Islamic establishment, who has the authority to interpret religious law as he sees fit. "He's probably the only leader in the Arab world who knows anything about Islamic epistemology and jurisprudence," Bernard Haykel, a scholar of Islamic law at Princeton University and acquaintance of MBS, told the *Atlantic*.

The prince was treated as a kind of rock star when he went to Silicon Valley in the spring of 2016 to sell Vision 2030. He pressed flesh with Facebook CEO Mark Zuckerberg and the founders of Google and dined with the venture capital titans Marc Andreessen and Peter Thiel. The charm offensive reflected MBS's two-faced approach to diplomacy: appear progressive to the international community while brutally suppressing dissent at home. In early 2016, as he was becoming a force on the world stage, Saudi Arabia executed a prominent critic, Shia cleric Nimr al-Nimr, and forty-seven others. Many were beheaded in Riyad's Justice Square, which has earned a grim nickname as the frequent site of state-sanctioned killings: Chop Chop Square. Activists were thrown into jail for calling for the same reforms MBS was championing publicly; their crime was not their ideas but rather giving voice to them. Change could come only from the royal family.

In May 2017, MBS ordered a blockade of Qatar, throwing energy markets into chaos and leading to a dramatic escalation in tensions throughout the Middle East. He was leading Saudi Arabia in previously unimaginable and sometimes reckless ways, yet he still had no claim to the throne. That finally changed a month after the blockade began. MBN, then fifty-seven, had seemed the obvious choice to be the future king. He had previously overseen Saudi Arabia's spy agency and led the domestic war against al-Qaeda; he was injured in 2009 when an al-Qaeda suicide bomber targeted him. MBN could survive terror attacks but, in the end, not his own cousin. Late one night he was summoned to a palace near Mecca and informed that the king had changed his mind and now wanted MBS to be the crown prince. MBN was handed a letter to sign renouncing his claim to the throne. He refused throughout the night but ultimately cracked, agreeing to resign orally. As the sun rose, MBN, a diabetic,

was led through the castle, presumably to go home to recover. Instead he was confronted by his cousin and an army of cameras. He
was forced to recite a pledge of loyalty to the new crown prince, who
sealed the deal with a kiss on the cheek. "Now I will rest," MBN said,
"and you, god help you."

Just like that, Mohammed bin Salman, then thirty-two, positioned himself for a fifty-year reign. To ensure that there was no
opposition to his meteoric ascension, he rounded up hundreds of
members of the ruling class and imprisoned them in the Riyadh
Ritz-Carlton, which overnight had been retrofitted with doors that
would not open from the inside. Among the detainees were billionaire tycoons, a dozen princes, and the head of the Saudi Arabian
National Guard. Officially, the aging king was conducting a corrup-
tion probe, but everyone knew that the so-called sheikdown was
merely MBS flexing. There were allegations of torture and abuse.
One detainee, Major General Ali al-Qahtani, died during an "interrogation." By the end of that unprecedented public humiliation, the
prisoners had transferred more than $100 billion back to the state
that they had supposedly obtained illegally. Many of the transactions
were overseen by Yasir Al-Rumayyan, a relative unknown who two
years earlier had been installed by MBS to oversee the Public Investment Fund. Al-Rumayyan's outsider status had been an asset, as
MBS was looking to weaken the influence of the old guard. Now Al-
Rumayyan's fealty at such a high-stakes moment secured his place in
the crown prince's inner circle.

MBS's iron grip on Saudi Arabia was complete. In just two years
he had turned himself into one of the two or three most powerful
people in the world. And now he had kindred spirits in the White
House.

As a money-hungry real estate developer in New York City, Donald
Trump did a lot of business with the Saudis, and later, as a politi-

cian, he described his affinity for them thusly: "They pay cash." On the day he launched his presidential campaign at Trump Tower in the summer of 2015, he said, "I love the Saudis. Many are in this building." Later that year, he bragged at a campaign rally that Saudis "spend forty million, fifty million dollars" buying his apartments. In fact, one of Osama bin Laden's half brothers, Shafiq, lived in Trump Tower just a few floors below the building's eponymous owner. In 1995, during one of his bankruptcies, Trump sold the Plaza hotel on Fifth Avenue to a group of investors led by Prince Alwaleed bin Talal Al Saud, who would later be ensnared in the sheikdown. Three years after declaring himself broke, Trump bought a $30 million yacht from the playboy arms dealer Adnan Khashoggi, reputed to be one of the richest men in the world. (His nephew Jamal would become a headline-making journalist.)

Despite his ties to the Saudi elite, Trump helped build his political brand with inflammatory anti-Muslim rhetoric. But MBS saw through the ugly bluster and after Trump's stunning electoral upset recognized a similarly transactional personality. In February 2017, a month after Trump was inaugurated, MBS visited Washington. What was supposed to be a short meeting with the president lasted for seven hours. They bonded over a shared antipathy for Trump's predecessor, Barack Obama, a persistent critic of Saudi Arabia's human rights abuses. MBS had considered it a betrayal when Obama forged a nuclear treaty with Iran, Saudi Arabia's sworn enemy. The young prince also connected with Trump's thirty-six-year-old son-in-law, Jared Kushner, who had been made envoy to the Middle East despite having no diplomatic experience. Both MBS and Kushner were callow scions of powerful families desperate to make a mark on the world. They became text buddies on WhatsApp, setting off alarm bells in Washington about cybersecurity and possible violations of the Presidential Records Act. (Kushner's attorney said his client took screenshots of the communications and forwarded them to the National Security Council to comply with the Presidential Records Act.)

Kushner persuaded Trump to make Saudi Arabia his first overseas state visit, in May 2017, over the vociferous objections of Secretary of State Rex Tillerson. Trump, whose administration was at
the same time defending his "Muslim travel ban" in court, received
Saudi Arabia's highest honor for a foreigner, the Collar of the Order
of Abdulaziz Al Saud. Tillerson was pointedly excluded when MBS
hosted Kushner and his wife, Ivanka Trump, for dinner, just as an
invitation to another meal with top officials from the United Arab
Emirates never came. Tillerson later testified to Congress that he
had been "angry" about the snubs and had thundered to his staff,
"Who is secretary of state around here?"

Two weeks after Trump's visit, Saudi Arabia and the UAE began
their boycott of Qatar, although in Doha it was referred to by a more
politically charged word: blockade. The stated reason was Qatar's allegedly fomenting terrorism, but one of the few official demands to
end the blockade was the dismantling of Al Jazeera, the state-owned
news network based in Doha, which provides clear-eyed coverage of
Saudi Arabia across the Arab world.

Trump and Kushner baffled most of the political class with their
very public support of the blockade, given Tillerson's calling for its
end and the U.S. government's stated position of neutrality toward
Qatar. Doha is home to the strategically critical Al Udeid Air Base,
where thousands of American troops are deployed. It serves as the
forward headquarters of the U.S. military's Central Command, overseeing combat missions, surveillance flights, and drone flights across
the Mideast, North Africa, and Asia. "We could not understand why
the Trump administration was so firmly taking the Saudis' side in this
dispute," said Senator Chris Murphy, a Democrat from Connecticut,
". . . because the United States has very important interests in Qatar."

Those who follow the money were happy to supply one theory:
revenge. In 2010, Trump had traveled to Qatar to try to raise capital
for a real estate fund but had been rebuffed by Sheikh Hamad bin
Jassim al-Thani, Qatar's prime minister and foreign minister. Just

a month before the 2017 blockade began, Qatar's sovereign wealth fund, the Qatar Investment Authority, had turned down the Kushner family's request for nearly $1 billion in financing as Jared and his father, Charles, desperately tried to stave off financial ruin. In 2007, the family real estate firm, Kushner Companies, had paid $1.8 billion for 666 Fifth Avenue, the highest price ever for a New York high-rise. It looked like a bad deal even before the economy collapsed a year later. In 2008, the Kushners accepted a huge loss and sold a 49 percent stake in the building for $525 million. Now they were staring down the gun barrel of a $1.2 billion mortgage payment due in February 2019, for which they remained on the hook for 51 percent.

The Qataris may have had $250 billion in their sovereign wealth fund, but MBS commanded two and a half times that through his Public Investment Fund. To many in Washington, it seemed as if Kushner was suddenly betting on a stronger horse. In October 2017, Kushner traveled to Saudi Arabia for a surprise visit with MBS. In a curious twist, he flew commercial. In a March 2018 article, the *Washington Post* reported, "Most people in the White House were kept out of the loop about the trip and its purpose. . . . intelligence officials were troubled by a lack of information about the topics discussed."

The Qataris apparently took notice: a month later, the Kushners received a $184 million loan from Apollo Global Management to refinance a building in Chicago; the Qatar Investment Authority is one of Apollo's largest investors. That transaction later sparked an investigation by the Office of Government Ethics and a review by the White House counsel. Three months later, Kushner's top secret clearance was downgraded.

Meanwhile, Kushner's father-in-law continued to provide political cover for MBS. After leaks about the sheikdown ripped through the news in November 2017, Trump felt compelled to tweet, "I have great confidence in King Salman and the Crown Prince of Saudi Arabia, they know exactly what they are doing. Some of those they are harshly treating have been 'milking' their country for years!"

Representative of much of the reaction was a tweet by Trita Parsi, an adjunct scholar at the Middle East Institute: "Trump just endorsed Saudi crown prince's Putin style purge. . . . Saudi has Trump exactly where they want him."

With loyal friends and allies in the White House, MBS must have felt he could get away with anything.

Jamal Khashoggi long held a unique place in Saudi Arabian society: a celebrated journalist in a country that brutally repressed the press and any public dissent by its citizens. He came from a famous family. In addition to his uncle Adnan, the arms dealer, Khashoggi's first cousin was Dodi Fayed, the Egyptian film producer who in 1997 died in a Paris tunnel alongside his girlfriend, Princess Diana. Khashoggi's grandfather was the personal physician of Ibn Saud, the kingdom's founder.

Khashoggi had an enduring love for his country. He supplemented his high-profile work as a writer and editor at a variety of media outlets throughout the Middle East by working as an official in the Saudi Embassy in Washington, DC, and reputedly serving the Saudi Arabian intelligence community. His deep connections and immense personal charm kept him in good graces with the royal family even as he occasionally published things that would have landed other journalists in jail, or worse.

Khashoggi initially supported MBS, impressed by the prince's modernization of the Saudi Arabian society, which would include opening movie cinemas and ordering the removal of the cinder-block walls that separated the sexes in restaurants. But he subsequently criticized in print the Saudi bombing in Yemen in 2015 and the blockade of Qatar two years later, earning back-channel warnings from the royal court. Unlike previous rulers, who had tolerated Khashoggi as a kind of distant family member who occasionally said impertinent things around the dinner table, MBS had zero tolerance for anyone who would dare question his authority.

Khashoggi was particularly aggrieved by the harsh treatment of those who offered even the slightest counternarrative in Saudi Arabia. When more than a dozen public figures were arrested in one fell swoop—including a prominent economist, Essam Al-Zamil, who had merely tweeted a critique of the Aramco IPO—Khashoggi registered his disgust in an interview with the *New York Times*, calling the crackdown "absurd." Friends and colleagues beseeched him to be more careful. In late 2017, just as the Saudi government was about to ban him from leaving the country, Khashoggi fled to the United States. He signed on as a columnist with the *Washington Post*, and his first piece carried an incendiary headline: "Saudi Arabia Wasn't Always This Repressive. Now It's Unbearable." He wrote, "I have left my home, my family and my job, and I am raising my voice. To do otherwise would betray those who languish in prison. I can speak when so many cannot. I want you to know that Saudi Arabia has not always been as it is now. We Saudis deserve better." MBS was incensed. He ordered one of his top lieutenants to bring Khashoggi home or "make arrangements," according to a later CIA assessment.

Throughout 2018, MBS continued to open up Saudi Arabia culturally and economically while becoming more ruthless at home. He was received as a head of state in the United Kingdom, where he met the queen and dined with the Russian owner of the *Evening Standard* and the *Independent*, Alexander Lebedev. Rupert Murdoch hosted a dinner for him in his home. After MBS arrived in the United States, he hobnobbed with Mark Zuckerberg, Bill Gates, Google cofounder Sergey Brin, Apple's Tim Cook, Oprah Winfrey, the CEOs of Disney, Uber, and Lockheed Martin, and Elon Musk. (The PIF would soon buy $2 billion worth of Tesla stock.) At the White House, President Trump said publicly, "It is an honor to have the crown prince of Saudi Arabia with us. The relationship is probably the strongest it's ever been—we understand each other." He added, "We have a really great friendship, a great relationship." Back home, MBS's henchmen arrested and tortured a young female activist named Loujain al-Hathloul, who was deemed a national security threat for advocating for women's rights. But the global ruling class was happy to ignore those faraway atrocities because there was so much money to be made with Saudi Arabia.

MBS had always been obsessed with the discourse on Twitter, one of the few ways that Saudis, mostly under the cloak of anonymity, can furtively express their opinions. The government built a sophisticated network of propagandists on Twitter. It also hacked into the direct messages of the dissident video blogger Omar Abdulaziz, who had fled to Canada. Spyware planted on Abdulaziz's phone allowed the Saudis to read his text messages with his old friend Khashoggi. They were discussing ways to organize MBS's critics into a previously unfathomable unified opposition.

In September 2018, Khashoggi, 59, went to the Saudi Embassy in Istanbul to fill out the paperwork necessary to wed a Turkish native, Hatice Cengiz, a bookish PhD candidate. He was told to return in a couple of weeks to retrieve the completed documents. Khashoggi had grown bolder in the year since he had left his homeland, and not just in his texts with Abdulaziz or the tone of his columns for the *Post*. He had met a couple of times with a private investigator working for the 9/11 families who were suing Saudi authorities. He had also founded the nonprofit advocacy group Democracy for the Arab World Now, or DAWN. The provocative name called to mind the Arab Spring, which had spooked despots throughout the Middle East. MBS feared, rightfully, that Khashoggi had become the face and the voice of Saudis who yearned for more freedom.

Unknown to Khashoggi, his surprise first visit to the embassy led to a phone call to intelligence officials in Riyadh, setting a deadly plan into motion. By the time he returned to pick up his documents, Saudi agents had swept the building for electronic listening devices—they missed many—and dispatched the Rapid Intervention Force, a special forces unit that reports directly to MBS. Overseeing the mission was one of the crown prince's most trusted fixers, Saud al-Qahtani. Among the assembled men was Lieutenant Colonel Salah Mohammed al-Tubaigy, a doctor with the Ministry of Interior. As they waited inside the embassy for Khashoggi to arrive, the fifteen-man kill squad chatted freely, unaware that their every utterance was being recorded by the Turkish government. "Has the sacrificial animal arrived yet?" one goon asked. Al-Tubaigy casually mentioned that he liked to listen to music and drink coffee while cutting up corpses.

Khashoggi knew that walking into the embassy carried risk. He had left both of his cell phones with his fiancée and instructed her to contact a top official in the Turkish government if he did not return immediately.

The Saudi workers at the embassy had been told to stay home that day, and upon arrival Khashoggi must have known something was about to go terribly wrong. He was taken to the consul general's office, where the Saudi agents had gathered.

"We will have to take you back [to Saudi Arabia]," one of the men told him.

After some back-and-forth, Khashoggi cried out, "This is against all kinds of laws. I am being kidnapped!"

It was worse than that. A needle was plunged into his neck, flooding his body with sedatives. Then he was strangled. Six minutes later, the whirring of a bone saw could be heard through the recording devices as al-Tubaigy began dismembering the corpse. The body of Saudi Arabia's most famous public intellectual was wheeled out of the embassy in two suitcases and flown home in a private jet owned by the Public Investment Fund.

Initially, the Saudi Arabian government tried to play dumb about Khashoggi's disappearance. MBS's brother Khalid bin Salman, the ambassador to the United States, tweeted that reports of Khashoggi being murdered in the embassy were "absolutely false." But Turkey's democratically elected government wasn't going to carry MBS's water and began leaking gory details and recordings of what had really happened, igniting international outrage about the inhumanity of Khashoggi's butchering. Saudi Arabia then switched to a counternarrative that attempted to absolve MBS of culpability, saying that Khashoggi had instigated a "quarrel" with his interrogators, who had accidentally killed him and then tried to cover up the evidence. No one bought that lie. A CIA report noted that MBS had sent numerous text messages to al-Qahtani on the day of the assassination, and, given his absolute control of his government, it defied belief that the crown prince had been clueless about the operation. Overnight MBS earned a new moniker: Mr. Bone Saw.

Just a few weeks after Khashoggi's murder, the second annual Future Investment Initiative, aka Davos in the Desert, was held in Riyadh. MBS, once the darling of the international business community, had suddenly become so radioactive that Jeff Bezos canceled his appearance, Hollywood superagent Ari Emanuel backed out of a $400 million investment from the PIF that he had been chasing for years, and Richard Branson pulled out of a $1 billion deal for his space travel company. Referencing Khashoggi's murder, Branson said that it "would clearly change the ability of any of us in the West to do business with the Saudi government."

Only two important allies stood by MBS's side: Trump and Kushner. The president opposed the releasing of the CIA report that enshrined MBS's involvement in the murder and vetoed a subsequent congressional bill to block arms sales to the kingdom. Meanwhile, Kushner reportedly counseled MBS through the tumult by way of WhatsApp messages. Trump issued a presidential statement saying, "Our intelligence agencies continue to assess all information, but it could very well be that the Crown Prince had knowledge of this tragic event—maybe he did and maybe he didn't!" Those were Trump's basest reality show instincts at work, in which a geopolitical crisis was turned into a tantalizing cliffhanger for his followers.

Given Saudi Arabia's convoluted internal politics, MBS was never a sure thing to become king; only one of the previous five crown princes had ascended to the throne. (Though it should be noted that MBS himself pushed aside two of them.) King Salman had plenty of other sons and nephews from whom to choose an heir. With the crown prince at his most vulnerable, Trump dispatched Secretary of State Mike Pompeo to Riyadh for photo ops and staged denials. "Mike, go and have a good time," Trump said, according to Pompeo's recent memoir. "Tell him he owes us." It was a make-or-break diplomatic rescue mission that blunted efforts to isolate MBS in the halls of Congress and around the world.

"There was a moment in time where the international community could have made it clear that the Khashoggi murder was the straw that broke the camel's back, and that we weren't willing to deal with MBS," Senator Chris Murphy said in 2022. "If he ultimately becomes king, he owes no one bigger than Jared Kushner." *A Lannister always pays his debts.* The day after Trump left office, Kushner founded a financial services company named A Fin Management, which led to his private equity fund Affinity Partners. MBS poured $2 billion into the fund, even though four members of his five-person panel of advisers were not in favor of the investment, citing Kushner's dodgy real estate record and lack of experience with private equity.

The crown prince's name would forever be tarnished for the slaying of his most vocal critic, but MBS survived, regrouped, and continued to remake Saudi Arabia in his own image. Trump knew the score, telling Bob Woodward, "I saved his ass."

Tyrannical politicians have been laundering their reputations through sports at least as far back as when Adolf Hitler presided over the Berlin Olympics in 1936. In 2014, in the midst of hosting the Winter Games in Sochi, Vladimir Putin sent his army to invade Crimea. In preparation for the 2022 Olympics in Beijing, China simultaneously built stadiums for the Games and concentration camps for Uyghur Muslims. MBS knew the playbook; during the Qatar blockade, Saudi propagandists accused Qatar of using the run-up to the 2022 World Cup to try to cleanse *its* dirty deeds. Now the crown prince went all in on his own sportswashing campaign. It began in September 2018, when the English boxers George Groves and Callum Smith clashed in the newly built King Abdullah Sports City in Jeddah. In December 2018, still reeling from the blowback of Khashoggi's murder, MBS presided over Saudi Arabia's first For-mula E ePrix race, part of a ten-year commitment to bring the elec-tric car circuit to the kingdom. Given that public entertainment had been banned for nearly four decades before MBS's rise to power, the race was the biggest sporting event Riyadh had ever hosted, and the crown prince turned it into a spectacle. Vision 2030 banners were draped throughout the city. Various B-list celebrities were paid to at-tend, including the English soccer star Wayne Rooney, and Enrique Iglesias played a concert.

A month later, Saudi Arabia hosted a Supercoppa Italiana soccer match in which Juventus took on AC Milan. MBS continued to court more splashy sporting events. A handful of prizefights followed, and December 2019 brought the Diriyah Tennis Cup presented by Aramco, featuring eight top players from the ATP Tour. The Saudi Arabia Snooker Masters events the following October kicked off a ten-year commitment with the World Snooker Tour. And then, in 2021, the Public Investment Fund led a consortium of buyers in spending $350 million to purchase Newcastle United FC, a proud old club in the English Premier League, touching off a frenzy of in-terest in soccer around Saudi Arabia. Newcastle's new ownership situation was not well received in jolly old England. At the first away game after the takeover, at Selhurst Park, the home of Crystal Palace, a banner was displayed with illustrations of a man dressed in tradi-tional Arabian clothing carrying a sword dripping with blood. The banner featured a list of alleged offenses carried out by the Saudi

Arabian regime: "terrorism, beheading, civil rights abuses, murder, censorship, and persecution." Despite that kind of blowback, Saudi Arabia's foray into big-time sports created a dizzying slate of distractions for its citizens. Golf became the unlikely showcase.

It started at the top, with MBS's close confidant, the golf-obsessed Yasir Al-Rumayyan, who pushed and prodded for the launch of the Golf Saudi in 2018. Majed Al-Sorour, a buffed former professional soccer player who radiates alpha energy, was tapped to run Golf Saudi. It had been wooing the European Tour for years, and Keith Pelley did Al-Rumayyan a monumental favor by not canceling the inaugural 2019 Saudi International, which was conducted just three months after Khashoggi's murder. "We are a global tour that plays all over the world," says Pelley. "Our board members and players were consistent in expressing the sentiment 'We don't mix politics with sport. You can't be hypocritical and single out one country now.'"

Determined to make its first tournament a smashing success, Golf Saudi earmarked an unprecedented $20 million for appearance fees, with Dustin Johnson and Brooks Koepka each receiving in excess of $1.5 million. Fellow Americans Bryson DeChambeau and Patrick Reed also made the trip and spouted the predictable pablum about "growing the game," and Reed even made a cringey visit to an elementary school, camera crew in tow, where he got the kids to enact the finger-to-the-lips shushing gesture that the erstwhile Captain America had popularized at the Ryder Cup. Other players were loath to be part of such publicity stunts. Rory McIlroy turned down a reported $2.5 million appearance fee, saying "One hundred percent, there's a morality to it." Paul Casey, a UNICEF ambassador who proudly carried the organization's name on his golf bag, noted Saudi Arabia's continued bombing campaigns in Yemen. "It just didn't sit well with me," he said of Golf Saudi's sportswashing efforts, ". . . signing a deal and being paid to be down there . . . I would be a hypocrite if I did that. Anybody who says sport isn't political, that's rubbish. Sport is very political. . . . I'm glad I took a stance, more so if it highlights the issues within the region, especially next door in Yemen. . . . I've seen the numbers. In Yemen, 22 million people are facing starvation, 11.5 million kids. I didn't want anything I do to get in the way of a great organization like Unicef."

The first Golf Saudi Summit was held in concert with the tournament. Inevitably, Greg Norman was a featured speaker, and he honored the commitment. One attendee of the summit spoke to me on the condition of anonymity, due to what he called the "lingering stench" of having been a guest of the state so soon after Khashoggi's killing: "It was quite interesting to watch Greg at work. He can be incredibly charming, if it suits his needs. He put the full-court press on Yasir and Majed—you never saw him without one or both of them, and he had them eating out of his hand. They were quite taken by Norman and his stardom. It was obvious they were cooking up something big, but nobody knew what." After the summit, Norman's business conversations became dominated by what he called "KSA"—Kingdom of Saudi Arabia.

For the 2020 International, Golf Saudi lured Phil Mickelson, who had traditionally been reluctant to play internationally. (He jilted the Crosby Clambake, where he was a five-time champion and always used as a ball marker an old silver dollar that his grandfather Al Santos had earned as a boy caddying at Pebble Beach.) The Saudis were still aligned with the Premier Golf League, and players and agents took turns visiting Al-Rumayyan's yacht, parked just offshore, to hear recruiting pitches.

Around the time of the 2020 Saudi International, the PGL lost an important early ally in McIlroy, who had initially encouraged Andy Gardiner in his efforts to modernize the presentation of professional golf. Near the end of a Player Advisory Council meeting at the Los Angeles Open, Jay Monahan was asked an off-agenda question about the PGL. After some back-and-forth, McIlroy stood up and announced, "This is easy, either you are about money or you're about legacy." The following week, at the WGC-Mexico Championship, he expanded on his thoughts to reporters: "Money is cheap. Money is the easy part. That shouldn't be the driving factor. The more I've thought about it, the more I don't like it. The one thing as a professional golfer in my position that I value is the fact that I have autonomy and freedom over everything that I do. If you go and play this other golf league, you're not going to have that choice." McIlroy also referenced Arnold Palmer renouncing Greg Norman's World Tour and said that he, too, wanted "to be on the right side of history." Norman, still bitter after all these years, fired off a pithy text message. Said McIlroy, "We had a pretty testy back-and-forth, and he was very condescending: 'Maybe one day you'll understand' and all this shite."

Throughout the first half of 2020, the Saudis explored ways to become more deeply invested in the sport. They announced the formation of the Aramco Team Series in partnership with the Ladies European Tour, which conferred crucial Solheim Cup points on the events. The series launched in the fall of 2020 and continues to run tournaments in the United States, Europe, Asia, and Saudi Arabia. The LPGA gave its blessing by allowing its top stars to compete, and America's sweethearts Nelly Korda and Lexi Thompson have been among the tournament winners. Women's golf has always struggled to attract sponsors, so no one appeared too bothered about the Saudis' underwriting the $1 million events; quite the opposite, actually. Said Thompson, "Honestly, these events are put on so well and Aramco has been a huge supporter of the Ladies European Tour and golf in general. We're all out there playing a game we love. Having the support from sponsors in Saudi Arabia and Aramco, it's great."

In addition to the pledge to back the PGL, Al-Rumayyan had two summer meetings with Pelley to forge a larger partnership with the European Tour. On the table was a ten-year, $500 million marketing deal in which Golf Saudi and the PIF would have branding and signage at every tournament and become presenting sponsors of the tour's Middle East swing. A capital fund would be created for joint commercial and charitable ventures.

But everything changed in the two and a half months between the announcement of the PGA and European Tour's strategic alliance and the February 2021 playing of the Saudi International. The Saudis had given up on the PGL, coming to the conclusion that if they wanted to be a part of professional golf, it would have to be from a position of strength, by organizing their own tour and forging a compromise with an existing circuit. The Saudis already had the relationships and, of course, unlimited resources. Now they brought in additional intellectual firepower in Gary Davidson and Jed Moore, whose Performance54 consulting group had been working alongside Gardiner for years. They switched sides late in 2020, going all in with the Saudis, who would ultimately buy 51 percent of Performance54. "When all this started I had one house, and now I have three," Moore confided to a friend at the European Tour after a couple of years serving the Saudis. Among the Shakespearean themes of this saga are betrayal, and not just among the players: Richard Marsh was once one of Andy Gardiner's best friends, but they haven't spoken since Marsh threw in with P54 in 2021.

Performance54 and the Saudis quickly cooked up their own version of a world tour, the details essentially cut and pasted from the PGL: forty-eight players, fifty-four holes, no cut, individual and team components, $25 million purses. Folks associated with the PGL were livid at the betrayal; one investor told me of the Saudis, "They're not our partners [anymore], they're now our competitors. They one hundred percent stole our idea."

The 2021 Saudi International was a crucial moment in the battle for the soul of professional golf. Following one of the practice rounds, dozens of golfers crowded into a conference room inside the Royal Greens Golf & Country Club clubhouse in King Abdullah Economic City. The gathering had the same crackling intensity as the player meeting Norman had organized twenty-seven years earlier at the Shark Shootout to sell his World Tour to his peers. But this time, Arnold Palmer was nowhere to be found. Al-Rumayyan offered a rah-rah speech, and Moore walked the players through a detailed presentation of how a Saudi Golf League underwritten by the Public Investment Fund could work. The players were fired up; you could almost hear the cash registers ringing. Says one of the men in attendance, "When we walked out of that room, it was a done deal. This was happening."

Al-Sorour and Moore established a beachhead in West Palm Beach, Florida, renting office space and a big house. Al-Sorour began hanging out at the Bear's Club, where McIlroy, Dustin John-son, Justin Thomas, Rickie Fowler, Keegan Bradley, Ernie Els, and other pros are members. He became omnipresent on the back patio, engaging players and agents in animated conversations. But before blowing up the structure of professional golf, the Saudis extended an olive branch. It has become an accepted part of the narrative that Jay Monahan "wouldn't take the call." In fact, he shut down the Saudis on a couple of occasions. In March 2021, Al-Sorour had a meeting with Jack Nicklaus at the Bear's Club at which he asked Nicklaus to reach out to Monahan to discuss how "they might work together going forward," according to a lawsuit Nicklaus later filed against a business partner. "Mr. Nicklaus reached out to Mr. Monahan later that week and was told that the PGA Tour had no interest in collab-orating with Golf Saudi."

Increasingly frustrated, Al-Sorour dashed off a letter to Mona-han dated April 17, 2021. That it carried Al-Sorour's name and not Al-Rumayyan's is, says someone close to them, "cultural," adding, "H.E. would never put his name on a request if there was the slight-est chance it would be turned down. He wouldn't put himself in a position where he could lose face." After some opening pleasantries, the letter, which has never before been made public, said:

I am writing in my capacity as lead advisor of a new golf enterprise. I want to introduce you to our proposition and outline its value as a prospective partner of the PGA Tour. We are proposing an innovative league featuring twelve "teams" of top talent competing head-to-head over 14 weeks, creating a new dimension for sports and stakeholders.

Al-Sorour talked a bit about the new league's potential "social impact" while pledging to "uphold the values and heritage of the sport." Then he got to the heart of the matter: "We have a very interested individual and group and are confident our approach will benefit all who participate. It is possible that the league should be operated on a schedule that is largely complementary to the PGA Tour. With the positive responses we have received, we have chartered our course to launch in 2022." All the formal language did not disguise the inherent threat: We are launching with or without you.

In closing, Al-Sorour wrote:

I have respect for the PGA Tour and we view this as an opportunity for a collaboration that would grow the game. We believe also it is the strategic development of a new investment opportunity for professional golf. This process would be realized as a partnership and add a positive new dimension for the game, the players, sponsors, communities, charities and fans alike. We'd like to arrange a sit-down with you to discuss our approach in more detail and highlight how this could represent value for you, your members, partners and community.

We look forward to hearing from you.

Yours sincerely,

Majed al-Sorour

The vision, as the Saudis hoped to explain, was that the PIF would underwrite the $25 million purses and pay the PGA Tour a hefty fee to handle tournament operations, rules, scoring, and so on. It would be a financial windfall for the players and provide a fresh revenue stream and a jazzy new product for the Tour. But how would players flow back and forth between the team and individual events? Would they have to commit to playing in each one? What would the tournaments be called? How would FedEx Cup points be allocated and TV revenue be shared? Those and many other details needed to be discussed, which was why Al-Sorour had proposed the meeting with Monahan.

This was the moment of truth for Hockey Jay. He had been masterful in guiding the Tour through covid, securing a game-changing TV deal, and thwarting the PGL. But the Saudis were proposing to fundamentally alter his business and force him to give up some control. They were threatening his dominion. He never responded to the letter or even brought it before his full board of directors.

In describing the letter to a colleague, Monahan called it "strange." It had come on a blank sheet of paper with no letterhead— not Golf Saudi or the Public Investment Fund. The postmark was from Oregon; after some digging, Tour sleuths discovered that Al-Sorour had a paramour there. The letter did not include his title at Golf Saudi. In this kind of high-level corporate correspondence, it would have been standard to include Al-Rumayyan and PGA Tour board members as addressees, but they were glaringly absent. No mention was made of the source of funding. Al-Sorour included no contact information. Of course, Monahan knew who Al-Sorour was, whom he worked for, how much money he was sitting on, and how to reach him. But the letter's curious lack of protocol and specificity gave Monahan just enough wiggle room to blow it off. Was Al-Sorour freelancing behind his boss's back? Was the project tied to the PGL or something else entirely? Monahan could have asked any of his top players for Al-Sorour's cell phone number—most were already in negotiations with him!—and given him a call. He could have hopped on his jet, bum-rushed the Bear's Club, and found Al-

Sorour on the back patio to engage him in discussion. But imagine Monahan's state of mind: he's the muthahfuckin' commissioner of the PGA Tour and one of the most powerful figures in golf. He was not duty bound to chase after a shadowy would-be competitor offering a nebulous deal. He was already pissed that the Saudis had set up shop in Florida—in his backyard!—and were trying to steal his players. If they wanted to talk, there was a right way to do it, and Al-Sorour's unorthodox letter wasn't it. It is true that Monahan could have taken a more nuanced view: that the Saudis—already partners of the European Tour and Ladies European Tour and friends of the LPGA—were potentially an asset, an opportunity, a windfall. But that would have taken a humility, perspective, and savvy that eluded Monahan. He responded to the letter like Sonny Corleone, not like Tom Hagen.

James Hahn was one of the four player directors on the PGA Tour Policy Board throughout 2021, alongside five independent directors drawn from the business world. (The jocks would be granted a fifth seat in 2022, for appearances' sake.) "We never saw the letter in any of the board meetings," Hahn says. "The letter was never brought up, it was never discussed."

Kevin Kisner, another player director of that era, says, "There was a large discussion on that matter, but Jay had made his decision not to have a conversation before that. He's our leader, and we have to be respectful to what he believes is the best way to run the PGA Tour, and he's pretty damn good at it."

But, Kiz, doesn't the commissioner work for the players?

"Absolutely he does. But just because some guy we don't really know decides to start a tour and pump billions of dollars into it doesn't mean it's going to work out for everyone, right? I think there's way too many coulda, shoulda, woulda maybes. Jay had a plan, and we followed it."

Says an adviser to Golf Saudi, "Not taking the meeting has to be one of the biggest mistakes in the history of golf. You're the commissioner of the PGA Tour and somebody wants to pour a billion dollars into the Tour to improve your product and make your players fabulously wealthy, and you won't even talk to them? In corporate America that's a fireable offense. Monahan needs to be responsible to his shareholders"—the players, metaphorically speaking—"but I don't think he knows he has any."

What was the response of Al-Rumayyan and Al-Sorour to being blown off?

"'Fuck those guys,'" says the adviser. "There are heads of state who will turn their schedule upside down to get a few minutes of Yasir's time. The Saudis are used to getting their way. They are not used to being told no."

The Saudis turned their attention to the European Tour and began by playing hardball. In June 2021, after two years of negotiations, the Dubai-based shipping company DP World signed a ten-year naming rights deal to turn the European Tour into the DP World Tour, for nearly $500 million. After the deal was consummated, Al-Rumayyan, who in addition to running the Public Investment Fund is the chairman of Aramco, began leaning on DP World to break the contract and instead sponsor the Saudis' breakaway tour, what was being referred to as the SGL, though no one was sure if it stood for Super Golf League or Saudi Golf League. That was no small ask: Aramco is DP World's biggest client. DP World felt compelled to pause the deal with the European Tour and explore its options with the SGL. A secret meeting was convened in Malta, bringing together Pelley, Guy Kinnings, and Paul McGinley, representing the European Tour; Al-Sorour and Al-Rumayyan's adviser Ismail Sharif, a Middle East power broker who turned Dubai into a golfing destination; Danny van Otterdijk, the chief marketing officer of DP World; and various assistants for each side. For the first time, Al-Sorour laid out a vision of the SGL teaming with the European Tour. Unofficial minutes from the meeting would subsequently be leaked throughout the golf world, leading to the narrative that the Saudis had offered the European Tour $1 billion. In fact, half of that was the DP World money; Al-Sorour said that as part of the new partnership, the Saudis would "allow" that (signed!) deal to go through. The other $500 million was merely equity in the SGL. The only cash the Saudis would be investing in the European Tour would be for the creation of a tournament in the kingdom to go on the Tour's schedule. To the European Tour leadership, that sounded suspiciously like the PGL deal it had vetted and declined the year before: lots of grand talk about future riches but not enough up-front money for it to take the gamble of fundamentally altering its business model and making an enemy of the PGA Tour. One of the folks representing the European Tour asked Al-Sorour if the Saudis had signed any players to contracts.

"A lot," Al-Sorour said.

"Which players?"

"I can't tell you that right now."

Eye rolls all around.

The European Tour, after a subsequent meeting of its board of directors, declined the SGL's overtures. Months of delicate diplomacy ensued, and in November 2021, the DP World Tour renaming was announced.

With all of the ongoing conversations at the Bear's Club and elsewhere, word soon spread through the golf world about the formation of the SGL. Rejected by the European Tour and ignored by the PGA Tour, the SGL's patrons finally accepted that getting a seat at the table would not be possible through partnership or compromise. No, they would have to buy it with the crushing weight of their money. (Not for nothing, a McKinsey report commissioned by Golf Saudi to assess the viability of a breakaway league was referred to as "Project Wedge.") Fantastical dollar amounts began to be thrown around, and this time it was guaranteed up-front money from a source that had an endless supply of it.

Monahan recognized the threat that the well-capitalized SGL

represented to his business. In the fall of 2021, the PGA Tour convened another board meeting. Player director Charley Hoffman asked Monahan, "Why don't we have a discussion with any of the Saudi guys who are putting together this tour?"

The answer to that simple query, according to Hahn and another person in the room, would shape golf history. "We are at war," Monahan replied. "We do not negotiate with another entity that is trying to put us out of business. We do not negotiate with people who are trying to ruin the golf ecosystem."

The PGA Tour board meetings were populated not only by the directors but also by Andy Pazder, then the chief tournaments and competitions officer; legal counsel; and a handful of other Tour suits. "Andy does not have a vote, but he is very vocal and always on Jay's side," says Hahn. "All of the other Tour people are on Jay's side, too, obviously. As a player, you feel outnumbered. When Jay said we wouldn't negotiate with the Saudis, as a player, that was it. End of discussion. It felt like a dad yelling at his son: 'This is how it is because I said so, and we're done talking about it.' There was no pushback, no follow-up questions. Every meeting we had from then on was about 'How do we combat this threat to our business?' 'We're at war here, fellas. These guys are trying to take over our business.' That's all we heard: 'We're at war, we're at war, we're at war.'"

With the battle lines drawn, the Saudis stepped up their offensive. The players who had been such a receptive audience at the 2021 Saudi International constituted a solid core of a new tour, but more top talent would need to be bought. In the wake of the PGL messiness, and with the leadership of the PGA and European Tours having closed ranks against the incursion of a breakaway league, getting big-name players to change their allegiance would be a complicated, delicate matter. The Saudis needed a sneaky double agent to do their bidding behind enemy lines.

6.

PHIL MICKELSON HAS ALWAYS BEEN OBSESSED WITH money, owing to a life of conspicuous consumption (his own Gulf-stream IV, etc.), a deep resentment of paying taxes, and a self-described gambling addiction. In 2013, he made a flippant comment to reporters bitching about California's state income tax, touching off one of the many uproars in his messy public life. Mickelson's next stop on the PGA Tour after that comment went public was at a pretournament press conference at Torrey Pines Golf Course in La Jolla, California. Before going into the media center, he huddled in the parking lot for nearly an hour with his publicist and a couple of Tour officials, plotting the best way to talk himself out of yet another jam of his own making.

One of the other assembled men said, "The problem, Phil, is that fans don't want to hear complaining from a guy making forty million dollars a year—"

Mickelson cut him off: "It's fifty million."

Mickelson had good reason to keep track of every dollar. In 2016, he became ensnared in the insider trading case of the renowned gambler Billy Walters. Named as a relief defendant, he repaid to the government $932,738.12 for his "ill-gotten gains" plus $105,291.69 in interest but was never charged with wrongdoing. As part of their investigation, government investigators conducted a forensic audit of his finances from 2010 to 2014. According to a source with direct access to the documents, Mickelson had claimed $40 million in gambling losses during that period. Billy Walters, Mickelson's former betting partner, estimated in his 2023 autobiography that Phil had wagered a billion dollars across three decades, and that his losses ran into nine figures. That may or may not explain why Mickelson chased the PGL money and then the Saudi dough so hard.

But Mickelson had other motivations for wanting to watch the PGA Tour burn while siding with the guys holding the matches. He had long butted heads with Tour commissioner Tim Finchem and his successor, Jay Monahan. He hated how bloated the Tour had become. Brandel Chamblee recalls a long-ago B.C. Open at which he and Mickelson had been paired. "Knowing that I was on the Player Advisory Council," Chamblee says, "he spent the whole time in my ear saying the PGA Tour should be reduced to only thirty players— nothing but the stars. He was totally oblivious to the fact that it would eliminate my job." Mickelson hated the opposite-field events conducted for the Tour middle class in the same weeks as the World Golf Championships, rightfully pointing out that they diluted the Tour's overall product. He hated putting on a show for the fans for two practice rounds and two tournament rounds, all the while signing a million autographs but not earning a dollar in the weeks he missed the cut. He really hated that the PGA Tour barred players from accepting appearance fees, whereas every other worldwide golf circuit allowed the top players to scoop them up. He hated that in his best year he had earned "only" $6.9 million on the Tour while the stars in team sports were making five and six and seven times that. As he became a snarky social media presence, he came to hate the Tour's stringent media rights policies, which prevented him from monetizing his own highlights. He hated that the NBA was making money for its players by selling NFTs while the Tour, per usual, lagged behind. Both in public and in private he raged against all of that, but Finchem and then Monahan simply patted him on the head and sent him on his way like a petulant child. Mickelson longed to be validated and even celebrated as an agent of change. He needed to be right and for the world to know it. The Saudis were the perfect bedfellows: desperate for star power and leadership to launch their breakaway league, they were happy to give Mickelson everything he had always wanted.

The week of the 2021 PGA Championship altered the trajectory of Mickelson's life—and of professional golf. Al-Sorour rented a big house near the Ocean Course at Kiawah Island Golf Resort in South Carolina, and a steady procession of agents and players swung by to listen to sales pitches. Many had been down a similar road with the PGL, but Andy Gardiner had been selling merely an idea and the dream of future riches; Al-Sorour had cash on the barrelhead, and loads of it. The numbers were so big as to provoke disbelief, even giddiness. On the putting green and driving range, in the locker room and parking lot, there was a new refrain: " 'What's your number?' " says James Hahn, the Tour veteran. "Everyone had a number." For many it was strictly theoretical but still a fun exercise.

With that as a backdrop, Mickelson summoned one of the defining performances of a legendary career, storming to victory at that PGA Championship and, a month shy of his fifty-first birthday, becoming the oldest man to win a major championship. It was the ultimate mic drop. His legacy complete—give or take a U.S. Open— he had only one thing left to do: reinvent himself. Golf Saudi had already been dangling a monster offer. According to a veteran agent who had many discussions with Al-Sorour and who ultimately sent a couple of players to LIV, "I have it on good authority that they had been offering Phil a three-year deal in the low nine figures. After he won the PGA, it went to four years and the dollars nearly doubled." That represented generational wealth and confirmed what Mickelson had always believed: he deserved LeBron money, Curry money, Mahomes money, Trout money.

Mickelson became increasingly enmeshed with the Saudis. He and three other players he declined to name—but whom insiders would later cite as Dustin Johnson, Brooks Koepka, and Bryson DeChambeau—hired lawyers to write the operating agreement for the new league, codifying that the players would get their way. That was either smart business or supreme disloyalty—perhaps both.

Throughout the 2021 season, the whispers grew louder: the Saudis are coming. Then, two days before Halloween, the pieces on the chessboard finally began to move when Golf Saudi announced that it had hired a CEO for a new venture called LIV Golf Investments: Greg Fucking Norman. Who else could it have been? For three decades, ever since his dreams of his World Tour had been shattered by Finchem and mocked by his peers, Norman had been waiting, lurking, hoping, praying for one last chance to stick it to the Tour. Making Norman the figurehead of whatever the Saudis were scheming wasn't merely a hiring; it was a declaration of war. "They could not possibly have selected a more divisive, controversial, or, frankly, disliked figure than Greg Norman," says Deane Beman, Finchem's predecessor and the man who built the modern PGA Tour. "It was a very clear signal that they did not want to work within the existing structures of professional golf."

In all the hoopla surrounding Norman's hiring, there was no mention of a top-tier new circuit with extravagant purses to compete against the PGA Tour, only that LIV Golf had committed $300 million over the next ten years to the Asian Tour to back a new ten-event series of tournaments. (LIV is the Roman numerals for 54, theoretically the perfect score in a round of golf if every hole is birdied on a par 72; but wouldn't a perfect round feature at least one eagle?) The investment in the Asian Tour provoked much confusion. It had long been a backwater of professional golf, a last chance for players not good enough to make it in the United States or Europe. Why on earth would anyone pour $300 million into a tour known for its bureaucratic inefficiency and sometimes dodgy tournament offerings? In fact, the Golf Saudi press release summarized the situation quite well, saying that the Asian Tour investment would "set in motion a number of momentous developments for professional golf world-wide."

Mickelson approved of Norman's hiring. The two have never been close but have always recognized each other as kindred spirits. "We respect each other's point of view," Norman says. "We understand market value and that the [PGA] Tour works for us, we don't work for the Tour. Phil asks tough questions. He's not here to placate anybody. He's got a mind of his own and his own opinions, which can be incredibly strong and poignant."

So the Saudis had made their first gambit. (One of Mickelson's favorite TV shows is *The Queen's Gambit*. "It fits his obsessive personality," his wife, Amy, told me.) Now all eyes were on Mickelson. Everyone in the interconnected golf world knew he was working both sides of the street; he had already quietly reached out to a variety of players to gauge their interest in the new Saudi superleague. "I think Phil recruited every player on the PGA Tour except for me," says one veteran who ultimately signed with LIV Golf. "I started wondering, *Do I have BO? Bad breath? Why won't Phil call me?* It sort of hurt my feelings."

After a dalliance with the PGL and amid a flirtation with the Saudis, Mickelson, incredibly, began pitching yet another breakaway tour, this one largely underwritten by a billionaire from the sports betting world and the private equity behemoth Silver Lake. The unnamed league proposed an eight-event team series that would be tucked into the PGA Tour schedule. Six of the events would have $20 million purses, whereas the other two would offer $50 million. Half of the league would be owned by investors and half by players. If this sounds familiar, it's because, a PGL source says, "Phil got access to all of our work and started shopping it around." Talks went as high as Monahan and Ed Herlihy, the chairman of the PGA Tour's board of directors. Herlihy is a leading mergers and acquisitions attorney and also an influential member at Augusta National. He ended further discussion of the new league with a succinct verdict:

"If it's not one hundred percent owned and controlled by the PGA Tour, it will be viewed as hostile."

The story about the thwarted league was broken by the *New York Post* in February 2022 in an article by Mark Cannizzaro, who has a close relationship with Mickelson. (Cannizzaro also covers the NFL, and Mickelson has been known to pump him for usable intel; Mickelson wrote the foreword to Cannizzaro's book about the Masters.) In the *Post* story all the sources were anonymous, but at least one sounded suspiciously like Mickelson: "The Tour could have ended the threat of the Saudi league had they done this. This would be a collaborative effort. It was all worked out . . . until [Herlihy] shut it down in one sentence. It undermines everything the Tour has been saying about who they are—that this is owned by the players, this is run by the players. That is complete b.s."

As he worked relentlessly in the shadows, the biggest question in the game remained "What does Phil want?" Nobody knew for certain.

Then, a few days before Thanksgiving 2021, he picked up the phone and called me; I was putting the finishing touches on a biography of Mickelson and had spent the previous year beseeching him for an interview. In our momentous phone call he admitted that the new Saudi circuit was nothing more than what he called "sportswashing" by a brutally repressive regime. "They're scary motherfuckers to get involved with," he said. "We know they killed [Jamal] Khashoggi and have a horrible record on human rights. They execute people over there for being gay. Knowing all of this, why would I even consider it? Because this is a once-in-a-lifetime opportunity to reshape how the PGA Tour operates. They've been able to get by with manipulative, coercive, strong-arm tactics because we, the players, had no recourse. As nice a guy as [Monahan] comes across as, unless you have leverage, he won't do what's right. And the Saudi money has finally given us that leverage. I'm not sure I even want [LIV Golf] to succeed, but just the idea of it is allowing us to get things done with the [PGA] Tour."

Mickelson enumerated many of his grievances: "The Tour is sitting on multiple billions of dollars worth of NFTs. They are sitting on hundreds of millions of dollars worth of digital content we could be using for our social media feeds. The players need to own all of that. We played those shots, we created those moments, we should be the ones to profit. The Tour doesn't need that money. They are already sitting on an eight-hundred-million-dollar cash stockpile"—a wildly exaggerated number that hinted at the truth. "How do you think they're funding the [nascent Player Impact Program, which would distribute $50 million to top players in a glorified popularity contest]? Or investing two hundred million in the European Tour? The Tour is supposed to be a nonprofit that distributes money to charity. How the fuck is it legal for them to have that much cash on hand? The answer is, it's not. But they always want more and more. They have to control everything. Their ego won't allow them to make the concessions they need to."

I couldn't believe what I was hearing. Mickelson loves the sound of his own voice, and it is often hard to know where the insight ends and the bullshitting begins. But after years of secret meetings and quiet conversations, he knew the state of play better than any other golfer. Was he really willing to blow up the PGA Tour if he didn't get his way? "I know twenty guys who want to do this," he said of the Saudis' breakaway league, "and if the Tour doesn't do the right thing, there is a high likelihood it's going to happen."

The fuse had been lit.

7.

ON NOVEMBER 30, 2021, A WEEK AFTER PHIL MICKELSON called me and opened a vein, I submitted the manuscript of his biography to the publisher. The copyediting and legal review proceeded at their normal leisurely pace, slowed by the holiday season. Mickelson's incendiary thoughts about the PGA Tour and his would-be Saudi patrons remained out of the public eye.

He continued to work hard behind the scenes, however. At the first PGA Tour event of 2022, the Tournament of Champions at the Plantation Course at Kapalua, Maui, Mickelson was paired with Harris English for the final round. They were miles behind the leader, Cameron Smith, setting up a low-stress Sunday stroll in paradise. English, then thirty-two, was coming off a career year in which he had won twice and played for the United States in the Ryder Cup. He would be a big get for LIV Golf, and Mickelson spent the entire round in English's ear, making his sales pitch. "Phil was relentless," says a caddie who was filled in on the details by English's looper; much of the information that flows through a professional golf tour is spread from caddie to caddie. "Apparently he wouldn't leave Harris alone the whole round. Poor Harris is this nice, quiet southern gentleman, so he was too polite to tell Phil to fuck off, but he apparently was really bothered by the whole thing."

Taking the high road, English says, "I always enjoy playing with Phil. He was talkative, as always. We did talk a lot about LIV. I had some questions, and he had all the answers."

Mickelson's advocacy for the players to get a bigger slice of the pie began to pay dividends in January 2022, when the inaugural Player Impact Program (PIP) bonuses were handed out by Monahan as belated stocking stuffers. Tiger Woods took first place and $8 million, despite having missed the whole season after smashing his right leg in a car accident; the money was a kind of emeritus recognition for all he had done for the Tour in the preceding two decades. Mickelson came in second ($6 million), Rory McIlroy third ($3.5 million), Jordan Spieth fourth ($3.5 million). One of the criteria for determining the PIP winners was the "MVP Index," which calibrates the value of engagement a player drives across social and digital channels; the metric is derived by a company founded by Shawn Spieth, Jordan's dad. Jordan was a member of the PGA Tour board when it approved the PIP and his old man's involvement. Hahn, the only player director not to vote in favor of the PIP, says of the Spieths, "How is that not a conflict of interest? I mean, let's just have a PIP of who cooks the best Korean barbecue and let my mom be the judge. Like, what the fuck?" Among all the Tour players who didn't get a PIP handout, frustration reigned that it was just a popularity contest divorced from tournament results. Says Hahn, "That got brought up at a board meeting, and Rory said, 'Anyone can win the PIP if they play better.' Patrick Cantlay won the [2021] FedEx Cup but didn't get a dollar of PIP money. How much better can you play than that?"

All the free money handed out by the PGA Tour for the PIP did nothing to slow the gathering momentum of a rival league. In early February 2022, Mickelson made what had become his annual pilgrimage to the Saudi International. Coming out of that week, the talk of a breakaway league turned into a low roar. The Saudis had set a benchmark: As soon as twenty-four players—half of the proposed field size for each event—committed, the new world tour would be announced publicly. Player agents and others in the know whispered that a twenty-fourth player signing was imminent.

While in Saudi Arabia, veteran scribe John Huggan buttonholed Mickelson for an interview, ostensibly about how the reigning PGA

Championship winner was gearing up for the new season. Mostly unprompted, Mickelson went on the warpath, airing a number of his business-related grievances with the PGA Tour. On February 2, Huggan's story was posted on the *Golf Digest* website. "When I did 'The Match'—there have been five of them—the Tour forced me to pay them $1 million each time," Mickelson said during one of his riffs. "For my own media rights." In fact, the network that had aired the made-for-TV spectacles, Turner Sports, paid the licensing fee, not Mickelson. But Mickelson was on a roll and not inclined to let facts get in the way. One of his quotes in the story spurred a number of racy headlines: "That type of greed is, to me, beyond obnoxious."

Mickelson has always been a rascal, a muckraker, and a shit stirrer. Now the Saudis had validated all of his maverick tendencies by offering to make him the centerpiece of the kind of transformational change to the golf world that he had always craved. His comments to Huggan left no doubt that he would continue to use the golf press as his bully pulpit. But the things he had told me, unseen and with the book release still three months away, provided a crucial context that was otherwise lacking about the biggest (non-Tiger) golf story of the century. After consulting with the publisher, we decided to drop a book excerpt on the website of the Fire Pit Collective, a media company at which I am the executive editor. It contained all of Mickelson's incendiary thoughts about Monahan, the Tour, and the Saudis, including his cynical riff about the "scary motherfuckers." The excerpt went live on February 17, on the morning of the first round of the PGA Tour's Los Angeles Open, and instantly began tearing through the Twittersphere. Players were packed onto Riviera Country Club's tiny range, with caddies, agents, swing coaches, trainers, and assorted other hangers-on milling about. Folks stared at their phones, and some players stopped hitting balls to huddle with colleagues. Disbelief tinged the air. "It was crazy, man," says Tour veteran Jhonattan Vegas. "People were shocked. It was like, what the hell? It had that confusing feeling, where everything you think you know turns out not to be true."

At PGA Tour headquarters in Ponte Vedra Beach, Florida, embattled staffers couldn't believe their good fortune. The collective feeling was that Mickelson's loose lips might do what the Tour appeared serially incapable of doing: stopping the Saudis. As one member of the media department puts it, "I'm not going to say people were running up and down the hallways spraying champagne, but you could definitely feel the energy in the building." This person adds, "For years, we had been under siege with questions about the PGL, then the SGL. Reporters, players, even some of our own staff were pushing us to take a more aggressive stance, but how can you publicly defend yourself against something that doesn't officially exist? Why give them that oxygen? Phil did a brilliant job of distilling the entire counterargument: 'They're scary motherfuckers you don't want to get involved with.' What a gift."

Among the LIV leadership, a funereal atmosphere pervaded. One executive later told me, "You almost single-handedly brought down the entire organization." Players who had committed to the tour, and their agents, began burning up the phone lines, expressing their misgivings and exploring exit strategies. Greg Norman, who already nursed a persecution complex, would later complain to the *Daily Telegraph* that I had been in cahoots with the PGA Tour on the timing of the book excerpt. "It was calculated—it's not like my 45 years in the game has left me on the outside," said Norman, who has, in fact, been on the outside looking in ever since his World Tour collapsed. "I have some pretty good intel that, you know, it was calculated in how it came out." That was laughable, given that when the excerpt dropped I had been battling with PGA Tour executives over what they believed to be violations of their outdated media policies and they were refusing to credential me to tournaments. The only LIV person who had a sense of humor about all of the hullabaloo was Majed Al-Sorour, who months later offered me a meaty handshake and said, "When the quotes came out, I called Phil and said, 'Am I really that scary? Because I'm the only Saudi motherfucker you know!'" Mickelson went underground.

Because so many of the conversations had been conducted in the shadows, some in the golf press had been slow to recognize the gathering magnitude of the Saudi breakaway league. (It's not as though there had been a press release when the Saudis moved their money out of the Premier Golf League.) But now, with Mickelson having provided a primer on what was happening behind the scenes, the players at Riviera were getting pounded with more pointed questions. Top stars were being asked to pick a side: Are you committed to the PGA Tour or not? Dustin Johnson became a crucial test case.

For most of his career, Johnson had been considered an extravagantly talented underachiever whose priorities were to make birdies, make money, and get laid, not necessarily in that order. In 2014, he was suspended by the Tour for six months for failing a third drug test, news broken by the ace reporter Michael Bamberger. (The PGA Tour doesn't comment publicly about disciplinary matters, and Johnson's excuse for previously disappearing from the Tour following his second positive test was that he had hurt his back lifting a jet ski.) DJ's salvation came in the unlikely form of Paulina Gretzky, the sexpot Instagram influencer and daughter of the greatest hockey player of all time. They began dating in early 2013 and were engaged by that summer. In the spring of 2014, they discovered that Paulina was pregnant. A few months later, Johnson took his leave from the Tour.

"I think for a long time Dustin had been struggling with the question 'Who loves me and believes in me, not as a golfer but as a person?'" says Joey Diovisalvi, Johnson's longtime personal trainer. "In that period of reflection he came to discover that Paulina and her family were his sanctuary. In the hardest of times they had his back. Love became the defining thing in his life, and when you're finally not afraid to love back, that's a life-changing shift." The couple's first son, Tatum, was born in February 2015. As a teen Johnson had lived through the acrimonious divorce of his parents; fatherhood gave him a purpose that had always been missing. (Another son, River, was born on the eve of the 2017 U.S. Open.) All of the pieces were coming together for Johnson, but the final push came from a man nicknamed the Great One. "I don't know golf," says Wayne Gretzky, an 11 handicapper, "but I know sports. There are great talents at every level. What separates the superstars is preparation and commitment. The notion that I'm some kind of guru to Dustin is overblown. He was a top ten player long before I met him. But if I've helped in any way, it's with the message that to be the best he has to pay the price. I've encouraged him to set very high goals for himself. Tiger-like goals. So this year you've won three tournaments and a major—next year make it five tournaments and two majors. Don't be afraid to be the best. Embrace it."

From the end of his drug suspension in early 2015 through the autumn of 2020, Johnson packed a Hall of Fame career into half a decade, piling up sixteen wins and spending long stretches at the summit of the world ranking. He conquered one of golf's toughest courses, the Oakmont Country Club in Pennsylvania, at the 2016 U.S. Open and shattered various scoring records in winning the 2020 Masters. The good ol' boy from South Carolina choked up upon being presented with the green jacket, the first time he had ever displayed any emotion in public other than ennui.

After Johnson won his second Saudi International, in 2021, he became LIV's primary target along with Mickelson. Johnson made for an easy mark in that he was never going to overthink what joining a breakaway league might do to his, ahem, legacy or the disquieting questions of where the money would be coming from.

Fast-forward to the 2022 Los Angeles Open and the publication of Mickelson's inflammatory quotes. Johnson missed the cut and had already departed the Riviera Country Club, but he overshadowed the final round when he released, through the PGA Tour's social media channels, a statement affirming his loyalty. "I am fully committed to the PGA Tour," he said. "I am grateful for the opportunity to play on the best tour in the world and for all it has provided me and my family. While there will always be areas where our Tour can improve and evolve, I am thankful for our leadership and the many sponsors who make the PGA Tour golf's premier tour." A smattering of pros was on the small putting green near Riviera's first tee when word of Johnson's statement began to spread. The players, including Justin Thomas and Collin Morikawa, bumped knuckles, and JT was heard exclaiming, "Fuck, yeah, Dustin."

A few hours later, Bryson DeChambeau released a statement of his own: "While there has been a lot of speculation surrounding my support for another tour, I want to make it very clear that as long as the best players in the world are playing the PGA Tour, so will I." He says now, "Did I feel pressured by the Tour? Yes, I did. My sponsors were definitely pressuring me. It was a high-pressure situation."

It was at Riviera that Rory McIlroy began to find his voice as the conscience of the Tour. He said of Mickelson's comments, "I don't want to kick someone while he's down obviously, but I thought they were naive, selfish, egotistical, ignorant. A lot of words to describe that interaction he had with Shipnuck. It was just very surprising and disappointing, sad. I'm sure he's sitting at home sort of rethinking his position and where he goes from here."

Indeed, two days later, Mickelson issued a nonapology apology that felt as though it was aimed mostly at mending fences with the Saudis. "Golf desperately needs change, and real change is always preceded by disruption," he wrote. "I have always known that criticism would come with exploring anything new. I still chose to put myself at the forefront of this to inspire change, taking the hits publicly to do the work behind the scenes." He added, "My experience with LIV Golf Investments has been very positive. . . . The specific people I have worked with are visionaries and have only been supportive. More importantly they passionately love golf and share my drive to make the game better. They have a clear plan to create an updated and positive experience for everyone including players, sponsors, networks, and fans."

As soon as the statement dropped, Mickelson's longtime endorsement partner KPMG announced that their relationship was over. (Callaway Golf, with which Mickelson had a lifetime contract, put its deal on "pause.") For the time being, Mickelson had become toxic.

McIlroy captured the prevailing feeling at Riviera when he asked, "Who's left? Who's left to go? I mean, there's no one. It's dead in the water in my opinion. I just can't see any reason why anyone would go. I mean, Greg Norman would have to tee it up to fill the field. Like, I mean seriously? I mean, who else is going to do it? I don't think they could get forty-eight guys."

The rhetoric intensified two days after Johnson and DeChambeau pulled the rip cord on LIV Golf, when Monahan hosted a players' meeting early in the week of the Honda Classic. At one point, a constituent asked Monahan what would happen if a Tour player signed with LIV. The commissioner pointed at the door. He went even further, telling his players that any of them who signed with LIV risked a lifetime ban by the PGA Tour. Afterward, he told the Associated Press, "We're moving on." That would go down as the golf equivalent of Neville Chamberlain's "peace in our time," though Monahan was not alone in the sentiment; that same week, on the NBC telecast of the Honda, Jack Nicklaus said of Mickelson decamping for LIV, "Apparently if he does, he'll be going alone."

As soon as word leaked about Monahan strong-arming his players, Norman released a two-page letter addressed to the PGA Tour commissioner. It began with the classic opening line "Surely you jest." He made a lot of noise about players' rights and threatened an antitrust lawsuit against the Tour. Amid all the saber-rattling, one bit in the letter rang particularly true: "Commissioner—this is just the beginning. It certainly is not the end."

8.

DESPITE THE PUBLIC POSTURING, LIV GOLF WAS REELING in the days after the Mickelson bombshell. Staffers had been deep in discussions with Dustin Johnson and Bryson DeChambeau but were blindsided by the players' public pronouncements of loyalty to the PGA Tour. "We first heard about it on Twitter," says one LIV executive. "It was complete and total panic and chaos. We went from the verge of launching to feeling like, Hey, it was a good run, but now it's over."

Then His Excellency Yasir Al-Rumayyan organized a group call. To that point in the process, Al-Rumayyan had been a low-key presence with the LIV people: soft-spoken, reserved, and happy to stay in the background while his swaggering lieutenant, Majed Al-Sorour, handled the day-to-day details. There were thirty or so people on the call, including a handful of Public Investment Fund employees and LIV consultants Andrew McKenna and Ari Fleischer, who had served as President George W. Bush's press secretary.

"I believe in all of you, I believe in what we are building, and we are going to press forward," Al-Rumayyan said with some steel in his voice. "We will do what we have to do to launch this. Just get me sixteen players."

His resolute tone galvanized the operation. "We all went into the call with our heads hanging low, feeling so defeated," says the LIV exec. "Then it became like in *The Wolf of Wall Street* when Leonardo DiCaprio gives that speech and the whole room goes crazy. When His Excellency finished speaking we were all high-fiving. It was like, *Let's fucking go! We're gonna fucking do this!*"

With PGA Tour loyalists already clucking about LIV's demise, Al-Rumayyan ordered an accelerated timeline to announce the schedule: staffers were given two weeks to lock down eight tournament venues. The initial plan had been to begin the season in Portland, Oregon, in early July, but that was deemed too far away. LIV Golf needed to launch and it needed to launch now; every day of delay felt like a retreat. To kick off the new alliance with LIV, the Asian Tour had planned to play an event in the United Kingdom for the first time, at the Centurion Club outside London in early June. LIV bigfooted its new partner and took over the date and venue for what would become its first tournament. The rest of the schedule flowed from there.

LIV's siege mentality only intensified when Jay Monahan held his annual state of the union press conference at the Players Championship three weeks after Mickelson's comments had gone public. "I'd like to emphatically reiterate what I told our players at our mandatory player meeting two weeks ago at the Honda Classic: The PGA Tour is moving on," Monahan said. "We have too much momentum and too much to accomplish to be consistently distracted by rumors of other golf leagues and their attempts to disrupt our players, our partners, and most importantly our fans from enjoying the Tour and the game we all love so much. . . . We are and we always will be focused on legacy, not leverage."

Legacy, not leverage. In the short term, that became the Tour's rallying cry. Eight days after those words were uttered, LIV Golf returned fire by announcing its inaugural schedule of eight tournaments, including the London event and stops in Thailand and Saudi Arabia. The other five tournaments would be played in the United States, a provocative challenge to the PGA Tour, though the season finale did not yet have a confirmed venue. (Trump National Doral in Miami would later be announced as the host site.) The total purse was a whopping $255 million: $25 million for the first seven events and a season-ending team extravaganza with a $50 million purse and

$30 million in bonuses for the top three individuals in a season-long points race. "Our events are truly additive to the world of golf," Greg Norman said in a statement. That word—*additive*—would be hotly debated in the months to come. "We have done our best to create a schedule that allows players to play elsewhere, while still participating in our events," he continued. "I believe players will increasingly make progress in achieving their right to play where they want."

One minor detail was missing in the schedule announcement: players. It remained unknown who would and would not be making that leap of faith. But no matter who turned up, the first LIV event was now less than three months away. Al-Rumayyan had put his reputation—and by extension, that of his friend and boss, the crown prince of Saudi Arabia—on the line. They had made available the full resources of their petrocracy kicking off the greatest gold rush in golf history. Left to do the prospecting was an array of khaki-clad smooth talkers who were quite comfortable operating in the shadows.

In 1958, Mark McCormack was a very bored junior associate at the Cleveland law firm of Arter, Hadden, Wykoff & Van Duzer. He had a wife and infant son and was looking for an escape hatch from the stultifying life of preparing loan documents. McCormack, who had been a college golfer at William & Mary, began reflecting on why professional golfers were so underpaid compared to athletes in team sports. He concluded that in the absence of a union, the golfers needed an advocate to fight for their fair market value. In November 1958, he traveled to Atlanta for the Carling Open. He spent the week wooing players to join his newly formed National Sports Management firm. McCormack oozed intelligence and passion, and by the following March he had signed seven players who had finished in the top ten of the 1958 moneymaking list, including Arnold Palmer, then twenty-nine. Palmer, the reigning Masters champ, was on the verge of becoming one of the biggest stars in sports. But by the end of 1959, a season in which he won three times, he had grown wary of being packaged with the lesser players in McCormack's stable. He gave his agent an ultimatum: me or them. McCormack threw in with his superstar, off-loading his interest in NSM and, in early 1960, creating the International Management Group. McCormack said he would draw up a contract to commemorate the new partnership. Palmer's reply created an enduring mythology: "You're going to tell me what you're going to do for me, and I'll tell you what I'm going to do for you, and then we'll shake hands and go ahead and do what we said." Sports marketing would never be the same.

By the mid-1960s, along with Palmer, IMG represented Jack Nicklaus and Gary Player, and the Big Three traversed the corporate world, vacuuming up dollars. McCormack became a cultural touchstone—a visionary who was symbiotic with the talent. The world of professional golf soon became awash with young, ambitious men (always men) who wanted to work with McCormack or compete against him. "The agenting business tended to attract guys who played competitive golf but couldn't make it to the highest level," says Mac Barnhardt, one of the deans of the industry and himself a college golfer. "Some had worked as accountants, some as lawyers, some in sales, but they all wanted to be close to the game."

By the mid-1990s, IMG was a behemoth employing hundreds of people and generating hundreds of millions of dollars in revenue. (Greg Norman was a key client in the 1980s until—no surprise—an acrimonious divorce.) In particular, golfers at the highest level needed agents because they're independent contractors competing in a global game without the structure and support of a team. And golf fans spend billions of dollars annually to play the same equipment as their heroes do, creating a robust endorsement market.

IMG extended its hegemony in 1996 by signing Tiger Woods and landing him a deal with Nike that paid $40 million over five years, an unheard-of sum for a boutique sport. The first TV contract negotiated in the Woods era kicked in for the 1999 season, and purses nearly doubled. "The Tiger money changed everything," says Barnhardt. "It shifted who came into the business. They weren't so much golf guys anymore, they were MBAs and business minds. The relationships became very transactional. It was no longer about managing a career and helping a player slowly become the best he could be. The name of the game became signing a bunch of guys; those who played well made everyone a lot of money, those who didn't, they got let go."

Woods's first minder at IMG was Hughes Norton, a veteran agent with a few rough edges but a knack for dealmaking. Mark Steinberg was a junior IMG staffer of that era. As an undergrad, he had been a walk-on for a legendary University of Illinois basketball team, the Flyin' Illini, that had reached the Final Four in 1989. He still carried himself with a jock's assuredness, even though he had never gotten off the bench.

Steinberg interned at IMG while working toward a law degree at Illinois and landed a job upon earning his diploma. He slowly, doggedly worked his way up in the women's golf division. He signed Karrie Webb and Annika Sörenstam, and by the mid- to late 1990s, both had emerged as Hall of Fame talents. Even as his star rose, Steinberg grew restless. Seeking to diversify beyond its core sports of golf and tennis, IMG courted the basketball star Vince Carter. One day, Steinberg strolled into the office of his boss, Alastair Johnston, who says, "Mark came in and told me, 'I'd really like to branch out and work with Vince Carter to build a basketball franchise, because I don't have a passion for golf.'"

But after two years with Norton, Tiger wanted a new advocate. At twenty-one, Woods had reshaped the game in his image with his record- and barrier-breaking 12-stroke win at the 1997 Masters, making himself one of the most valuable athletes in the world. Johnston chose Steinberg, then thirty, to run the Chosen One's career. "Tiger wanted someone younger," says Johnston. "They could speak the same language, and they had the same sense of humor, though I don't think either one is particularly funny. Mark was smooth, very ambitious, and very aggressive." Steinberg listened intently as Johnston delivered the news of his promotion. "Finally he spoke up," says Johnston. "He said, 'This is wonderful because I have such a passion for golf.' So that's Mark Steinberg."

Steinberg turned Woods into a multinational corporation unto himself over the next decade, ultimately raking in nine figures a year in endorsement income for his client. While Woods played the most dominant golf of all time, his agent was routinely celebrated as one of the most powerful figures in the game. Tiger always called him "Steiny" in public, and there was nothing Steiny wouldn't do for his guy. In 2007, he held secret meetings with David Pecker, the CEO of American Media—its most profitable title, the *National Enquirer*, had photographic proof of Woods's tryst in a church parking lot with the waitress at a diner where Tiger often took his wife for breakfast. Steinberg got the story killed in exchange for Tiger's doing an unlikely cover story with *Men's Fitness*, another American Media publication. (Close friends with Donald Trump, Pecker would later be implicated in the "catch and kill" scandals in which he had buried Trump's sexual indiscretions during the 2016 presidential campaign. Funny how the world works: when Mohammed bin Salman made his much-ballyhooed visit to the United States in 2018, to meet with President Trump, American Media flooded Washington, DC, with a nearly one-hundred-page commemorative magazine, the *New Kingdom*. On the cover, around a regal photo of MBS, were hyperbolic headlines such as "Our Closest Middle East Ally Destroying Terrorism" and "Improving Lives of His People & Hopes for Peace.")

The artifice that had been carefully constructed by Tiger and Steiny came crashing down on Thanksgiving 2009, touching off the most salacious sex scandal of the internet age. It is easy to forget now the intensity with which it raged: the steady stream of exceptionally graphic text messages that Woods's girlfriends leaked to the press; the front-cover treatment of the *New York Post* for twenty straight days; the furtive photograph of Woods at a sex addiction treatment facility in Hattiesburg, Mississippi, looking both haunted and hunted. Steinberg initially contended publicly that he had been clueless about his client's serial infidelity, though various paramours of Woods contradicted that. (The quid pro quo with the *National Enquirer* didn't come out until later.) The superagent gave a performative interview in which he said he had "had to do a lot of soul-searching" about remaining Woods's agent. Would Steiny really have divorced himself from the man who had made his career?

"I'm not sure much there is validity to that," says Johnston, his tone drier than the Sahara. "I would be skeptical of that."

Both the Woods and Steinberg brands were badly damaged by the scandal. It came at an inopportune time for Steinberg because his relationship had become frosty with the man who had bought IMG after McCormack's death in March 2003, Theodore Forstmann, a private equity superstar. Forstmann was also a legendary swordsman who counted Princess Diana, Elizabeth Hurley, and Padma Lakshmi among his conquests. He thought he understood Woods in a way that no one else at IMG possibly could, and he wanted to directly oversee Tiger's image reclamation. Steinberg remained overprotective of his client, and his cold war with Forstmann escalated. Eventually, says Johnston, "Teddy told Mark he was no longer welcome at IMG."

And thus Steinberg—and Woods— decamped for Excel Sports Management in May 2011. That was the beginning of the end of IMG's long reign. (After Forstmann died of brain cancer in November 2011, IMG was sold again, to William Morris Endeavor, which deemphasized player representation.) Smaller boutique agencies had already become more prominent across the landscape of professional golf, and now they proliferated. With the zeal of a spurned lover, Steinberg began building Excel into an industry power, luring the veterans Justin Rose, Gary Woodland, and Matt Kuchar and signing young talent: Justin Thomas, Collin Morikawa, Matt Fitz-patrick, and Daniel Berger, among others. Rival agencies carved out their own identities.

Impact Point became a factor by focusing on Europeans and Spanish-speaking international players, thanks to the genial presence of Carlos Rodriguez, a native of Spain, whose close relationship with José María Olazábal helped him land Sergio García. Rodriguez's business partner has long been the intense and pugnacious Irek Myskow. Approached at a tournament about doing an interview for this book, Myskow said, "Look around you, man. This is all make-believe bullshit. None of this matters. There are kids dying in Ukraine, who gives a fuck about any of this? I grew up in Communist Poland—we had it so bad it makes today's North Korea look like a vacation. How can you expect me to care about any of this? Go find another bozo."

An American counterpart of Impact Point was GSE Worldwide. GSE was born in 2019 when a private equity firm gobbled up the former TLA Worldwide and rebranded it. TLA had focused on baseball, with some 175 clients, but it had emerged as a scrappy force in golf by signing promising up-and-comers; in 2015, it had landed Bryson DeChambeau, the most coveted amateur to make the scene in years. In a highly competitive field, the firm's success rankled its counterparts. "They engage in what we call 'paper pushing,'" sniffs a rival agent. "They come in and tell a young player, 'Sign with us and we will guarantee you a half a million dollars a year in endorsement income.' Sounds great, and since no one other agency is guaranteeing that, the player signs. But now [GSE] has to cut a bunch of deals or they're going to lose their ass. So they chase every dollar, even if it's a bad fit for the player. And if the player hates the deal and turns it down, they say, 'Okay, fine, that money you would have made counts against the guarantee.' So then the player feels pressured to take the deal, even if it's for the wrong ball or the wrong driver. It's not a healthy dynamic."

Andrew Witlieb, the president of GSE, calls these "false accusations" that are "completely out of line," adding, "This is clearly an attempt to sabotage GSE due to the success of our clients. There are plenty of things we can say about other agencies and their business practices, but that is not how we do business. Our client roster speaks for itself."

GSE acquired Impact Point in 2019, creating a powerhouse agency with a roster that included Abraham Ancer, Sam Burns, Paul Casey, Branden Grace, Kurt Kitayama, Jason Kokrak, Sebastián Muñoz, Joaquin Niemann, Louis Oosthuizen, Carlos Ortiz, J. J. Spaun, and Jhonattan Vegas. When LIV Golf was launched, Excel and GSE found themselves in the middle of a once-in-a-lifetime bidding war for golf talent. Augusta, Georgia, became a key battlefield.

The Masters is always the biggest week of the year for golf's power brokers, who dine on the back veranda of the Augusta National clubhouse and huddle under the famous oak tree, to say nothing of the many corporate dinners and parties that are held every night. In April 2022, the air was alive with talk of LIV Golf; it was as palpable as the pollen. "As agents, we have a fiduciary responsibility to the client to pursue every opportunity under the sun," says Barnhardt. "If Krispy Kreme puts out the word they want to sign players, we would all be wooing them. Because of the money being offered by LIV, you can imagine the frenzy. It was nonstop. Every player you can think of got an offer."

As always, the meetings were conducted behind closed doors. But LIV still cast a stink cloud over the 2022 Masters. Mickelson, a three-time champion, was noticeably absent as his exile continued. At the traditional Tuesday-night champions' dinner, Gary Player ruffled a few feathers by offering a passionate defense of Mickelson; the Black Knight represented South Africa throughout the apartheid years, so he knows what it feels like to be a golfing pariah. It had not yet been made public, but Mickelson had been suspended for a year by the PGA Tour. (According to the player handbook,

"Public comments that a member knows, or should reasonably know, will harm the reputation or financial best interest of PGA Tour . . . shall be considered conduct unbecoming a professional.") It was the final breaking point in a fractious relationship. LIV Golf showed Mickelson mercy by not pulling its offer, but, according to a LIV executive, it did give Mickelson "a haircut" and he received "substantially less" than the $200 million that had previously been offered.

Mickelson was supposed to be LIV's key building block, but for the time being, he had become damaged goods. So more than ever, LIV badly needed box-office draws. With two months to go before the first event, efforts were redoubled to nab major championship winners and Ryder Cup heroes. LIV was also targeting young talent, with an emphasis on U.S. Amateur champions. In Augusta, LIV again hosted agents for negotiations. The talks were led by its player relations team: Jed Moore, a big man who talks in excited paragraphs; Gary Davidson, short and wiry, with a Scottish accent thicker than Turnberry fescue; and Richard Marsh, who has a vast hipster sneaker collection and looks like the actor Gerard Butler. The triumvirate had been engaging with agents going back to their consulting arrangement with the Premier Golf League. But the PGL offers were based largely on equity in the teams and thus had been mostly theoretical. Now shit had gotten real.

"Once LIV announced their schedule, they forfeited all of their leverage," says an agent who sent multiple clients to LIV. "They had to have players, and you could feel the desperation. The numbers started going up. Quickly."

As always, Steinberg was in the middle of everything. Over a period of a few months in early 2022, he had a series of meetings with Moore and Marsh, though he betrayed little interest in LIV. "Steiny was very careful to always protect the relationship he has with the PGA Tour," says a LIV executive. Moore and Marsh were trying to get an audience with Woods to present a blockbuster offer. Norman would later call it "mind-blowingly enormous," adding, "We're talking about high nine digits." That was typical Normanian hyperbole as it is hard to put an actual number on the deal since much of its value would be abstract. LIV was proposing to give Woods 100 percent equity in his own franchise; other would-be captains were offered only a 25 percent stake. "Whether it's Michael Jordan or Derek Jeter or Magic Johnson or now Tom Brady, a lot of GOATs wind up owning or buying into teams," says the LIV executive. "We wanted to make Tiger the GOAT of all GOATs and give him a piece of the league itself. What is five percent of LIV Golf worth? Potentially a lot." No number for the up-front money was ever settled upon because LIV could never get Steinberg to engage fully, mirroring the lack of interest of his boss.

After destroying his right leg in a one-car accident in February 2021, at a time when he was still recovering from yet another back surgery, Woods already knew he had a limited number of swings left in his brittle body; he was disinclined to waste a single one of them on a newfangled golf league, not when he remained stuck on eighty-two career PGA Tour wins, tied for the all-time record with Sam Snead. If LIV somehow could have signed Woods, it might have landed Steinberg, too. According to three LIV golfers, Steinberg was initially offered the CEO position to run the entire operation, the job that Greg Norman ultimately took. Justin Rose, a longstanding client of Steinberg, told me in January 2023, "I did hear that, a long time ago. I never talked to Steiny about it. I'm not sure it ever got to the stage of serious discussion. But there was definitely noise around it, and you can see how it would make sense from LIV's standpoint." For his part, Steinberg says, "Absolutely not."

As negotiations between an array of agents and LIV reached a fever pitch, Excel clients were largely absent from the discussion. Says a contemporary of Rose's who wound up with LIV, "If my name is not attached, I will tell you straight up that Rosey was fucking desperate to get out here. He was dying to make a deal. That it didn't happen tells me something went very wrong with the process and it had nothing to do with the player."

Rose, a proper English gent, sounds Churchillian in addressing the topic. "Who you talk to determines your point of view," he says. "If you're in a camp that's willing to have that conversation [about going to LIV], it becomes more real. There is safety in numbers. You see guys stepping across that threshold, it doesn't seem like such a crazy decision. So there's momentum within an organization, or there is a lack of it. From my point of view, Steiny has had an open dialogue [with LIV]. He's had his ear to the ground. Clearly, he has a lot of skin in the game in terms of who he represents, and he has to play it quite carefully given that. Listen, if I wanted to go in that direction, he wouldn't shy away from having to have those conversations on my behalf. I have considered it, and I will consider it."

Most of the skin to which Rose refers comes by way of Woods, who behind the scenes became a strong advocate on behalf of the Tour. I asked Woods if he has any influence on Excel clients' decision-making. "I do not, no," he said. "I certainly have had my opinion with Steiny and the company, but that's about Excel and what they want to do. No, I do not have any direct influence with them."

Aha, so you have indirect influence, then?

Woods couldn't quite suppress a smirk. "I have my opinions, yes."

Unlike at Excel, the GSE folks were drowning in LIV offers. That provided a distinct competitive advantage, as the GSE agents had a more complete understanding of the market. Says Alastair Johnston, "The reason IMG was so successful in the early days was because we represented so many players. We knew the rate cards, even though they were never written down. There is no stock exchange for a player's services, but there is a whole lot of intelligence you can glean from being immersed in the industry. As a player, you want your agent to have access to as much data as possible."

As more and more GSE players began leaning LIV, a certain peer pressure developed. "I think a couple of guys got pulled along, but only a couple," says a GSE golfer who signed with LIV. Rodriguez pushes back on the notion that he or his colleagues, enticed by mega commissions, nudged their players toward LIV. "My job is to present the good, the bad and the ugly to the player and let them decide," he says. "You can't lie to players, you can't steer them in one direction or the other. It's their life, and they have other people around them to help make decisions—financial advisers, wives, friends. They are going to do what's best for them, not what's best for their agent. Every time. They're the superstars. I'm replaceable, they're not. I know that, and they know that. So I'm only interested in what's best for them."

The dealmaking continued into May 2022. Steinberg's client Justin Thomas prevailed at the PGA Championship to return to the front ranks of the game, but the biggest thunderbolt of the week might have been Dustin Johnson's press conference musings about LIV: "I think golf is in a good spot, and I think what they're doing is—could potentially be good for the game of golf. I'm excited to see what happens here in a few weeks." That was the first public signal of what the LIV folks had known for weeks: DJ was back in play!

It had been three months since his pledge of allegiance to the Tour in the wake of the Mickelson comments, and Johnson, a man not normally prone to introspection, had been ruminating on his professional life. His emotional Masters victory in November 2020 was the twenty-fourth win of his PGA Tour career, a figure bettered by only sixteen players in the postwar era. He took a victory lap at the 2021 Ryder Cup, going 5–0 to lead the United States to a lopsided victory. Still, Johnson had taken his foot off the gas pedal ever so slightly after the Masters win, as 2021 was his first winless season on the PGA Tour. Off the course he seemed more content than ever. His long engagement with Paulina Gretzky certainly had its ups and downs; in 2018, Gretzky created tabloid headlines by deleting every photo of her fiancé from her Instagram account, and the *Daily Mail* subsequently reported that it was because of Johnson's peccadillo with a toothsome socialite and fellow member of Sherwood Country Club. But by all accounts Johnson had grown into a doting dad, and after nine years of being betrothed, he and Paulina finally tied the knot in April 2022. He was thirty-seven. Privately, he began telling intimates he was tiring of the grind and wanted to start tapering off his playing schedule. The plan was for LIV golfers to play ten events in 2023 and fourteen the following season. As Johnson would later say, "Pretty simple: If someone offered anyone a job doing the same thing they were already doing, but less time at the office and they're going to pay them more, pretty sure you're going to take it. And something's wrong with you if you don't."

If Johnson was looking for advice about breakaway leagues, his father-in-law knows firsthand about the life-changing money they can provide: in 1978, at seventeen, Wayne Gretzky signed a seven-year, $1.75 million contract with the Indianapolis Racers of the renegade World Hockey Association, He played only eight games for Indy before the floundering finances of the WHA led to his being shipped off to the NHL's Edmonton Oilers, which honored his contract and then extended it the following year. Says one LIV executive, "Sports history was on our side. If Dustin was relying on Wayne's advice, we knew he'd take the fucking money."

Johnson had a LIV offer on the table going back to the summer of 2021. Now, with the first event in London only weeks away, the signing bonus was sweetened to $150 million. The offer would expire at one second before midnight on May 31. The clock was ticking, and LIV's initial credibility would largely be determined by whether Johnson signed on the dotted line.

In the meantime, LIV continued to scramble to fill out its initial field. Tom Hoge is an example of how quickly a player's fortunes can turn. At the start of 2022, he was an anonymous journeyman on the PGA Tour. Then he outdueled Jordan Spieth to win the Pebble Beach Pro-Am for his first PGA Tour victory. Suddenly, in early May, a LIV offer materialized. "I had to strongly consider it for sure because it was a lot of money, and I came to the realization it's probably more money than I'll ever make in my career out here," says Hoge, whose career PGA Tour earnings to that point were $9.7 million.

Was the LIV offer eight figures?

"I got to do some math here," Hoge said.

Sir, that would be $10 million or more.

"Yes, it was," Hoge said. "You start thinking about really weird things at that point. What if I fall down the stairs and break my arm and never make a dollar playing golf again? And you look at supporting your wife and family, and you almost feel guilty by turning it down at that point. So I went through that thought process and kind of ran the whole spectrum of thoughts through my head."

LIV recruited another unlikely player in Andy Ogletree. He had won the 2019 U.S. Amateur as a sweet-swinging southern boy at Georgia Tech, but his professional career had failed to achieve liftoff due to injuries and his desultory play. LIV offered him only a spot in the London field, with no guarantees beyond the $120,000 that a last-place finish would pay.

Talor Gooch was another under-the-radar player whom LIV targeted. He grew up in Midwest City, a small Air Force town outside Oklahoma City. His home away from home became the John Conrad Regional Golf Course, a no-frills public track. An unusual feature of John Conrad was the convicts who performed community service by tending to the golf course in their orange jumpsuits. Many of Gooch's rivals attended a fancy high school in Edmond that was a golf powerhouse. Gooch would surreptitiously snap photos of the felons and send them to his adversaries with the message "I hope you're enjoying Oak Tree"—the very private club where the other team practiced. "I guess I've always had a little chip on my shoulder," he says, redundantly.

Gooch never won an individual title at Oklahoma State, but he got incrementally better each year, earning third-team All-America honors as a senior. Upon turning pro in 2014, he repeated the pattern of slow, steady progress. He played in Canada in 2015 and '16 and then graduated to the Korn Ferry Tour, where he won the 2017 Visit Knoxville Open. That shot him to the PGA Tour. He barely kept his job in 2018, gaining partial status by finishing 139th on the FedEx Cup list, but he improved to 101st in 2019 and to 60th the following year. In the fall of 2021, Gooch finally caught fire, culminating in a breakthrough win at the RSM Classic at the Sea Island Club on St. Simons Island, Georgia. After the victory, he broke ground on a dream house for his college sweetheart, Ally, and their baby daughter, Collins, in Oklahoma City's old-money enclave of Nichols Hills. "Growing up I thought, 'Gawd, those rich bastards,'" Gooch says with a laugh. "It's so crazy, my buddy who's a baseball player for the Phillies [J. T. Realmuto] bought a house about a block and a half from where we're building, and we talk about 'I can't believe we've turned into those people.' We never imagined that we would be thinking about private school for our kids and stuff like that. We're kind of disappointed in ourselves, but it's also cool."

As a former middle-class striver, Gooch found the LIV riches intoxicating. He was also seduced by the notion of being a trailblazer. "Talor always wanted to be in the limelight in professional golf," says his college coach, Mike McGraw. "I definitely think he believes it's good for his brand. Any notoriety must be good, right?" Now, having played the best golf of his life at exactly the right time, Gooch had a fat offer on the table with the first LIV Golf event just days away. But more money can lead to mo' problems. Individual deals vary, but the industry standard is that golfers keep all of their on-course earnings while their agents take 20 percent of endorsement income and appearance fees. The LIV offers, with guaranteed upfront money and tournaments with no cuts and thus built-in minimum paydays, created new gray areas. Because a last place finish would pay $120,000, some agents considered that a de facto appearance fee and planned to commission the first $120K of a player's winnings. What to do about the bloated signing bonuses? It wasn't exactly money won on the golf course or a traditional endorsement deal; who deserved what? "We basically met in the middle," says a GSE golfer who signed with LIV. "It wasn't their normal cut, but it was fair. They didn't gouge anyone. They knew they were going to be ringing the bell over and over, they didn't need to be greedy. And neither did I. There was plenty to go around."

Not every negotiation was so amicable. Gooch's career-long agent was Jeff Stacy. He had finagled the sponsor's exemption for Gooch's first start on the PGA Tour in 2014, when Gooch was fresh out of college, and had held his client's hand during the lean years in the minor leagues when he was struggling to find his footing on the PGA Tour. Now LIV was dangling more money than either of them could have ever dreamed of: $30 million. But just weeks before LIV Golf London was to begin, Gooch and Stacy parted ways, due to what the player calls "philosophical differences." If Gooch was heading to LIV, it would be with a new agent. Stacy became a cautionary tale among his brethren. Says one agent, "Cold fucking world, man."

9.

ON APRIL 20, 2022, AN UNUSUAL BIT OF NEWS WENT OUT on the wire: Jack Nicklaus was suing himself. Well, not exactly. The Nicklaus Companies, of which the man himself had sold 51 percent of his interest in 2007 for $145 million, was suing Big Jack for breach of contract, tortious interference, and breach of fiduciary duty. The lawsuit, filed in the Supreme Court of the State of New York, alleged that Nicklaus had scooped up appearance fees for himself and not the company and improperly engaged in negotiations with a video game developer. By far the most incendiary allegation concerned—what else?—Saudi money.

The complaint (which read more like a press release than a legal filing, seemingly by design) made the headline-generating claim that Nicklaus had been about to throw in with LIV Golf until his corporate minders stepped in. "Fortunately for Nicklaus Companies—and Mr. Nicklaus—the Company was eventually able to convince Mr. Nicklaus to stop exploring a deal for the endorsement of the Saudi-backed league," the suit charged. "The Company essentially saved Mr. Nicklaus from himself by extricating him from a controversial project that could have not only tarnished his legacy and reputation, but severely damaged the Nicklaus Companies' name, brands and business. Thanks to the intervention of Nicklaus Companies, the Company was able to minimize fallout from the situation and protect the goodwill and good name of both the Company and Mr. Nicklaus. . . . If not for the efforts of Nicklaus Companies, Mr. Nicklaus could have been pilloried in the news media for accepting payment for what could be characterized as betraying the PGA Tour."

Nicklaus had his first meeting with His Excellency Yasir Al-Rumayyan at the 2019 Masters, and those conversations led to a deal for the creation of Qiddiya, the first Nicklaus Design course in the Middle East to be overseen by Jack. His business partners didn't seem to mind the Saudi money back then: GOLF.com and Nicklaus Design are part of the same corporate family, and the website covered the project so enthusiastically that the wags at *No Laying Up* began referring to it as "Gulf.com."

Covid prevented Nicklaus from making a site visit to Qiddiya, but he continued having conversations with the Saudis. In May 2021, Al-Rumayyan, Majed Al-Sorour, and a coterie of assistants met with Nicklaus and his people at the Bear's Club in Jupiter, Florida. The legendary Hollywood producer Robert Evans liked to say, "There are three sides to every story: yours, mine, and the truth." Two people who were in the room at the Bear's Club tell very different stories. A member of the LIV team says, "Jack was lovely. He was very receptive. We explained our vision: to invest hundreds of millions of dollars into the Asian Tour to expand playing opportunities at the developmental level; to create a new global tour for the game's best players and pay them what they're truly worth; and to give back to the game through charitable endeavors. Jack said, 'I can see you have your hearts in the right place, and I'd like to be a part of it.'"

A person in Nicklaus's inner circle says, "Jack made it clear he wasn't interested. He said, 'Along with Arnold Palmer and Gardner Dickinson, I helped create the PGA Tour. I host a tournament on the PGA Tour. My legacy is through the PGA Tour.'" (Never mind that Nicklaus led a failed coup against commissioner Deane Beman in 1983, largely because he believed the Tour's expanding TPC network was hurting his golf course design business.)

About two weeks later, Nicklaus sent a letter to Al-Rumayyan saying that he would not take any role with Golf Saudi. "By accepting your offer I would be turning my back on what I created and have championed," he wrote. (He gave a copy of the letter to Jay Monahan, who still keeps it on his desk.) What did or did not compel Nicklaus to write the letter is the crux of the lawsuit. Nicklaus later told Michael Bamberger of the Fire Pit Collective, "I was offered something in excess of $100 million by the Saudis, to do the job probably similar to the one that Greg [Norman] is doing. I turned it down. Once verbally, once in writing." The LIV source says that the octogenarian Nicklaus was never in line for a day-to-day CEO job but rather a promotional, ceremonial role; there was talk of creating a Jack Nicklaus Trophy. This person scoffs at the $100 million figure, saying, "We never discussed a dollar amount he would be paid. It was a preliminary, conceptual conversation."

The Nicklaus v. Nicklaus lawsuits continue to drag on with bruising depositions and titillating headlines; in May 2023, the Golden Bear filed suit accusing the Nicklaus Companies of defamation relating to its public statements that he wanted the Saudi money. It's a sad state of affairs for the eighty-three-year-old living legend, but the unpleasantness has not been the only public controversy for late-period Jack. In October 2020, near the end of one of the most contentious presidential campaigns in U.S. history, Nicklaus posted on social media that he had just cast his vote for his golfing buddy Donald Trump and offered a ringing endorsement of the man. (Vice President Mike Pence had called Nicklaus to appeal for his public support; someone close to Nicklaus says, "I think the president was afraid to do it in case he got turned down.") In his post, Nicklaus wrote that Trump has "delivered on his promises" and "worked for the average person," while being "more diverse than any President I have seen and has tried to help people from all walks of life—equally. . . . If we want to continue to have the opportunity to pursue the American Dream, and not evolve into a socialist America and have the government run your life, then I strongly recommend you consider Donald J. Trump for another 4 years." Trump would narrowly carry Ohio, the state where Nicklaus had grown up, and Florida, where he has spent his adult life.

Nicklaus was hailed for the courage of his convictions in conservative circles while those on the other end of the political spectrum expressed disappointment, even outrage. Representative of this was a reply below Nicklaus's tweet by David Jones, a columnist for the *Patriot-News* of Harrisburg, Pennsylvania, who wrote, "I've had to listen to this guy's gibberish my whole life. We went to the same high school. What he knows about is . . . golf. Hard to find a more prosaic and simple-minded person who's had a greater opportunity to understand the larger world and yet grasps only his tiny sliver of it."

Why would Nicklaus wade into such an overheated debate, with no public prompting? In *All the President's Men*, Deep Throat provided an enduring road map for understanding political behavior: "Just follow the money." In the Trump administration's fiscal funding plan for 2020, $20 million was earmarked for a mobile children's hospital project at Miami's Nicklaus Children's Hospital. Jack had lobbied the president during one of their rounds of golf together, and Politico later reported, "Trump personally directed [the Department of Health and Human Services] to earmark the funds."

For the president, it was a small price to pay for the chance to sportswash his reputation through Nicklaus, just as Trump had laundered public opinion when he had flown in for the trophy presentation at the 2017 Presidents Cup; when he had spent three days at, and tweeted eight times about, the 2017 U.S. Women's Open conducted at his eponymous course in Bedminster, New Jersey; with his company's endorsement deal that had compelled Bryson DeChambeau to wear the word TRUMP on his sleeve; when he had presented Tiger Woods with the Presidential Medal of Freedom following the 2019 Masters; and, most especially, when he had awarded Gary Player and Annika Sörenstam the Presidential Medal of Freedom the day *after* the January 6, 2021, riots. For Trump, the loving embrace of professional golfers was especially valuable because so many other athletes publicly scorned him; championship-winning teams in various sports had declined invitations to the White House or never received one because the players noisily made it known that they wouldn't attend. In 2017, the Golden State Warriors fell somewhere in between: they received an invitation but, after the mild-mannered Steph Curry excoriated Trump in *USA Today* and said that the team would not go to the White House, the president, in a huff, withdrew the invitation on Twitter. That led LeBron James to tweet at Trump, "U bum[,] @StephenCurry30 already said he ain't going! So therefore ain't no invite. Going to White House was a great honor until you showed up!"

No wonder Trump found sanctuary in the gentleman's game. When he was in the White House, golf never seemed far from his mind. In perhaps the most cogent analysis of how he had taken the electoral college while losing the popular vote, he said, "If you're a golfer, it's like match play versus stroke play." To illustrate his contention of widespread voter fraud in the 2016 election, he cited to a gathering of lawmakers that two-time Masters champ Bernhard Langer had been unable to vote at a polling place in Florida, while several people "who did not look as if they should be allowed to vote" had been permitted to cast provisional ballots. One complication with that spurious anecdote: Langer, a German national, is not a U.S. citizen and is not eligible to vote here. In a meeting with business leaders at the White House, Trump coaxed Jeff Immelt, the CEO of General Electric, into telling the story of having witnessed the president make a hole in one years earlier. While TV cameras rolled, Immelt said, "President Trump goes up to a par-3 on his course. He looks at the three of us and says, 'You realize, of course, I'm the richest golfer in the world.' Then [he] gets a hole in one. So I have to say, I've seen the magic before."

Trump interjected, "It's crazy—actually, I said I was the best golfer of all the rich people, to be exact, and then I got a hole in one. So it was sort of cool."

Growing up in Queens as an outer-borough striver, Trump was attuned to the status markers of the ruling class. Private golf clubs were and remain a particular obsession of his. He could buy the gaudiest house in Palm Beach—Mar-a-Lago—and he did, but he would never be invited to join Seminole Golf Club in Juno Beach, where Ben Hogan wintered every year to prepare for the Masters. (According to club lore, Trump's chances of admission vanished when he dined there with his then wife, Marla Maples, and she breast-fed their infant daughter, Tiffany, in view of the ladies who were lunching.) As a real estate developer Trump may have reshaped skylines up and down the East Coast, but citadels such as Augusta National, Pine Valley, and Shinnecock Hills remain beyond his grasp, their memberships prizing discretion and old money. If building skyscrapers is pure id, creating golf courses is a chance to play God by reshaping the earth, so Trump created a series of monuments to himself, replete with man-made waterfalls. The perennial outsider now has nine eponymous private enclaves of his own to go to along with seven high-end public properties across three continents. Yet that wasn't enough; he hungered for the validation that would come with hosting major championships. Surprisingly, Tom Wolfe never wrote a book about Donald Trump, but he understood men like him on a granular level, once saying, "I think every living moment of a human being's life, unless the person is starving or in immediate danger of death in some other way, is controlled by a concern for status."

Hosting the 2017 U.S. Women's Open was a minor triumph for Trump, the culmination of more than a decade of intensive wooing of USGA officials. The Women's Open gets minimal media attention and is rarely a moneymaker for the host venue, but Trump gladly signed on, knowing that it could be a stepping-stone to what he covets most, hosting a U.S. Open at his crown jewel, Trump Bedminster. "I might be an old man being wheeled around or even dead," he told Bamberger in 2011, "but it'll happen."

He landed the next best thing, the 2022 PGA Championship. (It had been awarded in 2014, before Trump's foray into politics.) Hosting the PGA Championship took on extra significance when, in 2016, the PGA Tour took away its World Golf Championship from Trump Doral, as both the Tour and potential title sponsors were leery of the host overshadowing the event. The dis came in the midst of Trump's presidential campaign, which frequently featured inflammatory rhetoric about Mexican immigrants. That the Doral event was being moved to Mexico City led to much chortling, including by Rory McIlroy, who said, "We'll just jump over the wall."

And then the January 6, 2021, riots happened. The CEO of the PGA of America, Seth Waugh, said, "I watched it with overwhelming sadness, thinking how many people have died protecting the peaceful transfer of power. I felt revulsion, sadness, outrage, a bit of anger. I thought, This is a tragic moment for our way of life."

Waugh became CEO in 2018, inheriting the PGA Championship at Trump Bedminster. Four days after January 6, the PGA of America yanked its tournament from Trump and relocated it to Southern Hills Country Club in Tulsa, Oklahoma, a rare showing of backbone by a governing body. "Everybody wants to make this a political move, but we got put into a political place that was not of our own making," Waugh said. "My feeling was we could do existential damage to our brand by staying at Bedminster. If we stayed, the 2022 PGA would be about its ownership. People would think we were making a statement by staying there. I felt like we could do permanent damage to the brand if we stayed. As did the board."

Nicklaus was unhappy about the treatment of his friend and patron, saying "This move is cancel culture. Donald Trump may be a lot of things, but he loves golf and he loves this country. He's a student of the game and a formidable figure in the game. What he does in the future in golf will depend on what the cancel culture will allow him to do." "Cancel culture" has become an overly broad term employed in many ways, but a useful definition is "the consequences of one's actions."

Shunned by the PGA Tour and PGA of America, slow-played by the USGA, ignored by Scotland's Royal & Ancient (which refuses to bring the Open back to Trump Turnberry even though it is one of the best courses in the world and has a rich Open history), Trump had no options for hosting tournaments in the men's game—until LIV Golf arrived. He rushed into the embrace of the Saudis. Asked about the Trump-LIV nexus, Sergio García says, "Hey, we have to play where people want us." Indeed, a LIV executive says, "When putting together the schedule, the list of courses was not long, particularly in year one. Very few were willing to take the risk. But the Trump Organization raised their hand and they have a huge portfolio—not only of very good golf courses but venues with the necessary infrastructure to support the fan village, parking, the broadcast compound, all the things that go into a big tournament, which many courses can't accommodate." Then there is the marketing power of joining forces with the president of the United States. Says the LIV exec, "Does Trump bring ten or twenty times the global exposure? Abso-fucking-lutely. But we knew going in it could be a double-edged sword."

To serve as a host venue, Trump Bedminster was paid $2.9 million (according to Trump Organization COO Larry Glick), $4.5 million (per a well-connected member of the club), or less than $2 million according to another LIV executive, who says, "They could have held out for a lot more." (In Trump's financial disclosure released in early 2023, the exact number was obscured within broader revenue reporting for Bedminster.) But any seven-figure payday is an eye-catching number for a foreign monarchy to be funneling to the business of a former president, and the announcement of the LIV Golf schedule touched off renewed questions about Trump's (and son-in-law Jared Kushner's) financial ties to Saudi Arabia.

When subsequent court filings confirmed what everyone already knew—that the Public Investment Fund owned 93 percent of LIV Golf and paid 100 percent of its expenses—the advocacy group Jamal Khashoggi had founded, DAWN, called for a congressional investigation. "The revelation that a fund controlled by Crown Prince MBS actually owns almost all of LIV Golf means that MBS has been paying Donald Trump unknown millions for the past two years, via their mutual corporate covers," tweeted Sarah Leah Whitson, DAWN's executive director. "The national security implications of payments from a grotesquely abusive foreign dictator to a president of the United States who provided extraordinary favors to him are as dangerous as they are shocking."

Four years after his murder, Khashoggi continued to be part of the discourse around Saudi Arabia and, inevitably, LIV Golf. At a press event at the Centurion Club, a couple weeks ahead of LIV London being played there, Norman was asked about Khashoggi. He said, "Look, we've all made mistakes, and you just want to learn by those mistakes and how you can correct them going forward."

The outrage and condemnation came fast and furious, from Amnesty International and even from within LIV: chief commercial officer Sean Bratches resigned in protest. For a splashy event during the London tournament, LIV had rented Alexandra Palace, an iconic venue that dates to 1863. In the wake of Norman's comment, the palace pulled the plug on the party and LIV had to scramble to relocate. Now, *that* is cancel culture.

10.

MAY 31, 2022, WAS PERHAPS THE TENSEST DAY IN THE short history of LIV Golf. The contract offers that had been tendered to various players were due to expire at midnight, locking in the field for the inaugural event in London. The draft of the press release announcing the identity of the LIV pioneers was rewritten more than a few times. But throughout the long day and into the night, one question loomed largest: Whither Dustin Johnson? Phil Mickelson was still in the hurt locker, and his status remained uncertain. Talor Gooch, one of LIV's most intriguing potential prospects, had made it clear that he wouldn't leave the PGA Tour unless Johnson did. LIV needed a superstar to supercharge its inaugural field announcement, and DJ was the most viable candidate. Finally, deep into the night, the news arrived at the speed of light: Johnson was signed, sealed, and delivered. Minutes later, the Johnson-centric version of the press release went out, trumpeting the signings. Four years had passed since the news first broke about the initial stirrings of the Premier Golf League. The road to London had been circuitous but, at long last, golf had a breakaway league, with actual players.

As expected, Johnson starred in virtually every headline about LIV's announced slate of forty-two players. No Excel Sports Management clients took the plunge, but three GSE players did: Masters champion Sergio García (who had once dated Greg Norman's daughter, Morgan-Leigh; even after she broke his heart, García had remained close to the Shark); British Open champ Louis Oosthuizen; and Branden Grace, the winner of eleven tournaments across the European and PGA tours. (More GSE clients would soon be announced.) The final spots in the London field would be filled the following week through the top five finishers at an Asian Tour International Series event and one final "Commissioner's Pick." Given Mickelson's flair for the dramatic, everyone in golf believed that special invitation would go to Lefty. The suspense grew.

Besides Johnson, all of the players with any kind of name recognition came from outside the United States: García (Spain); Oosthuizen (South Africa); Masters champion Charl Schwartzel (South Africa); U.S. Open champ Graeme McDowell (Northern Ireland); two-time major champion Martin Kaymer (Germany); and English Ryder Cup stars Ian Poulter and Lee Westwood. For those international players, commuting among tours had long been a way of life, and they didn't have the same reverence for the PGA Tour as many American pros did. Of course, they were all thirty-seven years old or older. Instantly, the perception of LIV became that of a tour where veteran (read: past-their-prime) players were heading for a highly lucrative, low-stress farewell tour. It was the opposite of the PGA Tour's traditional meritocracy.

That context made Gooch's signing so impactful. Other than Johnson, Gooch generated the most buzz because he was youngish (thirty) and ascendant (thirty-fifth in the world ranking), meaning that he was risking the most by jilting the PGA Tour. *Golf Digest* called his jump "a legitimate shock."

LIV partially countered the over-the-hill-gang narrative with notable success in luring young talents at the outset of their careers, headlined by James Piot, the baby-faced reigning U.S. Amateur champion who had turned pro to sign a multiyear deal with LIV. So did David Puig, 20, a native of Spain who had been an All-American at Arizona State, and Turk Pettit, the 2021 NCAA champ from Clemson. Andy Ogletree, 24, the 2019 U.S. Amateur champ, took the LIV offer to play in London. Also announced was Ratchanon Chantananuwat, 15, the number eight amateur in the world, who had become the youngest winner of an event on an OWGR-sanctioned tour when he beat Tom Kim at an Asian Mixed Series event in Thailand. He would play as an amateur to gain experience, a refreshing concept given the nonstop talk about money. And then there was Chase Koepka. Brooks's kid brother, twenty-eight, had spent the previous half-dozen years struggling in golf's minor leagues. His signing felt like when a college basketball team hires as an assistant coach the dad of a superstar high school senior to aid in the recruiting process.

Beyond Johnson, Gooch, and Mickelson, LIV successfully wooed only two other Americans with long PGA Tour résumés: Kevin Na (age thirty-eight, five Tour wins, $37 million in career earnings) and Hudson Swafford (age thirty-four, three wins, $9.7 million). But there was another intriguing Yank in the mix: Peter Uihlein. A decade earlier, he had been the top-ranked amateur in the world, but Uihlein never found his footing on the PGA Tour and various other circuits. LIV offered him a needed fresh start, but what made the Uihlein signing noteworthy was the kid's dad. Wally Uihlein is a staunch traditionalist who, during his long tenure as the CEO of the parent company of Titleist and FootJoy, often bullied magazine editors by pulling or threatening to pull his company's vast advertising spending if a story didn't suit his old-school tastes. Hey, Peter, what does your dad think of your going LIV?

"I don't know, why don't you call him?" Uihlein said. "I'm sure he'll give you a detailed answer."

Wally Uihlein's cell phone number is one of the best-kept secrets in golf; a dozen well-connected folks came up empty. The younger Uihlein was called upon again and asked to provide his dad's number. "Hell, no," he said. "Absolutely not."

But, Peter, you're the one who suggested we call him!

"You gotta be kidding me," he said, laughing. "No way. You can DM him on Instagram if you want. Now get the hell outta here."

The European Tour, which had continued to wilt as the PGA

Tour pumped up its purses and bonuses, provided a more fruitful harvest as LIV plucked a handful of solid players still in their prime(-ish): Laurie Canter, Justin Harding, Sam Horsfield, Pablo Larrazábal, Adrián Otaegui, J. C. Ritchie, and Bernd Wiesberger, a member of the 2021 European Ryder Cup team. It made sense that European Tour players had little squeamishness about the oppressive political regime floating LIV, as they had learned not to worry about where the money was coming from; the European Tour would have gone out of business years before without the largesse of China, Qatar, the United Arab Emirates, and Saudi Arabia, which annually put on tournaments with the tour's biggest purses.

Once the London field dropped, two questions dominated the discourse: How much money did the players get to sign with LIV, and what would be the PGA Tour's retaliation? Jay Monahan reacted immediately and tepidly, releasing a short statement that was a nod to the fact that the Tour members had requested, and been denied, releases to play in LIV London. "As communicated to our entire membership on May 10, PGA Tour members have not been authorized to participate in the Saudi Golf League's London event, under PGA Tour Tournament Regulations," he wrote, and his insistence on calling LIV the Saudi Golf League was both petty and amusing. "Members who violate the Tournament Regulations are subject to disciplinary action." That was like an opera soprano inhaling before an aria; all the noise and melodrama was still to come, but the Tour would not act until the players made their betrayal official by striking their first tee shots in London.

As for the money, the deals varied wildly. The green jacket Schwartzel had won in 2011 still had intrinsic value, but he hadn't won anywhere in the world in six years, so he commanded only $4 million up front. Westwood and Poulter secured $10 million apiece. "They were among the first to sign," says a LIV executive, "and the longer you waited, the more you got." Na nabbed $25 million, García $55 million, Johnson $150 million. Every deal was structured differently, with the signing bonus usually spread across a couple of seasons. Players with maximum leverage, such as Johnson, got the vast majority up front; by the time he teed off in London, DJ had collected two-thirds of his bonus. Golf Channel's Brandel Chamblee tweeted, and a LIV lawyer subsequently said in court, that the signing bonuses had been advances against money won on the golf course, but numerous LIV executives vociferously deny this. "Every deal is different, so you never know," says McDowell, "but I've talked to many of the players out here, and none of them have that arrangement. Whatever you got up front, you keep, and then you chase down what you can and you keep that, too."

Players sought job security as well as money. Each captain received a four-year contract. Gooch did, too, and, like those of other top players, his includes a nonrelegation clause that he can't be demoted to the Asian Tour no matter how poorly he plays. But many players were guaranteed nothing beyond the 2022 or 2023 season. "There aren't as many long multiyear deals as people think," says one LIV executive.

On June 5, four days before the first round, LIV filled five more spots in the London field by taking the top finishers from the Asian Tour's International Series England. The next morning, LIV announced, to the surprise of no one, that Mickelson would be returning to public life in London: "I am ready to come back to play the game I love but after 32 years this new path is a fresh start, one that is exciting for me at this stage of my career and clearly transformative, not just for myself, but ideally for the game and my peers. . . . I fully realize and respect some may disagree with this decision and have strong opinions and I empathize with that." That last bit might go down as the biggest understatement in golf history.

In January 2001, President George W. Bush named Ari Fleischer the twenty-third White House press secretary. Nine months later,

Fleischer was by Bush's side as the 9/11 attacks unfolded. Fleischer would become a lightning rod in the tumultuous times that followed. He was one of the loudest voices selling the U.S. invasion of Iraq, presenting the American public with numerous lies and misleading claims about a cache of weapons of mass destruction that, it turned out, didn't exist. While the Bush administration subjected political prisoners to "enhanced interrogation"—a chilling term that came to include waterboarding, sleep deprivation, and forced nudity of detainees—Fleischer insisted, "The standard for any type of interrogation of somebody in American custody is to be humane and to follow all international laws and accords dealing with this type subject. That is precisely what has been happening, and exactly what will happen."

After leaving the White House in 2003, Fleischer cashed in with his own public relations firm. His initial foray into golf was ill fated. In March 2010, with his life aflame in scandal, Tiger Woods hired Fleischer for guidance. Fleischer left him in the lurch less than two weeks later, as Fox News reported that he had suddenly realized that "his very presence gave the impression that Woods was being stage-managed in his return to the public eye."

Even in private practice, Fleischer continued to fetishize 9/11, as every year on the anniversary he tweeted a minute-by-minute recreation of the events of the day through his own eyes. As a private citizen he didn't hold back his criticism of Saudi Arabia, the homeland of fifteen of the nineteen 9/11 hijackers. In a June 2011 tweet, he managed to disparage both the House of Saud and the sitting president, writing, "Obama copies Saudi Arabia. Has spent and is willing to spend hundreds of billions so he won't be overthrown."

The folks at LIV were clever enough to realize that their players needed media training ahead of their first tournament, but of all the flaks in the world, they somehow selected Fleischer. LIV desperately wanted to be seen as a sports league and not as a propaganda machine, but Fleischer was the most politically charged hire imaginable.

In the weeks before the London tournament, Fleischer held optional Zoom training sessions for the players. Graeme McDowell is a smooth talker and throughout his career has enjoyed an easy rapport with reporters, but he eagerly signed up. "I thought it was a great idea," he says. "We certainly were never offered that kind of support from the PGA Tour or European Tour. And Ari came with a big résumé, so I wanted to hear what he had to say." Much of the training consisted of a barrage of questions from Fleischer that McDowell calls "the craziest things you could imagine. It was helpful, honestly."

Prior to Golf Channel's launch in 1994 and the arrival of social media a decade later, pretournament press conferences were not a big deal. But now they are treated as events, filling the long days before there is any meaningful on-course action. For its first press conference in London, LIV went with a safety-in-numbers approach, bringing in McDowell alongside two of the mellowest characters in the game, Dustin Johnson and Louis Oosthuizen, and an excitable fifteen-year-old, Ratchanon Chantananuwat, whom no reporter was going to grill. Jane MacNeille, LIV's senior vice president of player communications, opened the press conference and, without any heads-up to the assembled reporters, introduced Fleischer as the moderator. "It was surreal," says Kevin Van Valkenburg, who was covering the tournament for ESPN. (He is now the editorial director at *No Laying Up*.) "If you came up with a *Saturday Night Live* skit about a LIV Golf press conference, Ari Fleischer would have been the perfect choice as the host. It seemed tone-deaf in such an obvious way: Here's a guy who tweets about 9/11 and has been supercritical of Saudi Arabia, and now he's taking LIV's money? It would have been one thing if he had been an established part of the PR rollout. But no, he was just sprung on us, like 'Live from London, with special guest star Ari Fleischer!'"

The opening minutes of the press conference were well choreographed by Fleischer, and the players' answers had a paint-by-the-numbers feel; you could almost hear the gears turning in their brains as they strained to remember their talking points. Johnson handled the tough questions with typical aplomb and brevity; like Forrest Gump, he can be accidentally profound. On the possibility of never getting to play in the Ryder Cup again, a reporter riffed, "Inevitably, people are saying on social media, and even in here, that you've chosen money over your country. What would be your reply to that?"

Johnson offered only nine words: "I chose what's best for me and my family."

London was a splashy town for a first tournament, but it came with one problem for LIV: the British press, spoiling for a fight on their home soil. "They brought the heat," McDowell says. He went off script with an honest answer about the financial realities of choosing LIV. "We have played all around the world for twenty years, chasing paychecks," he said. "It's a business. Yes, we love the sport, we love competing, but, you know, we're running a business here. It's like the sacrifice that we make being away from our families—I hate to use the word 'sacrifice.' We are all here playing golf for a living; it's a pretty sweet life. But still, you're away from your family thirty, thirty-five weeks a year. It has to be worth it financially, otherwise it's a big sacrifice you're making for no reason. You're always weighing up from a business point of view: What is the best financial outcome for me for my time spent? There are no promises on the PGA Tour. And an opportunity like this comes along where you can play the last three or four years of your career, in a very financially lucrative environment, it would be crazy to walk away from that as a businessman." Especially for a forty-two-year-old in danger of losing his PGA Tour card.

McDowell's gregariousness made him the center of the press conference. He was asked, "How do you reconcile your decision to be here with Saudi Arabia's human rights record?"

"This has been incredibly polarizing," he said. "I think we all agree up here, take the Khashoggi situation; we all agree that's reprehensible. Nobody is going to argue that fact. But we are golfers. Speaking personally, I really feel like golf is a force of good in the world. I just try to be a great role model to kids. I know what the game of golf has taught me. I love using the game of golf as something to kind of help grow around the world. That's pretty much what we've been for the last twenty years, being role models for kids and trying to use this game, like I say, as a force of good. We are not politicians. I know you guys hate that expression, but we are really not, unfortunately. We are professional golfers."

That was a solid answer, and if McDowell had stopped there, he might have escaped the press conference unscathed. But he just kept talking, straining to squeeze in another Fleischer-programmed talking point. That proved to be disastrous. Said McDowell, "If Saudi Arabia wanted to use the game of golf as a way for them to get to where they want to be and they have the resources to accelerate that experience, I think we are proud to help them on that journey using the game of golf and the abilities that we have to help grow the sport and take them to where they want to be."

Proud! McDowell's answer about money passed the smell test. But a U.S. Open champion expressing pride in providing public relations services for an autocratic foreign monarchy changed the energy in the room. Now a question was directed at the moderator, something I had never before seen in three decades on the golf beat: "Ari, you tweeted in [2011] about Saudi Arabia spending billions, hundreds of billions so they won't be overthrown. Is this golf series planned so Mohammed bin Salman won't be overthrown? Potentially to protect him? Is that what you're working towards?"

Fleischer responded, "I'm happy to talk to you about that offline. Anything I tweeted about prior to LIV, when you look at world relations, that was a long, long time ago."

Says Van Valkenburg, "The way he projected his response was

very haughty. It was like 'How dare you question me? You little people have no idea how complicated the real world is.'"

Now there was blood in the water. Rob Harris, a British writer
with the Associated Press, got in the last question, and it was a
doozy: "To the guys, particularly Graeme, you are now effectively
working as an extension of Saudi PR. You talked about how the
series is a force for good and the journey you've been told about
Saudi Arabia is on. How is that journey helping the women oppressed in Saudi Arabia; the migrant groups, their rights violated;
the LGBTQ individuals who are criminalized; the families of the
eighty-one men who were executed in March; and those being
bombed in Yemen?"

McDowell's voice had a low-grade anguish to it. "You know, I
think as golfers, if we tried to cure geopolitical situations in every
country in the world that we play golf in, we wouldn't play a lot of
golf. It's a really hard question to answer. You know, we're just here
to focus on the golf and kind of what it does globally for the role
models that these guys are and that we are, and yeah, that's a really
hard question to get into."

"Thank you very much," Fleischer said wanly, ending the press
conference. "Thank you for being here. We look forward to playing
some golf."

No doubt he did. He had to know in that moment that he had
already become a liability for LIV Golf; he would conduct no more
press conferences after the London tournament, though he remained on the LIV payroll as a "consultant." For an expert in communications, Fleischer is not very good at communicating: He didn't
respond to multiple emails requesting comment for this book.

The blowback began immediately for McDowell, as "proud" became a staple of scolding headlines and his social media channels
were filled with fury and even a few death threats. "It was ugly," he
says. "I wish I had that skill of answering questions without saying

anything at all, but that's not me. What I realized afterward was that no matter what I said, it was going to be the wrong thing. I played poorly for months after that because I was wounded by the criticism. I learned about myself that I really do care what people think of me. My skin is a little thicker now, but I'm not going to lie, it hurt."

The ensuing press conference featured Kevin Na, Talor Gooch, James Piot, and Sihwan Kim. Reporters had been told that each presser would last for thirty minutes, but after the pounding the players had taken in the first one, Fleischer and MacNeille appeared to be trying to run out the clock. They asked the players a number of gentle questions before finally calling upon reporters, who continued to press the players about the Saudi question. At the twenty-four-minute mark, shortly after another query about "sportswashing," MacNeille abruptly ended the press conference. Harris, of the Associated Press, had been raising his hand, waiting to be called upon. Now he loudly pointed out that it had not yet been thirty minutes and he still had questions to ask. MacNeille talked over him, saying "Excuse you. Excuse you. Calm down." At a high volume, Harris continued to try to ask a question. MacNeille ignored him and thanked the players for coming. They rose from their chairs and shuffled toward the exit, looking a little sheepish. Harris quick-walked toward the dais, calling out a question about "blood money." LIV director of communications Allen Barrett, a buffed former basketball player who is ordinarily mild mannered, stepped in front of Harris, and for a moment they were nose to nose, jawing at each other. A security guard materialized and nudged Harris out the door. That kind of press conference anarchy was unheard of in the normally staid sport. Other reporters began tweeting that Harris had been kicked out. Ten minutes later, having cooled off, he returned to his seat and began pounding his keyboard.

"I would say both sides were to blame," says Bob Harig, who was covering the tournament for *Sports Illustrated*. "They were trying to shut down the press conference early, but he still had questions. They could have just let him ask one or two. That would have defused it. But Rob's overreaction caused a scene that was unnecessary. We've all had press conferences end early on us—he needed to read to the room better. Everyone was already on edge, so things escalated."

The wild opening press conferences set the tone for the enduring, antagonistic vibe between LIV players and reporters. The tension did not abate the next day when the English lads, Lee Westwood and Ian Poulter, arrived in the media center. James Corrigan of the *Telegraph* often enjoys good-natured Twitter banter with each player, but he didn't come to play at the press conference, asking, "On the moral dimension as independent contractors, is there anywhere in the world you wouldn't play? If Vladimir Putin had a tournament, would you play there?"

When Poulter refused to answer such "speculation," Corrigan kept going. "Lee, would you have played in apartheid South Africa, for example?"

Westwood demurred on what he called a "hypothetical question which we can't answer."

Fleischer broke in plaintively, "Next question?"

After taking time to reflect, Westwood says, "Of course I wouldn't play in Russia. We've all seen the suffering of the Ukrainian people. But I think it's important to note that there have been professional golf tournaments in Russia [as recently as 2015], and they were conducted by the European Tour, not LIV Golf. Putin had already shown the world who he was by then, but none of the players who competed over there were criticized or belittled by reporters. Interesting, isn't it?"

The London press conferences would serve as a kind of taunt for every other golf scribe: Can you ask the tough questions, or are you a pussy? For the players on the receiving end, "it felt like we were under siege," says Westwood. One unexpected effect was, he says, that "It bonded all us together." Seemingly overnight, it became LIV against the world.

After all the early-week melodrama, the first round in London brought an unexpected relief: golf! For all the talk about LIV as a game-changing, disruptive force, at its core it's still just golfers hitting golf shots, which is a pleasant and often dull diversion.

The shotgun start had led to much derision, and in its first iteration it created a few awkward moments. "I was standing on the third tee box for about ten minutes, and there was nobody with me," says Charl Schwartzel. "And eventually I took my phone out, and I was phoning Graeme [McDowell]. I said, 'Graeme, mate, where are you? Am I on the right tee box?' That made it very different for me than what you would be used to, being announced on the first tee. But then once you got going, it was just golf for me." Except minus the architectural integrity of the design. All good courses have a rhythm like a well-crafted concerto. Think of Pebble Beach, with its gentle opening, raucous middle, and then a crescendo on the final two holes. Starting willy-nilly on a random hole destroys the architect's intent. The eighteenth at Centurion is a watery, do-or-die par 5, but Schwartzel would not end his round there. Instead he would finish on the second hole, a nondescript par 3. The benefit of the shotgun was that all the players were on the course at the same time, leading to a flurry of action. Fans (and reporters) were liberated from having to endure morning and afternoon waves, providing a condensed, easily consumable product. LIV had clearly put a lot of thought into the spectator experience, which featured fun activities for kids (face painting), excellent food (paella!), and drinks at surprisingly reasonable prices. (A few weeks earlier, Justin Thomas had taken to Twitter to scold PGA Championship officials for gouging fans $18 for a beer. LIV's lagers cost less than a third that.)

The opening round had a freewheeling, slightly chaotic energy; spectators repeatedly ducked under the ropes to get a better view of the action. Schwartzel led with a 65, but the biggest story of the day was Mickelson's return to the course. He dapped up His Excellency Al-Rumayyan on the first tee and then put together a surprisingly solid round of 69, which left him tied for seventh. Mickelson competed with the determination of a man who knew that his legacy is riding in part on the success of a renegade tour he helped launch. Is his name destined to be spoken with reverence like that of baseball's free agent pioneer Curt Flood, as an agent of change who reshaped the sports landscape? Or will the last act of his career evoke Jake La-Motta in Las Vegas, a past-his-prime palooka serving as a curiosity for fans drawn by spectacle and not sport?

I had not planned to cover LIV Golf London, but once Phil announced his return to public life, I felt compelled to be there. I caught an overnight flight and landed in London on the morning of the first round. MacNeille met me at the entry gate of the Centurion Club to hand-deliver both my media credential and a message: "Just so you know, Phil doesn't want to talk to you." Other than a text volley three months earlier on the day the book excerpt dropped, I had not enjoyed any contact with Mickelson since the book had complicated both of our lives. But I was noncommittal with MacNeille. I had crossed an ocean to do my job, and I wasn't going to let LIV or Mickelson dictate the terms.

After his first round, Mickelson went to an interview area outside the press tent. Just as he began answering the first question, I felt a meaty hand on each of my arms; I had been bracketed by a pair of beefy security goons. "We need to scan your badge," one of them said.

I knew in that moment that tomfoolery was unfolding. But I didn't want to make a scene, so I walked on my own volition about twenty steps to the woman in charge of checking credentials; the security henchmen shadowed my every move. My credential got zapped, and it confirmed what all of us already knew, that I had every right to be in the interview area. I strode back toward Mickelson, but one of the security guards stepped directly in front of me, blocking my path. We stood there bickering for a while. Mickelson's brief press conference ended, and suddenly my accosters floated away. I was hacked off. I didn't get to listen to Mickelson's comments or ask him a question. I texted Greg Norman, "Are you aware that I just got muscled out of Phil's press conference by a couple of your goons?" He didn't immediately respond.

I retreated to the pressroom to type my dispatch about how the golf landscape had been forever altered. I didn't mention the incident with the security guards because I didn't want to inject myself into the story. Once I reached my hotel, my phone began chirping. A video of my confrontation with the security guards had begun making the rounds. Shot by Alex Thomas, a sports anchor for CNN International, it captured the moments when I was being obstructed by the meatheads after having my badge scanned. Its Zapruder-like value comes from what can be glimpsed in the background: Standing directly behind me was Greg Fucking Norman, his face contorted into a soulless scowl. I had no idea he had been standing right there, a witness to the abuses of his security lackeys.

I was watching the video again when my phone bleated. It was Norman, finally responding to my text message, an hour and a half later. "Did not hear," he wrote. "Thanks for letting me know."

I hadn't gone public with the events of the press conference, but Norman's bald-faced lie was too outrageous to let slide. I responded to him with an image from the video showing him lurking directly behind me and then snapped a screenshot of the exchange and put it on Twitter. It inevitably went viral, getting traction because it confirmed the widespread belief that Norman is a putz. (Though in fairness, after talking to various folks, I came to believe it was Mickelson's overzealous minders who had sent in the bouncers, not Norman. That said, LIV's commissioner clearly could have interceded.)

My ejection from an otherwise innocuous press conference also fed the all-too-easy narrative of the Saudis' aggressive disdain for a free press. Even on a day when LIV offered actual golf, the on-course action was inevitably overshadowed by drama.

The final two rounds of LIV London were enlivened by choreographed announcements of new player signings. Pat Perez was a decent get, a credible veteran who would bring depth to the team element. He is also noisier than a junkyard dog and would undoubtedly create headlines, which appeared to be part of the LIV business model. His wife, Ashley, added some fanfare to the signing when she had a mini-meltdown on Instagram. Fighting back tears, her voice quivering with emotion, she said she had already blocked three hundred people for their anti-LIV abuse. (*New York Post* headline: "Pat Perez's Wife Goes on Bizarre Instagram Rant After Golfer Defects for LIV Tour.") But the real thunderbolts were the announcements of Bryson DeChambeau, 28, and Patrick Reed, 31. They exploded the notion that LIV was a kind of gilded golf retirement home; DeChambeau had battled wrist and hip injuries in the first half of 2022, but both he and Reed were squarely in their prime and had won major championships more recently than had Rory McIlroy and Jordan Spieth, to name just a couple. "Bryson and Reed leaving, that's when shit got real," says James Hahn, who in the summer of 2022 was one of the PGA Tour's player board members. Including Perez, they would all make their debut at LIV's second tournament, in Portland.

But first, LIV had to crown an inaugural champion. Charl Schwartzel continued his stellar play and ultimately led by five shots heading into the closing nine of the final round. He made some nervy swings coming in, and his palpable struggle to get his first win in six years confirmed that watching pressure golf on a fiddly course will never not be entertaining. After he closed out the victory, talk inevitably turned to money. His win was worth $4 million, and his hastily assembled Stinger team (including fellow South Africans Louis Oosthuizen, Branden Grace, and Hennie du Plessis) also prevailed, so they split the $3 million first-place prize. The $4.75 million Schwartzel collected for three days of work would have placed him nineteenth on the season-long 2020–21 PGA Tour money list. Du Plessis, 25, who finished second, cashed a total of $2.875 million, tripling his career worldwide earnings. Peter Uihlein won $1,050,000 for finishing fourth, more than seven times what he had earned in fifteen starts on the PGA Tour in the first half of 2022. Andy Ogletree finished DFL (in golf parlance, "dead fucking last"), but he won $120,000 anyway. For a kid keeping his golf dreams alive with credit cards, that was career-changing money.

In a cute touch, LIV organized a podium ceremony for the top three individual and top three team finishers, and the players awkwardly showered one another with champagne. Al-Rumayyan was called to the stage to give his speech, followed by Norman. Afterward, they joined other top LIV officials and the players for a private party in the Centurion clubhouse. (At pretty much every other professional golf tournament, the players can't split fast enough.) The air was tinged with giddiness and disbelief. "All the players were on their phones," says one LIV exec. "They were all calling and texting their friends on the PGA Tour, saying 'You gotta get over here, this is un-fucking-believable.' We all had that feeling: *I can't believe this is actually happening.*"

The London event ended on Saturday to give players an extra day to travel to the U.S. Open. LIV chartered, and paid for, a jumbo jet so they could ride in style. As the plane touched down in Boston, the final round of the PGA Tour's Canadian Open was playing out. Rory McIlroy and Justin Thomas offered a manifesto with four plus hours of riveting golf as they battled for an old, proud national championship. The winner would earn less than a third of Schwartzel's haul from the day before, but Rory and JT radiated a palpable hunger to put on a good show for their embattled tour. After McIlroy dropped a 62, he couldn't resist taking a shot at Norman, telling the world, "The guy that's spearheading that other tour has twenty wins on the PGA Tour and I was tied with him and I wanted to get one ahead of him. And I did."

McIlroy's feud with Norman had heated up that spring, after McIlroy watched a new documentary about the Shark's wrenching collapse at the 1996 Masters. Twenty-five years later, McIlroy had blown his own big lead on Sunday at Augusta. In the days after, Norman had sent a heartfelt note that tugged at McIlroy's heartstrings. Those feelings were rekindled as McIlroy watched the documentary, after which he sent Norman a text: "Hopefully it reminds everyone of what a great golfer you were. Watching it reminded me of how you reached out to me in 2011, and I just want to say that I'll always appreciate it. It meant a lot. I know our opinion on the game of golf right now is very different, but I just wanted you to know that and wish you all the best."

Norman replied, "I really think golf can be a force for good around the world. I know our opinions are not aligned, but I'm just trying to create more opportunities for every golfer around the world."

"Fine. Really nice," McIlroy said, picking up the tale. "Then, a couple of weeks later, he does an interview with the *Washington Post* and says I've been 'brainwashed by the PGA Tour.' We've had this really nice back-and-forth, and he says that about me. I thought, *You know what? I'm going to make it my business now to be as much of a pain in his arse as possible.*" It is amusing, and telling, that McIlroy's relentless campaign against LIV and Norman stems from that fit of pique.

No one was immune to the LIV-related blowback. During nearly a decade on the PGA Tour, Hudson Swafford had aroused little passion—a good player and a nice guy who just kind of blended into the scenery. He settled on Sea Island, Georgia, a cloistered enclave that is home to more than a dozen PGA Tour pros. Swafford had a deal to endorse Sea Island Golf Club and proudly carried its logo on his golf bag. After he joined LIV, his honorary membership at Sea Island was revoked; not only was it where he worked on his game, but its beach club served as the social center in the lives of his wife and young children. Davis Love III, the two-time Ryder Cup captain and staunch Tour loyalist, is the patriarch of Sea Island, and in that incestuous community he is widely believed to have played a role in Swafford's ostracism. "It was tough on Hudson and his family," says agent Mac Barnhardt, a snowboarding companion of Love's and a Sea Island local who negotiated Swafford's endorsement deal with the club. "It was sad. I was hoping Davis would step in. But he's a strong opponent of LIV, and he didn't put a stop to it."

Many of the players who signed with LIV couched their move as strictly a business decision. It was becoming increasingly obvious that their defections were, in fact, intensely personal.

11.

BESIDES THE OBVIOUS REASON—MONEY—WHAT DRIVES
a player to LIV Golf? Some foreshadowing could be found on Masters Sunday in 2018, on the northern edge of Augusta in a tidy two-story house with black shutters identical to those on the National's clubhouse. A daughter who was away at college had driven home from Athens, Georgia, to share the Masters with her parents. A dozen friends had dropped by, everyone settling into the outside seating area in the backyard by the pool, where there is a big TV. The family mutts, Murphy and Cooper, scampered underfoot. It was a Masters party just like every other with one wrenching difference: a few miles away, the hosts' son was on his way to winning the green jacket.

Bill and Jeannette Reed and their daughter, Hannah, were not welcome at Augusta National. Patrick had made that clear, the final twist of the knife in an estrangement that dates to 2012. So the Reeds gathered at the house their son had lived in while leading Augusta State to two national championships. Memorabilia from his playing career are still scattered about: crystal trophies, photographs on the walls, a couple of commemorative golf bags. The bedroom he hasn't set foot in for so long is still referred to as "Patrick's room." As the Masters played out, the soundtrack was buzzing and beeping phones; Bill alone had awakened to 152 text messages. The Reeds lived and died with every shot on the back nine, hooting and hollering at the TV. When the final putt dropped, they clung to one another like survivors on a life raft. Struggling to catch her breath, tears streaming down her cheeks, Jeannette said, "I can't believe my son is the Masters champion. It's surreal."

It was a dizzying mixture of pride and pain.

In a tense exchange in the champion's press conference, I asked Patrick if it was bittersweet not to be able to share the most triumphant moment of his life with his parents and baby sister. "I'm just out here to play golf and try to win golf tournaments" was his cold-blooded reply.

Every family has its own dysfunction. The Reeds' is key to understanding one of the most polarizing players in golf, a complicated man who arrived on LIV still trying to outrun his shadows.

Patrick grew up in Texas in a family of golfers. As Jeannette said on that Masters Sunday, "My sister was an excellent player, my father was a big golfer—he's in Heaven enjoying a Manhattan watching his grandson contend for the green jacket." Plastic golf clubs were among Patrick's first baby gifts. By age nine, he was taking lessons from Peter Murphy, a Hank Haney disciple. His boyhood hero, Tiger Woods, was sometimes at the same practice facility working with Haney, and Reed studied him carefully and modeled himself after a golfer who has always been a lone wolf. By the time he was ten, Reed was wearing trousers at tournaments, the better to prepare himself for the PGA Tour, while all the other kids wore shorts in the blazing Texas heat.

Bill worked in the health care industry, and the family moved to Baton Rouge, Louisiana, for Reed's high school years. Everyone who came into contact with the young Patrick was struck by his fierce determination. "In the summers and on the weekends he would show up by himself and hit balls for eight hours straight, with maybe one break in the middle to drink a Powerade," says Mike Johnson, the head pro at LSU Golf Course in Baton Rouge, where Patrick spent most of his teenage years. "Nobody had to push him, because he had an incredible drive to succeed. I don't think you can make a kid that way—it comes from inside."

The University of Georgia won a fevered recruiting battle, and Reed, a pudgy, baby-faced seventeen-year-old, joined a veteran team stacked with the future pros Hudson Swafford, Harris English, Russell Henley, and Brian Harman. Having grown up a golf nerd with few friends, he cut loose at Georgia, resulting in an arrest for underage drinking and possessing a fake ID. He pleaded guilty to the misdemeanor and was put on probation, fined, and sentenced to sixty hours of community service. Plenty of college kids make similar mistakes. What doomed Reed at Georgia was committing golf's original sin. As Shane Ryan wrote in his book *Slaying the Tiger: A Year Inside the Ropes on the New PGA Tour*, "During a qualifying round prior to a tournament, according to sources close to the team, Reed hit a ball far into the rough. When he approached the spot, he found another ball sitting closer to the fairway, and was preparing to hit it when several of his teammates confronted him. Reed pleaded ignorance, but the other Georgia players were convinced he had been caught red-handed trying to cheat." Ryan detailed a second alcohol-related offense during Reed's freshman year, which hastened the end of his career at Georgia.

Reed transferred to Augusta State University and moved back in with his parents, but he quickly squandered the fresh start with his immature, abrasive behavior. Stories are legion of how he rubbed his new teammates the wrong way, to the point that they considered taking a vote to kick him off the team. Yet Reed was such a blue-chip talent that he pushed the team to unprecedented heights. He went 3–0 in the match-play portion in back-to-back years to carry the Jaguars to consecutive national championships even as he was all but estranged from his teammates. In 2011, Augusta State took down Georgia to win the title. A Bulldogs loyalist told ESPN that Reed's triumph was the "death of karma."

Reed found comfort in the arms of a pert blonde named Justine Karain, who was four years older. By the time he turned pro in June 2011, she had completed two undergraduate degrees and was working as a nurse, but Justine couldn't resist the siren song of competition, so she volunteered to be her boyfriend's caddie. At Klein Forest High School in Houston, Justine had been a standout swimmer and soccer player, and she turned out to be a natural as his caddie. Patrick and Justine wed in December 2012, when he was only twenty-two. His parents had expressed misgivings about his getting married so young and urged him to slow down. The advice was not well received, and Bill, Jeannette, and Hannah were not invited to the wedding. Patrick cut off contact with his family, instead surrounding himself with Justine's people: her brother, Kessler, took over the caddying duties; her sister, Kris, served as a nanny for the Reeds' daughter, Windsor Wells; her mom, Janet, regularly traveled with the family, acting as a kind of chief of staff and helping with her granddaughter and her grandson Barrett, who was born in December 2017. The whole brood liked to share a rental house, with Patrick cooking most of the dinners, charring a variety of meats on the grill and occasionally whipping up his signature dish, shrimp Alexander, having pried loose the recipe from a chef at Morton's, his favorite restaurant. Janet is not a moderating influence on the complicated family dynamics; in an interview with me, she made a series of disparaging remarks about Bill and Jeannette and the way they had raised their son, even though she had never met them.

The Reeds have had no contact with Patrick since he got married, despite repeatedly emailing him and reaching out through intermediaries. Jeannette's Twitter feed chronicles her longing for her son:

> If I had a flower for every time I thought of you, I could walk in my garden forever.... #PatrickReed

> Dose of reality ... thinking an unknown caller is actually you ... heart goes pitter patter, then reality sets in ... crash and burn.

Justine has long been the source of conjecture on Tour, a mysterious figure draped in gold jewelry and flashy clothes who, like her husband, keeps to herself. The family drama spilled into the open in late 2016, when Justine wrote a Facebook post about her in-laws that included the line "They are sick people and need help." Hannah responded with a long, anguished post of her own, writing "I have sat back and watched the numerous and disgusting accusations his wife, mother-in-law and everyone now associated as his family have made. Patrick is not the same person he used to be. This is not a brother anymore, but a selfish, horrible stranger and it's heartbreaking. . . . It is devastating seeing my parents hurt and suffer from what is being posted about them."

Golf fans have picked up on the bad juju. Even though the Masters is played in a town to which Reed brought so much golf glory, the crowd was never on his side when he was in contention in 2018. When he won, the feeling around the eighteenth green was subdued to the point of being awkward. In a lounge outside the locker room, a couple of green jackets were watching the telecast and they exchanged mournful looks, like *Awww shit, now we're stuck with this guy forever.*

Winning the Masters only seemed to heighten the Reeds' sense of entitlement. That summer, when the Tour was in Boston, Patrick and Justine attended a Red Sox game and he took to Twitter *and* Instagram to complain about the seats the Tour had supplied them. At the ensuing Ryder Cup, Jordan Spieth dumped Reed as a playing partner—can you blame him?—and after going 1–2–0 in the lopsided loss, Patrick ripped his teammates and captain Jim Furyk to the *New York Times* and Justine took to Twitter to amplify the message. She stopped tweeting under her own name after that but eventually became linked to a burner account (@useGolfFACTS) that had a peculiar obsession with the notion that the PGA Tour was intentionally giving Reed disadvantageous tee times. (When I asked Justine if she would ever acknowledge that she was behind @useGolfFACTS, she demurred, "I don't know about that. Thank you for asking.") The Reeds were so high maintenance that the Tour put one of its media relations staffers permanently on call to deal with them.

But there was no way to finesse a couple of high-profile rules controversies that besmirched Reed's reputation and further estranged him from his colleagues. At the 2019 Hero World Challenge, Reed was assessed a two-stroke penalty for improving his lie in a waste bunker by moving sand during his practice swings; he insisted he would have been exonerated if the TV cameras showed a different angle. At the San Diego Tour stop, in 2021, Reed sought relief from an embedded lie in the rough but curiously picked up his ball before a rules official could arrive to inspect the scene. Reed's errant shot had bounced on a cart path, killing most of its speed and making it almost impossible for the ball to embed in the long grass. (Reed claimed not to have known about the cart path bounce.) The rules official, clearly taken aback that Reed had picked up his ball, granted relief, leading to howls of protest. Reed told reporters that he had handled the situation "perfectly," which happens to be the same word Donald Trump used to describe his fateful phone call to Ukrainian president Volodymyr Zelenskyy that led to Trump being impeached for a second time. That Reed went on to win at Torrey Pines fueled the outrage among his colleagues.

"It's sad," said Lanto Griffin, who tied for seventh. "Kind of pisses us off."

"You always view golf as a game of integrity above all else," says Tour veteran Tom Hoge. "Anytime there is a close call on a rule, I think the rest of us err on the side of doing the right thing. There have been so many incidents stacked up against Patrick, he's showing his true colors, I would say. I don't know why no tours have stepped in and played a more active role to try to stop some of this. I don't know what it would take for them to jump in there a little bit. You can see it with your own eyes."

Jhonattan Vegas, who plays out of the same course in Houston (TPC Woodlands) as Reed, says, "Dude, nobody would say they are his friend. He mostly practices and plays alone. From my experience, he's not a bad guy, he just cannot help himself when he gets on the golf course. I feel he likes the drama; there are people that way. It feeds him. He loves it."

Reed has won nine times on the PGA Tour, including two World Golf Championships and two FedEx Cup playoff events, but along the way he became a kind of traveling carnival act. "In 2021, I played with him three straight days in Charlotte," says Stewart Cink. "The things the fans yelled at him made *me* embarrassed. I told Patrick, 'Man, I don't know how Justine hasn't murdered somebody.' He said, 'Yeah, I guess I'm used to it.'"

Given all of this, it's easy to imagine that Reed craved a fresh start. Somehow, he and his wife still harbored the delusion that they could be the heroes of their own story. As Justine told me years ago, "He didn't grow up at a fancy country club. He was a Monday qualifier who's had to fight for everything he's ever gotten. Why can't we have that fairy tale, too?"

Besides the obvious reason—the need for a clean slate—what drives a player to LIV? A few clues can be found in a vinyl tent on the edge of a beat-up driving range at Dragonfly Golf Club, a scruffy public course surrounded by farmland in Madera, California. The 1,600-square-foot tent is the home of the Mike Schy Golf Performance Institute, and even the eponymous founder chuckles at how discordant the grandiose name is given its humble setting. The tent is stuffed with disfigured golf clubs that have been sacrificed in the name of progress, as well as all manner of jerry-rigged teaching contraptions. The trappings of the tent are of a piece with Madera, a tiny blue-collar town in the Central Valley, a hardscrabble swath of California that would've been the perfect setting for John Steinbeck's novels if he hadn't wound up just a little farther west.

Schy, 62, is a big sweetheart who tries but fails to put on a gruff exterior for his young pupils. The mad scientist's lab is devoted to *The Golfing Machine*, a dense tome by Homer Kelley in which the swing is scientifically broken down into twenty-four components. The Machine has a cultlike following among its disciples, but Schy despairs over what he considers the inaccurate and unfair popular perception of his bible. Kelley was certainly eccentric, and the ramblings of his wing-nut student Mac O'Grady helped cement the notion that the ideas in *The Golfing Machine* were not for the well adjusted. "We're used to being laughed at, criticized, called weirdos," says Schy.

He found the perfect pupil in Bryson DeChambeau, who grew up on Bellaire Avenue in nearby Clovis, amid the tidy middle-class homes that form a landscape of beige stucco and palm trees. "Team sports didn't work for Bryson," said his late father, Jon. "He simply couldn't understand why his teammates didn't give maximum effort at all times, like he did. It drove him crazy."

Golf turned out to be perfect for the socially awkward teen, and when Bryson was fifteen, Schy finally slid him his own well-thumbed copy of *The Golfing Machine*. "Mind blown," says DeChambeau. He carried the book everywhere and memorized pretty much every word. One sentence changed him forever. Chapter 10, section 7 covers what Kelley termed "customized" swing planes. With his quirky punctuation, Kelley wrote about a "Zero Shift" swing: "one Basic Plane Angle is to be used throughout the stroke without 'a Variation'—that is, No Shift." Those eighteen words raced through Bryson's mind for days. Was it possible to have a one-plane swing? He queried Schy, who said that the concept was intended for chipping and pitching.

Having been raised as a golfer to think untraditionally, DeChambeau came up with a solution that seemed blindingly obvious to him: make every iron the same length with the same weight, the same shaft flex, and the same lie angle (72 degrees), allowing the same swing plane to be repeated over and over. (He would continue to use a traditional-length hybrid, 3-wood, and driver.) Schy was supportive of the experiment, so a set of stray Nike VR heads was sacrificed in the name of science. In each they put a 37½-inch shaft, which is the length of a traditional 6- or 7-iron. In any set of clubs, the heads of the wedges are chunkier and heavier than those of the long irons. After running a series of calculations, DeChambeau determined that an ideal uniform weight for the heads in a single-length set would be 282 grams. Lead tape was used to make the heads on the longer irons heavier; the extra mass made up for a shorter swing arc. To shed weight on the wedges, holes were drilled in the back of the head and chunks of metal were gouged out of the backline of the sole; losing that mass was counteracted by the increased swing speed that came with the longer shaft. When the work was complete, DeChambeau raced to the first fairway at Dragonfly. From 160 yards he selected an 8-iron. The club felt a little long and light but not overly so. He hit a lovely draw pin high. On the second hole he dropped a ball 210 yards from the flag and reached for his reconstituted 5-iron. That was the moment of truth: if the shorter, heavier long irons worked, the underlying theory of the single-length set was sound.

He flushed the shot. "It was in the air for what felt like forever," he says. The suspense was awful. Was the ball going to be twenty yards short? Twenty yards long? It landed three feet from the flag. The revolution had begun.

Using his one-of-a-kind clubs, DeChambeau went on to a historic career at Southern Methodist University, joining Jack Nicklaus, Tiger Woods, Phil Mickelson, and Ryan Moore as the only players to win the NCAA Championship and the U.S. Amateur in the same year. During the U.S. Amateur telecast, Brad Faxon, a former Tour player, said of DeChambeau, "I think he is going to change the game." Said Jon DeChambeau, "That was surreal, because when Bryson was just a kid, I asked him his goals in golf, and he said, 'I want to change the game.'" In a game of copycats, DeChambeau had blazed his own trail.

He turned pro following the 2016 Masters and within two years was a dominant force on the PGA Tour, winning four times. Still, he hungered to be transcendent.

DeChambeau was already a long hitter but wanted to turn a strength into an overwhelming advantage, as the Golden State Warriors did with their emphasis on three-pointers. Typically, DeChambeau took it to the illogical extreme. During covid, he packed on nearly fifty pounds working out in his home gym and with a diet that in a typical day included a half-dozen eggs, a heaping serving of bacon, toast (half a loaf), peanut-butter-and-jelly sandwiches, a handful of granola bars, an enormous steak, a bag of potatoes, eight protein shakes, and various snacks. A couple of months into the experiment, he went to a grand old Donald Ross course in Detroit and turned it into a pitch-and-putt en route to victory. The revolution was accelerating. Two months later, DeChambeau overwhelmed one of the most feared courses in the world, Winged Foot in Mamaroneck, New York, en route to a 5-stroke laugher at the U.S. Open. He had changed the game in a profound way.

Inevitably, questions swirled around how DeChambeau had been able to reshape his body so radically in such a short amount of time. At the 2020 Travelers Championship outside Hartford, Connecticut, the reporter Michael Bamberger asked Jay Monahan if the PGA Tour had been testing for performance-enhancing drugs (PEDs) during covid.

The commissioner offered a one-word answer: "No."

The Tour had that exchange scrubbed from the official interview transcript. DeChambeau vociferously denied using PEDs.

DeChambeau's post–Winged Foot superstardom only seemed to embolden him to speak out, no matter the cost. At the 2021 Open Championship, he struggled off the tee and huffed to reporters, "If I can hit it down the middle of the fairway, that's great, but with the driver right now, the driver sucks."

Cobra PUMA Golf engineers had spent incalculable hours indulging DeChambeau's every whim, and Ben Schomin, the company's Tour operations manager, ripped his star endorser in a way that was unprecedented for an equipment manufacturer to go after its own player. "It's just really, really painful when he says something that stupid," he declared. "He has never really been happy, ever. Like, it's very rare where he's happy." That was the beginning of the end of a very lucrative endorsement deal.

Goofy, obtuse, strident, DeChambeau always had trouble connecting with his peers; the iconic eye roll that cameras captured from Brooks Koepka at the 2021 PGA Championship only hinted at the collective irritation. Feelings curdled at Torrey Pines in 2022, when DeChambeau began launching drives into the caddie parking lot beyond the end of the range. A tournament official beseeched him to aim into the tall nets down the side of the range. He ignored the plea and kept bombing his driver. Two cars were left with smashed windshields.

No wonder DeChambeau could never get any traction in his repeated bids to assume a leadership position among his colleagues on the PGA Tour. "A lot of my time out there was difficult," he says. "I was trying to get on the [Player Advisory Committee] for six years, and it never happened. You get voted onto it by the other players, and nobody liked the way I thought. I felt I had an interesting perspective on a lot of issues, I'd love to have been part of it, but they didn't want me."

As an avowed nonconformist, DeChambeau was among the easiest marks when a would-be breakaway tour began seducing Tour players.

LIV's signings of DeChambeau and Reed could both be traced to the DJ effect. A LIV executive says, "Without Dustin, I don't think we sign either of them." DeChambeau confirms as much, saying, "The big question was 'Who's going to jump first?'" The underwhelming slate of players for LIV London tilted the market in DeChambeau's favor. He had been negotiating with the Saudis for more than a year, but in the days after the London field was announced they came back to him with an even bigger offer: $130 million. "It's a business," says DeChambeau, a client of GSE Worldwide. "Stuff started happening. Ultimately we got to a place where it made total sense for me."

Before DeChambeau and Reed could make their LIV debuts in Portland at the end of June, they had to play in the U.S. Open at the Country Club outside Boston. That initial mixing of LIV loyalists and staunch Tour supporters made the national championship crackle with tension. The LIV players could feel all the eyes on them. "I felt like the hot chick," Talor Gooch says with a smile. "It was funny. It was unlike anything I've ever experienced."

Open week was also infused with the geopolitics that were now an inevitable backdrop to professional golf tournaments. American Airlines Flight 11, which had crashed into the North Tower of the World Trade Center on 9/11, had departed from Boston's Logan International Airport. Arriving in Beantown, the LIV golfers were greeted by the public release of a letter written by Terry Strada, the national chair of 9/11 Families United; Strada's husband, Tom, worked on the 104th floor of the North Tower and died in its collapse. The letter was a succinct recitation of why so many folks found the very idea of LIV to be objectionable.

> As a 9/11 widow, I feel compelled to help you understand the level of depravity the Kingdom engaged in when it knowingly sent government agents here to establish the support network needed for those hijackers.
>
> As you may know, Osama bin Laden and 15 of the 19 September 11 hijackers were Saudis. It was the Saudis who cultivated and spread the evil, hate-filled Islamist ideology that inspired the violent jihadists to carry out the deadly

9/11 attacks. And, most egregiously, it is the Kingdom that has spent 20 years in denial: lying about their activities, and cowardly dodging the responsibility they bear. Yet these are your partners, and much to our disappointment, you appear pleased to be in business with them.

Given Saudi Arabia's role in the death of our loved ones and those injured on 9/11—*your fellow Americans*—we are angered that you are so willing to help the Saudis cover up this history in their request for "respectability." When you partner with the Saudis, you become complicit with their whitewash, and help give them the reputational cover they so desperately crave—*and are willing to pay handsomely to manufacture.* The Saudis do not care about the deep-rooted sportsmanship of golf or its origins as a gentleman's game built upon core values of mutual respect and personal integrity. They care about using professional golf to whitewash their reputation, and they are paying you to help them do it.

That was the harsh reality now facing DeChambeau, Reed, Mickelson, and other LIV golfers: many people considered them traitors not only to the PGA Tour but also to their fellow countrymen.

The temperature at that U.S. Open went even higher on Monday, when Mickelson met the golf press in a hot, sweaty tent adjacent to the Country Club's yellow clubhouse. In the moments before Mickelson arrived, there was an unmistakable electricity in the air. He showed up dressed in black, as if for a funeral. For twenty minutes, he was pounded with questions about the outrage of the 9/11 families, Saudi sportswashing, how much he had been heckled in his practice rounds, how the move to LIV might taint his legacy, the frosty reception from his colleagues, LIV's alliance with Donald Trump, and sundry other thorny topics. He spoke in a dead monotone; there was no mirth from a consummate showman who had always treated press conferences as performance art.

Mostly he looked forlorn and defeated. Removed from the enablers and apologists on his payroll and away from the carefully cultivated artificial reality of LIV, Mickelson seemed to be feeling, for the first time, how much ill will he had stirred up. For the first two rounds he was paired with Shane Lowry, perhaps the most amiable man in golf. Privately, Lowry was furious at the USGA for making him part of the spectacle. If your very presence agitates Shane Lowry, you're probably doing something wrong.

Another notable pretournament press conference came by way of Koepka. From 2017 to 2021, he emerged as the best U.S. Open performer of his generation, going 1–1–2–T4. (He missed the 2020 Open due to injury.) But Koepka, previously celebrated for his brawny biceps, increasingly appeared to be held together by paper clips and chewing gum, as a series of injuries had left him winless since 2019. In private, he grew ever more emo, despairing that he would never again be a dominant force on Tour. His insecurity was born of his untraditional road to stardom.

A great-nephew of former Pittsburgh Pirates shortstop Dick Groat, whose team had won two World Series and who had been the 1960 National League MVP, Koepka grew up in Wellington, Florida, dreaming of playing in the major leagues. But when he was a boy his nose and sinus cavity were fractured in a car accident; baseball was deemed too risky, so he switched his focus to golf. Lightly recruited, he wound up at Florida State, where he didn't win a tournament until his senior year. After flunking out of the PGA Tour's Q-School in 2012, he lit out for the Challenge Tour, the minor league of the European Tour. Representative of life on the road was a tournament in Kazakhstan where Koepka slept in his car and dined on horse meat. Hardened by his travels, he went on to win in Spain, Italy, Scotland, and Turkey. A victory at the 2015 Phoenix Open secured his place on the PGA Tour. Koepka carried himself with a certain swagger even before he became a headliner. He became celebrated in golf circles for his brash civil disobedience at the 2015 British Open at

St. Andrews; as high winds caused balls on the greens to twitch, Koepka refused to continue playing despite the admonishments of a tweedy R&A rules official, who made it known that he carried the title "Sir." "I don't give a fuck who you are," Koepka responded. "I'm not playing until my ball stops oscillating."

In 2015 and '16, Koepka had three top tens in the majors, but something was still missing. Enter Dustin Johnson, who broke through at the 2016 U.S. Open. That same year, Koepka mentioned to his pal that he was going to rent a house while renovating his home in Jupiter, Florida. "DJ says to Brooks, 'Bro, stay with me, I've got plenty of space. I'll teach you how to drive a boat,'" says Johnson's trainer, Joey Diovisalvi. Koepka crashed with Johnson for six months and got a close-up look at his ascent to the top of the world ranking. After a long courtship, Koepka finally persuaded Diovisalvi to take him on as a client in the spring of 2017. "He came in as such a cocky little bastard," says Diovisalvi. "At the time Brooks was eighteenth in the world, and he says to me, 'I only have seventeen spots to go to relieve DJ of his position.'" But Koepka backed up the trash talk. Within a year he had summited the world ranking, and when he dusted Johnson in mano a manos at both the 2018 U.S. Open and 2019 PGA Championship, the pupil became the master.

With four major championship victories by the age of twenty-nine, Koepka was threatening McIlroy, Spieth, and Johnson as the best player of the post-Tiger era. But the next two and a half years were a washout due to injuries to his neck, wrist, hip, and, most seriously, right knee, which required surgery in March 2021 to repair ligament damage and a dislocated kneecap.

Koepka's burst of wins in the major championships brought him belated fame and fortune, but still he held on to old memories of how quickly it could be scattered to the wind. "I grew up with nothing," he says. "When I was a kid, a hurricane blew our roof off and it still wasn't fixed by the time the *next* hurricane came through. We had bug-infested walls." LIV's guaranteed money could certainly alleviate any material concerns, but in February 2022, Koepka pledged his loyalty to the PGA Tour, not a surprise given that he had a leadership role as a member of the Player Advisory Council. "I'm happy with the PGA Tour," he said. "I think everybody out here is happy." As for LIV, he had this withering analysis: "They'll get their guys. Somebody will sell out and go for it."

Koepka can be standoffish even in the best of times. At his U.S. Open presser at the Country Club he was downright salty, especially when queried about LIV. He admitted that he had watched some of the London tournament but, curiously, had not spoken to his kid brother about his experience. (Chase finished thirty-third.) As more questions came, Koepka snapped, "I don't understand, I'm trying to focus on the U.S. Open, man. I legitimately don't get it. I'm tired of the conversations. I'm tired of all this stuff. Like I said, y'all are throwing a black cloud on the U.S. Open. I think that sucks. I actually do feel bad for [the USGA] for once because it's a shitty situation. We're here to play, and you are talking about an event that happened last week."

He was asked, "Why have you decided to stay on the PGA Tour, and is that a permanent decision?"

Koepka's answer was not a ringing endorsement: "There's been no other option to this point, so where else are you going to go?"

Everyone has a price, and Koepka was asked if he would jump to LIV Golf if the PIF ponied up enough dough. "I haven't given it that much thought," he said.

That was poppycock. Koepka had been having high-level conversations with the folks at LIV for a full year; several executives refer to him as one of the "founding members" along with Mickelson, Johnson, and DeChambeau. But you have to respect his dedication to the bit.

Once again, playing golf was a welcome relief. Johnson was tied for seventh after the first round, just two strokes off the lead. But even once the scores started counting, there was bitchiness behind the scenes. Rory McIlroy had been a groomsman at Sergio García's wedding in 2017, but LIV had created a deep rift in their friendship. McIlroy hadn't known that García was defecting until they bumped into each other on the range at the Wells Fargo Championship in Charlotte, North Carolina, a month before the U.S. Open; García woofed that he had a new plane and offered McIlroy a ride to London for the first LIV event. That was typical of García's grating sense of humor. McIlroy had kept up his war of words in his pretournament press conference at the U.S. Open, but he did allow that, "I don't think it will strain any relationships. I'm still going to be close with the guys that have made the decision to play those events. It's not as if you agree on absolutely everything that all your friends do. You're going to have a difference of opinion on a lot of things. That's fine. That's what makes this a great world. We can't all agree on everything." Now, on the morning of the second round of the national championship, McIlroy awoke to a text from García "basically telling me to shut up about LIV, blah, blah, blah, blah, blah," McIlroy says. "I was pretty offended and sent him back a couple of daggers, and that was it." A fifteen-year friendship was kaput.

LIV golfers made a lot less noise between the ropes; Johnson ultimately faded to twenty-fourth place, but that still made him the highest finisher among his brethren, which PGA Tour honks delighted in pointing out. (Reed finished forty-ninth, DeChambeau fifty-sixth, and García missed the cut.) In the end, the Tour minted three new stars during a taut final round: Matt Fitzpatrick, the boyish, bookish champ who produced an all-time classic shot out of a fairway bunker on the seventy-second hole; Will Zalatoris, who for the second straight major championship battled to the final green, impressing again with his grit and stellar all-around game; and Joel Dahmen, a likable veteran who had played his way into the field through qualifying, lubricating his swing with a couple of White Claws between rounds at the qualifier. Dahmen held a piece of the thirty-six-hole lead at the Open and was a wisecracking delight.

Netflix cameras were there to capture all of it for the docuseries that was being filmed throughout the season. Fitzpatrick and Dahmen were already under consideration to be protagonists on the show, and their star turns at the Open guaranteed that they would be featured prominently. McIlroy, Koepka, and Johnson also nabbed starring roles. Netflix thought it was making a sports show, but it was quickly turning into a *telenovela*.

Two days after the U.S. Open, LIV Golf signed Abraham Ancer, arguably the biggest star in Latin America. (Ancer was the seventh GSE Worldwide client to go to LIV, and more were on the way.) At number twenty in the world ranking, he became the seventh player in the top fifty to jilt the PGA Tour. That same day, Tour commissioner Jay Monahan presided over a rowdy closed-door meeting with a hundred or so of his players at the Greater Hartford Open. The LIV threat had gone from theoretical to very real. The PGA Tour members wanted reassurances, and they wanted more money. Monahan delivered both. The Tour had hoped Tiger Woods would fly in to rally the troops at the players meeting, and went so far as to draft talking points for its biggest star. Woods didn't show, but the leaked memo offers insight into the Tour bureaucrats' mounting panic, and their hamhandedness. They wanted Tiger to begin with a testimonial to Monahan: "He's the right guy for this war. He's a fighter." Then Woods was scripted to leverage his son, Charlie, a teenager with a gorgeous swing, by saying, "I want him to experience the Tour that Jack and Arnie built, and that we've each contributed to and left better than when we found it." Finally, the money shot, Tiger's instructions to his colleagues on how to thwart LIV: "First, do what I did: tell the Saudis to go fuck themselves. And mean it." One can only imagine the whoops that went up in the Comms Department when Woods's ghostwriter typed those words.

The next day, Monahan held a press conference to state his case, a rare public appearance for a leader who preferred to do his bidding in private. (Critics would say that he was running scared.) Moments after he began speaking, LIV announced on social media that it had signed Koepka, a masterful bit of corporate trolling. Two weeks earlier, Monahan and his wife, Susan, had attended Koepka's lavish wedding in Turks and Caicos. Now he read his prepared opening remarks, unaware that Koepka had eloped to LIV for $130 million.

"Let me be clear: I am not naive," Monahan said. "If this is an arms race and if the only weapons here are dollar bills, the PGA Tour can't compete. The PGA Tour, an American institution, can't compete with a foreign monarchy that is spending billions of dollars in an attempt to buy the game of golf. We welcome good, healthy competition. The LIV Saudi Golf League is not that. It's an irrational threat; one not concerned with the return on investment or true growth of the game.

"Currently no one organization owns or dominates the game of golf. But when someone attempts to buy the sport, dismantle the institutions that are intrinsically invested in its growth, and focus only on a personal priority, that partnership evaporates. I doubt that's the vision any of us have for the game. Now, I know legacy and purpose sound like talking points that don't mean much, but when I talk of those concepts, it isn't about some sort of intangible moral high ground. It is our track record as an organization and as a sport."

He went on to celebrate the Tour as a "meritocracy" and concluded, "It's damn good and it's worth fighting for."

Monahan's fighting words were an amplification of something he had said two weeks earlier on the CBS telecast from the Canadian Open, when he had snarled, "I would ask any player who has left, or is thinking of leaving, 'Have you ever had to apologize for being a member of the PGA Tour?'"

Monahan's new offensive continued his muddled messaging. His first salvo, months earlier, had been "legacy, not leverage." But he had badly overvalued what PGA Tour membership meant to many of his players. One of the glum realizations in this war between tours is that certain professional golfers—who, by definition, play the game for money—are not romantics like the rest of us. Surely Mickelson would always play Pebble Beach to honor his beloved grandfather who caddied there, right? No way Reed would jilt his hometown event in Houston! Hilton Head had given DeChambeau his first sponsor's exemption when he was trying to secure his PGA Tour card, and he had vowed to always support the event in the future—his word is his bond! Turns out that for many big names, the tournaments between the major championships are just filler to keep themselves sharp and build their brands, and they don't have the emotional attachment to the towns or the venues that we presume. Swapping out a Tour event in Hartford for a LIV event in Portland isn't a big deal—if the price is right. "What you have to understand about professional golfers is that they are all whores," says a longtime agent. "That is the starting point."

With his legacy argument having fallen flat, Monahan was reaching for the moral high ground by painting a partnership with the Saudis as unethical, if not evil. But in 2021 (post-Khashoggi, in other words), the Tour's biggest sponsor, FedEx, announced a ten-year, $400 million investment to better service Saudi Arabia's domestic and international shipping needs. Jack Muhs, the regional president of FedEx Middle East, said, "This strategic expansion in the Kingdom will help Saudi-based businesses connect to new markets and customers around the world, supporting Saudi Arabia's Vision 2030 goals to diversify the national economy." Morgan Stanley is a presenting sponsor of the Tour's flagship event, the Players Championship, and it has played a crucial role in the Saudi Arabian economy; it oversaw the first IPOs of companies listed on the Saudi stock exchange, the Tadawul, and later became the first investment bank to enter into a swap agreement with nonresident foreign investors, opening up the Tadawul to the world. Along the way, it collected billions of dollars in fees and commissions. Coca-Cola sponsors the

Tour Championship, the season-ending crescendo, but well after MBS came to power, it spent $100 million on a new bottling plant in Sudair City for Industry and Business. "Coca-Cola is committed to investing in the Saudi market, considering the vast economic opportunities as well as the large consumer base," said Samer Al Khawashki, the managing director of Coca-Cola Bottling Company Saudi Arabia. In all, two dozen PGA Tour title sponsors have direct business ties to Saudi Arabia.

A longtime Tour player who ultimately went LIV says, "Tour sponsors love to take the Saudis' money. The CEOs who do those stupid interviews on Sunday afternoon TV, they love the Saudi money. The U.S. government and Lockheed Martin take hundreds of billions of dollars every year from the Saudis to sell them weapons of war. Race car drivers and tennis players and soccer players and boxers gladly take their money. So do musicians and Instagram influencers. You're telling me that the only job in the world that can't benefit from Saudi money is professional golfers? Get the fuck outta here."

Demonizing the Saudis was a high-risk ploy by Monahan, given how much business his sponsors do in the kingdom. And having just admitted that the Tour couldn't compete with the PIF's resources, it followed that LIV was likely to win a war of attrition; it would be a lot harder to forge a compromise with the people he had been openly disparaging. Or, a lot harder to sell such a compromise to the players and the public. But those were concerns for another day. Monahan's moves in Hartford made it clear that he had belatedly realized that quaint concepts such as legacy and morality were not going to save his Tour. Only money could do that. Despite his professed misgivings about joining a financial arms race, he announced exactly that: beginning in 2023, the Tour would boast eight (unnamed) tournaments with $20 million purses. At that moment, the Tour conducted only four events with purses exceeding $12 million, and three-quarters of the tourneys were offering less than

$9 million. (The major championships don't count, as they are not run by the PGA Tour.) Ever since LIV's launch, Monahan had been defensive and reactive. Now, at last, the Tour was punching back, with LIV-esque new purses. On Twitter, Talor Gooch offered some playful trolling by posting a GIF of the Rock crooning, "You're welcome." That inspired Tron Carter, the *No Laying Up* provocateur, to label him "a huge twat," representative of a significant chunk of the Gooch-related discourse.

On the other side of the Atlantic, there was more strife. During the second round of the BMW International Open in Munich, the European Tour announced that any of its members who competed in LIV London (among them Sergio García, Lee Westwood, and Ian Poulter) would be fined £100,000—roughly equivalent to last-place money at a LIV event—and suspended for three upcoming tournaments. That was just the opening salvo in a larger battle, as LIV had already pledged to file a lawsuit over any such suspensions. Still, García didn't take the news well. In the locker room at Golf-club München Eichenried, he loosed a tirade that included shouting at his colleagues, "This tour is shit! You are all fucked! You should have taken the Saudi money!" Robert MacIntyre, a young, promising Scot, was among those who witnessed the tirade. James Corrigan of the *Telegraph* broke the story and later approached MacIntyre for comment. He declined but tweeted cryptically, "Amazing how fast you can lose respect for someone that you've looked up to all your life." When I caught up with MacIntyre, he didn't want to talk, saying, "The less said about [García] the better."

C'mon, Bob, put a name on it! Was the tweet in fact directed at García? MacIntyre laughed, he sighed, he looked toward the heavens. He did a quick cost-benefit analysis in his mind, weighing the valor of authenticity versus the potential blowback of calling out García's petulance. Walking away, he offered only one word: "Yes."

12.

IN THE RUN-UP TO LIV GOLF'S FIRST TOURNAMENT IN the United States, in North Plains, Oregon, beginning on the last day of June, the league signed three more players: Carlos Ortiz and Eugenio Chacarra, both GSE Worldwide clients, and Matthew Wolff. Ortiz, 31, had a solid but unspectacular résumé, having won the Houston Open in 2020 and cracking the top fifty in the world ranking early the next year. The other new recruits generated more intrigue. Chacarra, 22, was the number two player in the World Amateur Ranking; he had previously announced that he would return to Oklahoma State as a red-shirt senior, but instead he turned pro to sign a three-year deal with LIV. In the battle for the next generation of stars, LIV was making continued inroads.

Only a few years earlier, Wolff, 23, had also been a can't-miss kid. In 2019, he had won the NCAA Championship, and later that year, as a PGA Tour rookie, he had taken the 3M Open, joining Ben Crenshaw and Tiger Woods as the only players to win the NCAA Championship and a Tour event in the same year. The following season, Wolff made strong runs at the PGA Championship and U.S. Open, finishing second to Bryson DeChambeau at the latter. (With his unique homemade swing, Wolff exhibited a style of play is as idiosyncratic as DeChambeau's.) But his results slipped precipitously in the two years that followed. Wolff later bravely went public with the mental health challenges he had faced during his slump. Reflecting on when he had hit rock bottom, he said, "I just want to stay in my bed and not be in front of everyone and not screw up in front of everyone." LIV Golf was either a fresh start or an act of escape, depending on one's bent.

As was fast becoming the norm for LIV, the pretournament press conferences were more electric than the golf that followed. Rory McIlroy, continuing his emergence as the voice of the establishment/preeminent shit stirrer, set the table during the Greater Hartford Open by calling Brooks Koepka's abrupt turnabout on LIV "duplicitous." On Tuesday of LIV Portland, Koepka swaggered into the media center along with fellow LIV newcomers Patrick Reed and Pat Perez. It's hard to think of a more polarizing trio in all of golf, and their defensive, sour demeanor called to mind something the Tour loyalist Peter Jacobsen had said: "It can't be a coincidence that all the assholes went to LIV." Tour player Harry Higgs used the word *villains*, but the same principle applies. Either way, it should be noted that during the press conference, Koepka addressed a reporter as "chief," which is always a leading indicator of a douche canoe. Of his flip-flop, he said, "Opinions change, man." He's certainly entitled to have a change of heart. It was the subterfuge, misdirection, and smug tone—indeed, the duplicity—that grated.

Throughout the press conference, all three players trotted out a new Ari Fleischer–approved talking point: joining LIV Golf means enjoying more family time! For the forty-six-year-old Perez, content to play just the LIV events after a lifetime of heavy schedules on the PGA Tour, that turned out to be true. Reed also offered an endorsement for a limited schedule, saying, "Being the guy who's played 30 to 35 events [per year] my entire career and basically living through Facetime watching my kids grow up, I wanted to spend more time with my children. I wanted to be a dad." Those were moving words and, given Reed's estrangement from his own parents, deeply humanizing. Alas, six weeks later, he looked like a craven hypocrite when he played back-to-back Asian Tour events in Singapore and South Korea, chasing world ranking points (and dollars). Then, the following month, he added three European Tour tournaments to his

LIV commitments and played five tournaments in as many weeks, crossing the Atlantic four times to barnstorm from Boston to London to Chicago to Paris to St. Andrews. So much for having more family time.

In Portland, geopolitics once again intruded on LIV's carefully curated artificial reality. The management company that runs Pumpkin Ridge Golf Club, the host venue in the Portland suburb of North Plains, had gladly scooped up the $3 million site fee without consulting the club's members, leading more than a dozen of them to resign in protest. In the weeks and months before the tournament, the dissident country clubbers were happy to air their grievances in both the local press and national golf media. Four days before the first round, North Plains mayor Teri Lenahan released a letter condemning LIV that had also been signed by ten other mayors from surrounding towns. "We oppose this event because it is being sponsored by a repressive government whose human rights abuses are documented," the letter said. "We refuse to support these abuses by complicitly allowing the Saudi-backed organization to play in our backyard."

Senator Ron Wyden, a Democrat from Oregon, jumped into the fray, too, telling reporters, "It's just a page out of the autocrats' playbook covering up injustices by misusing athletics in hopes of normalizing their abuses."

The optics became even worse for LIV on the day of the first round, when a group of 9/11 surviving family members held a protest a couple of miles from Pumpkin Ridge. Brett Eagleson, whose father, John, had died in the collapse of the South Tower of the World Trade Center, spoke at a lectern draped with an American flag. "I think one important message to these LIV golfers [and] the kingdom is that we're not going anywhere," he said. "Every tournament you're going to have to deal with us in bigger numbers. More stories from the families are going to be in your face, for every tournament that is on U.S. soil. This is an attack just like they attacked us on American soil." Eagleson had some choice words for Mickelson, whom he called one of his boyhood heroes: "Now to see him kowtowing to the Saudis and saying he doesn't give a crap about the struggles and the pain and the misery. . . . Three thousand dead Americans. He doesn't care because he got offered a paycheck? It's just the worst form of greed."

LIV golfers and their benefactors were learning a hard lesson about sportswashing: some stains are particularly hard to erase. If LIV had been created as nothing more than a wildly expensive PR campaign, the early returns suggested that it had been a colossal failure. Prior to 2022, many golf fans hadn't given a lot of thought to the House of Saud's role in the world at large or its brutal treatment of citizens who dared to speak out. Now the conversation was inescapable and the critiques were withering. At one point, after watching players get pounded in another press conference, LIV's Jane Mac-Neille asked wearily, "Why do they keep asking the same questions? Do they think the players are going to start saying the Saudis are bad people? It's not going to happen." By the end of the season, Mac-Neille could quantify the stress: tests revealed that she had lost 15 percent of her hair density.

Yet once the tournament began, a festive feeling filled the air. Portland was a shrewd choice as the first American beachhead because it is an enthusiastic golf market that has been ignored by the PGA Tour; the Seniors, LPGA, and top amateur events have regularly visited, but the last time any of the best male pros competed in Portland was in 2012 for Jacobsen's off-season charity event. LIV did not release attendance figures, but educated guesses put the daily crowds at three to four thousand. More interesting than the raw number was the demographic profile. "The type of fan was like, 'Wow,'" says one curious spectator, Paul Regali, a former club pro at Columbia Edgewater Country Club, which hosts the LPGA's annual tournament in Portland. "It was very different from the traditional golf fan. It was a young crowd—lots of tattoos, lots of piercings, zero golf apparel. Usually you can spot golf fans from a mile away: Foot-Joy shorts, white belt, Peter Millar polo. This was a T-shirt crowd." Regali has a lot of friends who are club pros, but none of them joined him at the LIV event. "Some of them are traditionalists and felt an allegiance to the PGA of America," he says. "Some couldn't get past the source of the funding, which is the squeakiest wheel. I understand all of that, but I was curious and wanted to go with an open mind." Regali has long been a contrarian voice on Twitter under the handle @TheGhostofHogan. When he tweeted some enthusiastic thoughts about LIV, his mentions turned into, he says, "a cesspool of negativity. People were really upset that I would even dare to go, but it felt like they were mad without even knowing why. I think LIV does that to people, but then again, so does Twitter." Despite all of that, he says, "I thought [the LIV event] was cool. I'm glad I could go and have an informed opinion instead of being just another asshole shouting from the rooftops without really knowing what I'm talking about."

Ortiz led after the first round with a 67, one stroke ahead of Dustin Johnson. DJ caught him the next day with a 68, while Reed crept within 3 strokes of the lead. But during the final round, they were all blown off the course by Branden Grace, best known as the first man to shoot a 62 in a major championship, at Royal Birkdale Golf Club during the 2017 Open Championship. Grace's closing 65 in Portland carried him to victory. For a tour that's supposed to be built on star power, the low-key Grace (like Schwartzel before him) was not the dream winner. The team element created more intrigue, even if it remained the source of many jokes: Jacobsen already had a well-practiced bit about the "Master Blasters" and "Ace Holes." In fact, with the onboarding of new players, the various team identities were beginning to become more clear. Ortiz, Chacarra, and Ancer joined Sergio García's Fireballs, creating a hot-blooded quartet of Spanish speakers. The Majesticks featured four Brits: Lee Westwood, Ian Poulter, Sam Horsfield, and Laurie Canter. The Torque flew the

flag for Japan with Yuki Inamori, Ryosuke Kinoshita, Jinichiro Ko-
zuma, and Hideto Tanihara. Only the most relentless Golf Channel viewer had heard of any of them, but LIV was still wooing 2021
Masters champion Hideki Matsuyama, and having fellow Japanese
golfers for teammates was an important sales pitch for a player who
still speaks limited English.

In Portland, Johnson's 4Aces prevailed in the team competition,
scooping up 60 percent of the $5 million team purse. It was easily
the most top-heavy team, with DJ, Patrick Reed, and Talor Gooch
all in the top forty of the world rankings—for the time being. After
being sprayed with the victors' champagne, Gooch was so drunk on
the moment that he said, "I haven't played a Ryder Cup or Presidents
Cup, but I can't imagine there's a whole hell of a lot of difference.
This was as cool as it gets. We've been saying it all week. The energy
is just different, it's awesome." He was trolled relentlessly by fans, reporters, and fellow players, including PGA Tour winner MacKenzie
Hughes, who tweeted, "I've had lots of LOL moments with LIV, but
this is undisputed number one."

Among the Aces, the aging Perez was the outlier. He laid an egg in
the final round at Portland, shooting 80, but still collected $750,000,
one-fourth of his team's haul. (For each round, only the three best
individual scores are counted toward the team tally.) Perez making
a fortune in team money while struggling on his own ball would
become one of the recurring punch lines of LIV's beta test season.
"It's just been an unbelievable experience for me," he said in victory.
"Even though I've won three times [on the PGA Tour], it doesn't
matter. This was so cool. It was so different. I've always wanted to be
a part of a team, whether it was a captain or vice captain, whatever it
was. It's been the greatest experience I've had in golf."

That was quite an evolution for one of golf's angriest men. In
2016, Perez had earned his second career PGA Tour win in just his
third start back after left-shoulder surgery had put his future in golf
in peril. To hear him tell it, the victory was the feel-bad story of the

year. "I was so excited to come back, and then I got a call from Callaway," he says of the equipment company that had sponsored him for the preceding three years. "They said they had nothing for me. I said, 'Okay, fine. You don't believe in me, you don't believe in my comeback, then fuck you.' I loved those irons, but I couldn't wait to put something else in the bag and then shove it up Callaway's ass. It was such a motivator. I thought about it all day and all night, month after month. All I could think was, *I am going to bury these people, and nothing is going to stop me.* So you ask me how it felt to win? That's how it felt to win."

Perez's bad-boy reputation dates all the way back to his days at Arizona State, where he achieved the rare feat of leading his team to a national championship in 1996 and then getting kicked off it a year later because, he says, "the coach was bringing in all these hot-shit recruits, and I guess he thought I would be a bad influence on them." (That coach, Randy Lein, concurs, saying, "Pat would have been our only senior, and he was too immature to be in a leadership position.") The rebel image solidified at Pebble Beach during his rookie year in 2002 when, after slicing a shot out-of-bounds on the fourteenth hole, Perez excavated vast swaths of the fairway as part of a nationally televised tirade. He still came to the eighteenth hole with a 1-stroke lead but kicked away the tournament by pushing his drive out of bounds and then hooking his fourth shot into Stillwater Cove en route to a fatal triple bogey. "I'll never forget talking to Pat a little while after Pebble," says former Tour player Jason Gore, who grew up playing junior golf with Perez. "He says—and you'll have to excuse my language—'The fucking commissioner wants me to go to anger management classes. If they make me go do that, I'm gonna be so fucking pissed.' That's Pat." Adds Gore, "For Pat the F-word is like a comma. I fully understand that from the outside he comes off as an obnoxious schmuck you want to punch in the neck. But deep down he has a good soul. He just doesn't want anyone to know it."

It didn't help that his first mentor on the Tour was John Daly and that Perez adopted his hard-living ways. After a bender during the Las Vegas Tour stop, Perez was so close to missing his tee time that at a stoplight he popped his trunk, jumped out of the car, and grabbed his spikes so he could put them on while driving, saving the precious seconds that would allow him to make it to the first tee on time. During the 2005 Byron Nelson Championship outside Dallas, he was bunking at the house of another iconoclast, Tommy Armour III, and after the third round the two stayed out partying until 5:30 a.m. Perez returned home and passed out on the couch but was awakened a short time later by Armour's brother with the disconcerting news that his tee time was less than an hour away. "[Caddie Mike Hartford] sees me on the range and says, 'Have you been drinking?' I say, 'How can you tell?' He says, 'I can smell it from twenty feet away.' When I went to tee up my ball on the first hole, I almost fell flat on my face."

With his taste for the high life, Perez became pals with a bevy of rock stars, professional athletes, actors, and various other bold-faced names. It took 198 tries, but he finally won a Tour event, the 2009 Bob Hope Classic, with a kick-in eagle on the seventy-second hole. About two dozen friends and family members engulfed him in a melee on the final green, including Gore, Armour, Major League Baseball player Pat Burrell, and NHL veterans Brian Savage and Branden Gracel. Says Perez, "Arnie [Palmer] was there, and he was looking around like, 'What the hell is going on?' I promise you, he'd never seen a celebration that crazy before."

But Perez was embraced by the Christians as well as the pagans. He played innumerable practice rounds with Aaron Baddeley, who these days rarely cuts his hair or bathes, citing an idiosyncratic interpretation of Scripture. Before he had kids, Perez often roomed on the road with Jason Kokrak, filling the rental house with groceries and cooking every night. "About the only thing Pat won't do is bake me cookies and tuck me into bed at night," says Kokrak.

Perez is fiercely loyal to his friends. He played high school golf in San Diego with Hartford, who hired Perez for his landscaping business at $5 an hour. Perez has, in turn, employed Hartford (also known as "H") as his caddie and says the job is his for life, a brotherhood built on contrasts. "I drink, he doesn't," says Perez. "I smoke, he doesn't. I spend money, he doesn't. I cuss, he doesn't. I'm a motherfucker, he isn't." Unlike every other player on Tour, Perez leaves club selection to his caddie. "I put my entire trust in H," he says. "He'll say, 'You've got 158 [yards] front, 172 hole, 165 over this corner, wind off the left, give me a three-quarter six-iron.' Bang. Done. He can see it more clearly than I can. With all the pressure and the nerves, it's easy to lose your head out there."

The other key member of Team Perez is Ashley, whom Pat met in Las Vegas in 2012, when he dined with a large group at STK steakhouse. He was seated next to Ashley, a friend of a friend, but "We had already been drinking for a while, and I was so housed I didn't even notice her," Perez says. He tucked into a skirt steak and immediately demanded that the waitress bring the chef to the table. He nervously approached, and Perez shouted, "This steak is so good I want to give you a hand job right here. I mean it. Drop your pants."

"That was the moment when I started liking him," says Ashley. "I appreciated the weirdness." They've been together ever since. At their wedding, they served the entree that had brought them together, and it was given its proper name on the printed menus: HAND JOB SKIRT STEAK.

Ashley also gets the credit/blame for her hubby's luxurious mullet. "I think it's sexy," she cooed over a pork chop dinner in their home. "Look at that picture," she added, pointing to an image on the dining room hutch of a short-haired, boyish-looking Perez. "That's boring as shit. This guy with the long hair looks like he's ready to party."

Indeed, on the driving range at LIV Portland, Perez couldn't stop talking about the luscious Bordeaux served at a player shindig hosted the night before by Majed Al-Sorour, the head of Golf Saudi.

That wasn't the only delicious aspect to pledging with LIV; he had wangled a four-year deal that included a $10 million signing bonus. "My money is in," he said. "I got it all. It's fucking incredible." And then came the $750,000 gift from his 4Aces teammates.

From Portland, Perez returned to his 9,000-square-foot house in the hills above Scottsdale, Arizona, which Ashley has decorated in a style so over-the-top that Liberace would blush. The script on the dinner plates serves as a tidy rebuttal for those who would question Perez's new love affair with LIV: *Fuck who doesn't like this place.*

During the week of LIV Portland, the PGA and European Tours strengthened their alliance by announcing a thirteen-year "operational joint venture partnership." The PGA Tour took another 25 percent of European Tour productions but this time didn't put any cash into the deal. Instead, the Tour committed to underwrite purses in Europe for the next five years, with guaranteed annual increases. After that, the European Tour has an option to extend the relationship for eight more years. As part of the deal, the top ten finishers on Europe's season-long points tally, the Race to Dubai, would gain PGA Tour membership for the following season. More money and more access was a win for the players on the European Tour, but the tour had doomed itself to servitude, as its ten best players every year were now sure to bolt to the New World, with its much bigger purses. Under the guise of partnership, Jay Monahan had bought himself an effective delivery system for fresh talent at a bargain price. That was the new Darwinian reality of professional golf, in which the top tours were now competing for the scarcest of resources: star golfers.

Paul McGinley, a European Tour board member when the deal was consummated, pushes back on the notion that the tour sold its soul. "People say we've gotten fucked by the PGA Tour, but they don't understand the situation," he says. "The European Tour has always been the little guy. Our best players have always gone to America, because the money was two to three times better. Always! You'd have to go back to Monty"—Colin Montgomerie in the 1990s—"the last time our best player stayed home. More recently the money had become four to five times bigger, so how were we ever going to hold on to our players? Then the Saudis came in. What does that mean for the little guy? We had to fight for our survival. You can say we've been turned into a feeder tour [for the PGA Tour] if you want, but the fact is, the Saudis gave us just enough leverage to get the financial security we needed. All told, the PGA Tour is going to be into us for well over three hundred million dollars. The only way they get their money back is through European Tour productions, and for that to be profitable we need to have healthy tournaments, so the PGA Tour can't let us fail. So it's a very clever deal that gives us thirteen years of stability with no risk. We had to pick sides, and we chose security."

In the LIV Golf era, professional golf had become brutally tribal. With that as the backdrop, the game's most enigmatic icon was finally ready to pick sides, too.

13.

ON FEBRUARY 23, 2021, SOMETHING DARK VISITED TIGER Woods. He was in southern California, having just served as the ceremonial host of the Genesis Invitational at Riviera Country Club while recovering from yet another back surgery. On that fateful Tuesday morning, he had to be up early to film some content for *Golf Digest* at Rolling Hills Country Club. Woods was traveling east on a hilly, winding portion of Hawthorne Boulevard in Palos Verdes; the street curved right but he went dead straight, plowing through the median, careening across the two oncoming lanes of traffic, hopping a curb, knocking down a wooden sign, plunging down an embankment, and smashing into a tree. "There were several rollovers during that process," said Los Angeles County sheriff Alex Villanueva. Two days earlier, Woods had made a cameo in CBS's eighteenth-hole tower, sending shock waves through golf Twitter with his glassy eyes, bloated face, and slurred speech, particularly troubling signs given his previous treatment for an addiction to painkillers. In the wake of the crash, he steadfastly refused to fill in any details, batting away questions by saying, "It's all in the police report." Indeed it is: at the time of the crash he was traveling an estimated eighty-four to eighty-seven miles per hour, more than double the speed limit in the residential area. The most troubling detail? The car's black box revealed that Woods had kept stepping on the accelerator throughout the crash and that the pressure applied to the pedal had remained at 99 percent. That could not have happened if he had fallen asleep at the wheel or been momentarily distracted by his phone.

From 1997 to 2009, Woods played the most dominant golf of all time and became maybe the most famous athlete on the planet and probably the richest. The car crash was the culmination of a very different dozen years: tabloid infamy, sex addiction therapy, divorce, repeated injuries, DUI, leaked dick pics, rehab, and finally a near-death experience. We will never know the depth of his emotional pain, the shame and loneliness, the crushing weight of being Tiger Woods. The physical wounds are easier to quantify: there are twenty-six bones in the human foot, and according to someone close to Woods, he broke twenty of them in his right foot during the crash. He had multiple open fractures to his tibia and fibula, requiring a rod to be inserted into his right leg, and screws and pins were inserted into the foot and ankle. There was also trauma to the muscle and soft tissue of the leg, necessitating surgery to relieve the pressure brought on by extensive swelling. Woods says that for a while it was touch and go if the leg would have to be amputated.

Even before the crash, he had been grappling with his golfing mortality, owing to a series of back surgeries. Before the injuries, Woods had been unwilling to reveal the well-guarded fortress of his inner self, lest it lessen his advantage over the mere mortals who were cowed by his presence on the leaderboard. But from 2014 to 2017, he was a nonfactor between the ropes, sidelined for ten of the sixteen major championships and missing the cut in four of the six at which he teed it up. As he sat alone playing video games in the dream house he had built for his now ex-wife, the isolation was profound; the people he called friends were mostly on his payroll. If he was going to become a beloved elder statesman, like his idols Arnold Palmer and Jack Nicklaus, he would have to try a lot harder to build relationships. "We saw a different Tiger in that period," says his contemporary Stewart Cink. "He became more open, a little more vulnerable. You could feel he wanted to connect with people in a new way. I was so happy to see that from him. We all knew Tiger

Woods the player, but it felt like we were finally getting to know Tiger Woods the man."

The lone wolf became more engaged in the politics of professional golf. After Phil Mickelson torpedoed captain Tom Watson at the 2014 Ryder Cup during a charged press conference after another lopsided U.S. loss, Woods became a vocal member of the ensuing task force that reshaped the way the U.S. team groomed its leaders and chose its players. He volunteered to be a vice captain at the 2017 Presidents Cup and impressed everyone on the U.S. side with his openness and generosity. "I would say that's when we started to get a little bit closer," says Justin Thomas, who has since become like a kid brother to Woods. "I just remember I couldn't wait to ask him to go make me a sandwich, like, 'You're my vice captain this week; you have to do whatever I say.' I never in my life thought I would be bossing Tiger Woods around, and he had to listen to me because he's a vice captain."

Asked to supply a good story about Woods from that week, Thomas says, "Daniel Berger went to [vice captain Fred Couples] and said, 'Tiger can't come with our group.' 'What do you mean?' 'I'm too nervous playing in front of him.' Freddy was like, 'Dude, he's on our team. Like, he's our vice captain.' Berger's like, 'I can't do it, you have to send somebody else with our group.' So we thought we had Tiger to use to our advantage, to make the other team nervous, but actually he made some of our own team members nervous. So there's that."

After spinal fusion surgery in April 2017, Woods made the fifth swing overhaul of his career, finagling a new way to deliver the club to the back of the ball. He still had magic in his hands and unparalleled competitive instincts. His stunning victory at the 2019 Masters, the fifteenth major championship victory of his career, left a different feeling swirling in the dogwoods: he had always been revered, but now the all-too-human Tiger was beloved at last. He shared the moment in a joyous celebration with friends, loved ones, and even the fellow players he had once lorded over. He kept building on that win. In October 2019, he won another Tour event, the Zozo Championship in Japan, the eighty-second win in his incomparable career, tying Sam Snead for the all-time record. Then, as a playing captain at the Presidents Cup at the wondrous Royal Melbourne Golf Club in Australia, Woods was presented with the ideal canvas for his touch, creativity, imagination, and tactical genius. His thrilling play led the United States to victory. Somehow, someway, he willed himself into once again being the best player in the world. He had climbed so many mountains, but that was the tallest one yet. Thus began what was supposed to be a wondrous final act as Woods resumed the chase for what had once felt like his birthright: a nineteenth major championship victory to usurp Big Jack.

The car crash changed everything. Woods's iron will would not be able to reconstitute the powderized bones in his foot and ankle. His back remained balky, and now the simple act of walking had become onerous; how could he possibly haul himself up and down hills and swales and mounds and into and out of bunkers as he trudged twenty to twenty-five miles during four rounds of competitive golf? With such a brittle body, how could he endure the physical grind to keep his game tournament sharp? Woods's days as a serious contender were over. At age forty-six, he would have to reinvent himself yet again—not as a player but as a different kind of force in the game.

J. P. McManus grew up in humble circumstances in Limerick, Ireland. As a teen, he began hanging around the track, betting on horses. He had a nose for sniffing out proprietary information and enjoyed enough success that eventually he bought his own horse and then many more, which he raced and put out to stud. "There was a saying among card players," he says, "that money was made round to go around, but my mom had her own take on that: 'Money was made flat to build upon.'" He became a celebrated "punter," his reputation greatly enhanced after being dubbed "The Sundance Kid" by the *Observer*. He built an empire with an array of business interests, including as a private foreign exchange trader operating out of Geneva, Switzerland, where he established residency for tax purposes. At the 2006 Jewson Novices' Handicap Chase, McManus put £100,000 on his own horse, Reveillez, at six to one odds with a well-known Scottish bookie, "Fearless" Freddie Williams. Reveillez won, earning its owner a whopping £600,000. Later the same day, he placed a £5,000 each-way bet on the 50-to-1 shot Kadoun, one of four horses he had running in the Pertemps Network Final Handicap Hurdle. When Kadoun pulled off the upset, Fearless had to fork over another £325,000. Just another day at the office.

McManus loves golf and for decades has been a fixture at the Crosby Clambake at Pebble Beach and the Alfred Dunhill Links Championship at St. Andrews, usually playing alongside his best friend, Dermot Desmond, another of Ireland's wealthiest citizens. Everywhere McManus goes, he collects friends. "JP is wonderful company," says McGinley, the 2014 European Ryder Cup captain. "He's smart, he's measured, and for all of his success he is very modest. He is a good listener and a wonderful storyteller. It's always an education to be with him. What's the word I'm looking for? Endearing! There is something so endearing about JP."

Top pros like to be around McManus because, unlike almost every other person they encounter, he needs nothing from them. Every five years or so, he throws an eponymous charity fundraiser that attracts a better field than most PGA Tour events do. "No appearance fees, no fees to go and play in the JP McManus Pro-Am," said Padraig Harrington. "But JP asks nicely, and he will support every player who comes to his Pro-Am. JP will support them for the rest of their life and their charitable endeavours. That really is it. Whenever they're running a charity event, JP will be first on that list to support them, right around the world. Anybody who helps JP out will become a friend to JP, and JP will always remember that."

In the 1990s, McManus became close with Mark O'Meara, an American of Irish descent who began bringing his new pal Tiger Woods to the great links of the Emerald Isle to tune up their games en route to the Open Championship. McManus handled all the logistics, including providing helicopters to get the lads around the island. Woods, famously miserly, volunteered his time to play in his first JP McManus Pro-Am in 2000. Four years later, he married the Swedish bikini model Elin Nordegren at Sandy Lane in Barbados, a resort co-owned by McManus, who fussed over the details as if he were the father of the bride. In 2005, Woods said from the pro-am, "We come together for JP and for him only." In a tweet he would later call McManus "one of my dearest friends."

In the summer of 2022, the hobbled Woods skipped the U.S. Open but two weeks later turned up for the JP McManus Pro-Am, an utterly baffling turn of events unless you understand the depth of his devotion to the tournament host. McManus has so much juice that, without his having to ask, LIV Golf moved up by one day its Portland dates and chartered a jumbo jet to whisk players from Oregon directly to Dublin. The pro-am was held at Adare Manor in County Limerick, a course and a castle on which McManus has spent a reported £100 million to transform it into the host venue of the 2027 Ryder Cup. The tournament at Adare marked just the second time LIV and PGA Tour golfers would come together, and the situation became more fraught when, two days before the first round, LIV announced the signing of one of the pro-am competitors, the Englishman Paul Casey, at that moment the twenty-sixth-ranked player in the world. That continued the gutting of Team Europe, as Casey was the fifth member of the 2021 Ryder Cup team to bolt to LIV. For decades, the self-image of European players (and fans!) had been built largely on Ryder Cup successes. For so many of those heroes to turn their back on the Cup set off an existential crisis across the continent. On the morning of the first round of the pro-am, the golf world was further roiled by the news that the International Dispute Resolution Centre, a nonprofit, independent UK body, had granted three LIV players—Ian Poulter, Adrián Otaegui, and Justin Harding—an injunction against the European Tour's decision to fine and suspend them. The rebel golfers were granted spots in the Scottish Open, which would begin later that week. (A fourth LIV golfer, Branden Grace, would also be added.) Expressing the outrage of many, Rory McIlroy said, "I think at this stage, if you've gone over to play on another tour then go and play on that tour. You've basically left all your peers behind to make more money, which is fine. But just stay over there. Don't try to come back and play over here again. The whole cake-and-eat-it type of attitude is where the resentment stems from within the PGA Tour and DP World Tour membership. That's the tricky part."

McManus's guests tried to be on their best behavior to honor their host, but the tension could be felt in subtle ways: Jay and Susan Monahan were having dinner in the manor when Koepka walked across the room to shake the commish's hand for the first time since changing tours (and hosting him at his wedding). Caught a little off guard, Monahan stood up as Koepka pulled him close. A witness to the conversation describes Koepka's message as "Sorry, but a man's gotta do what a man's gotta do." As a loyal wife, Susan emitted a vibe so chilly that Koepka is lucky he didn't get frostbite.

With all of that awkwardness as the backdrop, the JP McManus Pro-Am was where the top players began an uprising that would reshape the PGA Tour as profoundly as the Nicklaus-Palmer rebellion of 1968. Woods and Monahan had hashed out in advance the idea of gathering loyalists at the pro-am for a brainstorming session on how to remake the Tour in response to the LIV threat. In addition to Woods and the commissioner, the meeting included McIlroy, Jordan Spieth, Justin Thomas, Jon Rahm, Scottie Scheffler, Collin Morikawa, Adam Scott, Shane Lowry, Matt Fitzpatrick, Xander Schauffele, Patrick Cantlay, Sam Burns, and Rickie Fowler. That's a heckuva lot of star power. Monahan was deferential to the players, posing questions but mostly ceding the floor. "I think it was important with what was going on in the world of golf to basically show unity to ourselves, right?" says Rahm. "To show some sense of vision for the PGA Tour as players ourselves. I think that was important. Not only for the Tour itself but just for us players to see that, okay, where is everybody else and where do we want the shift to be going to? That was the beginning of obviously a long process. I think I'm glad we did it, and it was needed. I don't remember the last time that, let's say, the top ten, fifteen players of the PGA Tour got together to discuss the future. I think it was something that was really good for all of us."

A consensus began to build among the Tour's leading men: They needed more money, of course, but the product would have to be refreshed. A bedrock principle in the Premier Golf League proposal, which LIV had put into practice, was that every player would compete in every tournament, ensuring more head-to-heads among the top talent. The bloated PGA Tour schedule made that impossible, but what if certain tournaments were structured with wildly elevated purses to be shared among a smaller pool of players? In exchange, all the top stars would be compelled to turn up at each one, ensuring box office. The Tour already had unofficial tiers of tournaments, with a handful of invitational fields smaller than others; those changes would simply codify it. "Obviously it was big-idea stuff and pie in the sky, and not all the details were fleshed out," says McIlroy, "but at least it created a framework that we could work from." There was an obvious downside to cleaving the Tour into the haves and have-mores: the nonelevated tournaments would wither and perhaps have difficulty attracting corporate sponsorship. But that was a concern for another day. To fend off LIV Golf, the PGA Tour would need to placate its most important players. The nonstars could only muck things up, which was why midlevel players at the JP McManus Pro-Am, such as Tom Hoge, weren't invited to the secretive confabs. "It's fine, whatever," says Hoge. "Those guys earned the right to be there. You're only as smart as your place on the money list, or at least that's the perception."

It has always been a fundamental question on the PGA Tour: Does the commissioner work for the players, or do they work for him? The activism of the golfers in the summer of 2022 answered that—for the time being. Newly empowered, Woods called a second meeting at the pro-am but pointedly excluded Monahan. It's not a coincidence that Woods, a lone wolf and introvert, found his voice while in the company of McManus. "JP never gives an opinion without being asked," says McGinley, "but he's always in the backwaters, watching, learning, asking questions. When you're ready, he's the guy to go to for answers. His life is about assessing odds and managing risk. Tiger goes to JP for advice. Of course he does. They are closer than people know. I don't think many people have Tiger's trust, but certainly JP does." In that second gathering, the players hatched the idea of bringing in "outside counsel," says McIlroy, though "not in a legal sense, but someone to bounce ideas off that's not within the Tour to sort of maybe bring a little bit more clarity. I think when you're in something, it's maybe hard to take a step back and see the bigger picture in a way. So to have someone come in and do that; that was definitely the initiation of those discussions."

McIlroy had someone in mind: Colin Neville. He's the boardroom Zelig from Raine Capital who led the Premier Golf League's unsuccessful negotiations with the European Tour. Throughout the process, Neville had impressed various folks with his love of golf and mastery of granular details. Because Raine had not lost any money when the PGL deal collapsed, Neville had no axes to grind, and he was happy to jump back into the arena, albeit for a different team.

Amid all the palace intrigue at Adare Manor, the LIV guys were living it up. Deep into the night following the closing party—at which Woods stood and offered heartfelt words about McManus— Koepka, Jason Kokrak, Pat and Ashley Perez, and Dustin Johnson and his bride, Paulina, repaired to a small, private bar tucked into the Manor. The drinks were flowing, and Paulina, spilling out of a tight black dress, was having trouble balancing atop a leather barstool. Perez, wearing a backward baseball cap, pointed at Johnson, who had recruited him to LIV, and shouted, "I owe everything to that man!" DJ was too busy tending to his wobbly wife to notice. Despite the relaxed setting, Koepka radiated some heat when reflecting on his career change. "Fuck all of those country club kids who talk shit about me," he said, referring to the likes of Justin Thomas, Jordan Spieth, and others. "You think I give a fuck what they think? You think I care what people say about me? I just had three surgeries, and I'm supposed to turn down $130 million? I grew up with nothing. After signing that contract, the first person I called was my mom. We both cried."

From Adare Manor, many of the players traveled to the Scottish Open in North Berwick. Woods and McIlroy skipped it, resting up for their date with destiny at St. Andrews.

When covid canceled the 2020 Open Championship, the stewards at the Royal & Ancient juggled the rota to ensure that the Old Course would host the 150th Open in 2022. It was supposed to be a joyous celebration of the game's oldest championship and most historic venue, but everyone was edgy during Open week. It marked Paul Casey's first real tournament since the onetime UNICEF ambassador had gone to LIV. The cohosts of the influential *No Laying Up* podcast had been staunchly anti-LIV from the beginning but they were particularly riled-up about Casey's turnabout: D.J. Piehowski called him a "historic, historic, historic pussy," while Tron Carter referred to Casey as a "cunt." With this as the backdrop, Sky Sports reporter Jamie Weir approached Casey on the practice chipping green at the Old Course to see if he would do an on-camera interview. "He said, 'Oh, hello, mate,' in his usual smug, insincere tone," says Weir. "I asked about having a chat, and right away he was defensive and wanted to know the questions. I told him I wanted to talk about the 150th Open, his good history at St. Andrews, how his back was feeling, and then finish off with a question about LIV." Casey asked what the LIV question would be. Says Weir, "I said that he was twenty-ninth in the world but had just joined a tour without ranking points and would surely fall out of the top fifty, so, given that, had he given serious consideration that this Open could be the last major championship of his career? His face darkened. He said, 'Fuck off. Go fuck yourself. What a fucking shit question. Go fuck yourself. That's a shitty fucking question from a shitty fucking reporter.' I said, 'Paul, you're massively overreacting to this.' He was like, 'No, I'm not. Go fuck yourself. Fuck you, and fuck your interview.'"

Says Casey with a laugh, "That's a fairly accurate recounting. But what is missing is the fact he sauntered over, invaded my space, and interjected himself into an environment where he was not invited. And what he actually said was, 'This is probably going to be the last major championship you ever play.' He's just assuming I'm going to fail! I could have won that Open and been exempt for another twenty-five years. I was there grinding on my game, and it was his smugness that got me. I can debate with anybody, but he was just being a dickhead. You know what, Jamie Weir can go fuck himself. Again."

The tension seeped into all of the week's pomp. The R&A hosted a "Celebration of Champions" in which thirty-eight male and female winners of various British Amateurs and Opens played in a four-hole exhibition. It was a glittering roll call of living history, featuring Woods, McIlroy, Jack Nicklaus, Tom Watson, Lee Trevino, and Nick Faldo, among others. Louis Oosthuizen also played; he had pledged his allegiance to LIV but is so amiable and innocuous that no one objected to his presence. One two-time Open champion was not invited: Greg Norman. The golf establishment was going out of its way to punish and humiliate him. Mickelson also skipped the exhibition. "[The R&A] said, 'Look, we don't think it's a great idea for you to go, but if you want to, you can,'" he said. "I just didn't want to make a big deal about it, so I said, 'Fine.' We both kind of agreed that it would be best if I didn't."

More hurtful was his snub from a private dinner for Open winners held in the R&A clubhouse. Woods orchestrated that. "He talked to a handful of other [past champions] to get their blessing and then went to the R&A and told them, basically, no one wanted Phil there and it would make the night weird and awkward," says one of the men at the dinner. "Whose side were they going to take, Tiger's or Phil's? That's an easy choice."

Woods's pretournament press conference was his first state of the union since LIV had been launched. He wasted no time twisting the knife into Norman, saying of his exile from St. Andrews, "Greg has done some things that I don't think is in the best interest of our game, and we're coming back to probably the most historic and traditional place in our sport. I believe it's the right thing."

Speaking more generally, Woods made it clear that LIV offended his worldview and his belief in the fundamental meritocracy of tournament golf: "I disagree with it. I think that what they've done is they've turned their back on what has allowed them to get to this position. Some players have gone right from the amateur ranks into that organization and never really got a chance to play out here and see what it feels like to play a Tour schedule or to play in some big events. And who knows what's going to happen in the near future with world ranking points, the criteria for entering major championships. Some of these players may not ever get a chance to play in major championships. That is a possibility, that some players will never, ever get a chance to play in a major championship, never get a chance to experience this right here or walk down the fairways at Augusta National. That, to me, I just don't understand it. What these players are doing for guaranteed money, what is the incentive to practice? What is the incentive to go out there and earn it in the dirt?"

Throughout Open week the rumors grew louder as to which player would be the next to jump to LIV. One name kept coming up: Cam Smith, the vastly talented twenty-eight-year-old Aussie who four months earlier had won the PGA Tour's flagship event, the Players Championship. Smith didn't exactly quiet the loose talk when, during one of the practice rounds, he jogged across the first fairway to crash a photo op of LIV players on the Swilcan Bridge. He remained the center of attention after a first-round 67, tied for third, four shots behind the leader, Cameron Young, a young ball basher from New York. McIlroy was alone in second with a 65. Those were stellar scores, but all eyes were on Woods.

Throughout the 2022 season, he displayed an almost maniacal desire to return to competition, which would provide a kind of closure from his car crash, though not necessarily redemption. That he limped his way to making the cut at the Masters and the PGA Championship deserves to be remembered among the most impressive accomplishments of an unparalleled career. (He withdrew after three rounds at the PGA Championship because of the intense pain he was in.) But all along, Woods trained his focus on St. Andrews. He believed in his heart that he could contend on the flat course, which is a much easier walk than Augusta National or Southern Hills, the site of the PGA Championship. More to the point, the Old Course is a chessboard as much as a golf course. Woods has repeatedly broken his body, but it's comforting to think that this master tactician's golfing intellect remains intact. In the run-up to St. Andrews, he pushed himself harder than at any point since the accident. Could he somehow summon one more performance for the ages?

The delicious anticipation lasted about seven minutes into Woods's first round, when he fatted his approach shot on the first hole so badly that it bounced into a burn that is rarely in play. He blamed the divot his ball had been in and, spuriously, a gust of wind; in his prime, Tiger never made excuses, and he never would have missed short on a watery hole when he had all of Scotland long. He grinded hard during the first round but, plagued by imprecise short irons, faulty lag putting, and myriad maladies, could not produce any magic. He looked rusty in the extreme during a 78 that left him in 145th place. The only cure for play like that is tournament reps, but those now have to be parceled out judiciously.

Still, Tiger has always had a way of elevating our expectations. Overnight rain made the Old Course less fiery for the second round. *If he could get off to a hot start and get the putter working, maybe shoot a sixty-s—* no. He bogeyed the fourth hole, failed to birdie the par-5 fifth (missing a five-footer), and then foozled one out of the rough on number six, leading to another bogey. The crowd went limp, and Woods became more inward. It was now a certainty that he would miss the cut, setting up a three-hour requiem.

By the time Woods arrived at the eighteenth tee, all of St. Andrews had gathered to see him off. He roped a 3-wood into the Valley of Sin and headed home. (Having recently been made an honorary member of the R&A, he now has a locker within the stone fortress behind the eighteenth green.) As he walked toward the Swilcan Bridge, he suddenly became aware of how lonely it is at the top; the other players and caddies in his group had lingered by the tee, ceding him the stage. He marched down the rumpled fairway, tears welling in his eyes. Sheila Walker, the great-great-granddaughter of Old Tom Morris, watched from the window of her second-story apartment near the eighteenth green, which Old Tom had redesigned during his four decades as the steward of St. Andrews, beginning in 1864. Tweedy gents with gin-blossomed noses crowded the balcony of the R&A clubhouse. The vast grandstands shook with applause for Woods. McIlroy, walking down the adjoining first fairway, gave his boyhood hero a nod and a subtle tip of the cap, and something broke loose inside Tiger. The tears tasted of more than salt: pride, regret, passion, wistfulness, willfulness.

Woods has vowed to try to keep playing the Open, but he will be in his mid-fifties the next time the tournament returns to the Old

Course. "It's hard just to walk and play eighteen holes," he said after his round. "People have no idea what I have to go through and the hours of work on the body, pre and post, each and every single day, to do what I just did." This was goodbye. Even he knew it.

Woods was determined to play hard until the bitter end, and the crowd hushed as he approached his ball near the eighteenth green. St. Andrews is always bathed in sound, including the sodden chatter emanating from the pubs. Now seagulls could be heard shrieking. So could the evocative, faraway sounds of a bagpiper busking on nearby North Street. It had been a blindingly bright afternoon, but just then the sun disappeared behind a puff of clouds, the temperature dropped, and suddenly it felt like Scotland again. U.S. Open champion Matt Fitzpatrick, who had driven his ball close to Woods's, played first. On such a touch shot he normally employs a wedge, but, feeling the magnitude of the moment and knowing the whole world was watching, he went for a safer play with a putter. Woods followed with a lovely pitch to within three feet. The crowd roared again. But he missed the birdie putt, one more letdown during a bittersweet day. To use one of his pet phrases: *It is what it is.*

Afterward, Woods talked movingly of the emotional goodbyes that Nicklaus and Palmer had made from the Open. They had been almost two decades older than Tiger is now, yet haler and heartier. That is the thrill and the tragedy of Woods's career: he gave so much to the game, and to us, but it came at a steep cost. The Open was a chance to remember and celebrate—and to anguish.

With Woods exiting stage right, the 150th Open belonged to McIlroy. The wee Northern Irishman had been a towering figure in the game throughout 2022. During the third round he shot a scintillating 66, tying for the lead at 16 under with young Viktor Hovland, four strokes clear of their nearest pursuers. In one fell swoop McIlroy was going to win the 150th Open Championship, end his brutal eight-year drought in the majors, and singlehandedly thwart the Saudis. Storybook stuff.

On Saturday night at the Rusacks St. Andrews hotel, McIlroy's father, Gerry, ducked into an elevator carrying a pizza.

"He's playing beautifully," a reporter said to him. "It would be good to see him finish this off."

"Aye, it would be good for the game," Gerry replied.

The magnitude could be felt the next afternoon on the first tee. Rory's expression was impassive, but as he played his opening drive, a baby-faced standard-bearer stood at the edge of the tee box, struggling to keep his sign steady. It wasn't the wind. "My hands were shaking," the kid said a few minutes later. "I don't know why I'm so nervous, but I am."

The whole golf world was equally aflutter. Rarely have a man and a moment seemed so perfectly aligned. Following McIlroy's group, in tartan pants, was Jamie Weir, the Sky Sports reporter from Northern Ireland whose sister had gone to school with McIlroy. He did not try to hide his partisan interest. "In my entire life I've never wanted any outcome at any sporting event as much as I want Rory to win this," Weir said. He had nothing on the kid in the gallery carrying a handmade sign that said, "Rory I'm named after you!"

But across the front nine, McIlroy looked tense and edgy, and his discomfort showed on the greens as he squandered numerous scoring chances. Hovland retreated, ceding the chase to the two Camerons playing in the group ahead: Young, a young American who wields his driver like a sledgehammer, and Smith, the relentless Aussie whose genius with the wedge and putter threw into sharp relief McIlroy's shortcomings. While Rory was sizing up a hundred-foot eagle putt on the tenth hole, Smith was rolling in a sixteen-footer on eleven for a birdie that momentarily sliced the lead to a lone stroke. But McIlroy deftly cozied his putt to tap-in distance for a much-needed birdie, pushing to 18 under. The crowd released two hours of bottled-up tension with the loudest roar of the day. McIlroy had yet to miss a green in regulation and still had two very short par 4s (on twelve and eighteen) and a par 5 (on fourteen) coming. It felt as though he already had one hand on the Claret Jug. At the farthest point from town, the mood was festive, trending toward giddy.

But Smith just kept coming, raining in another birdie on thirteen to snatch a share of the lead. As McIlroy reached the fifteenth tee, there were the familiar cries of "Let's go, Rory!"—but the tone had curdled: it was now plaintive, even desperate, as Smith had just made his fifth straight birdie to take the lead. Sitting cross-legged under the rope line on the fifteenth tee were a half-dozen little boys. Their eyes never left McIlroy. His drive peeled toward the left rough, and the crowd murmured its concern. In the quiet, one of the boys said softly, "You can do it, Rory." It was touching in its tenderness. McIlroy slashed his ball out of the long grass, but it trickled forty feet too far. He missed the putt and was now running out of holes.

After a sloppy wedge at sixteen and a blown eight-footer at the Road Hole, McIlroy trudged to the eighteenth tee. He watched in the distance as the Camerons putted on the final green. Whistling and buzzing accompanied Young's eagle, which momentarily tied him with Smith, one shot ahead of McIlroy. From a thousand feet away, it was hard to tell how short Smith's birdie attempt was, but the ball rolled for only a split second before disappearing. The denouement was stunning in its swiftness. Six holes earlier, McIlroy had led by 2 strokes. Now he was down 2 and needed a miracle at eighteen, which would not come. Smith had shot 64—including a rousing back-nine 30—in ideal scoring conditions, while McIlroy had labored to a 70.

Earlier in the week, McIlroy had called an Open Championship at the Old Course the crown jewel of the sport. Smith had burgled what seemed like McIlroy's birthright. Afterward, McIlroy conducted himself with his usual dignity in his press conferences and then retreated to his suite at the Rusacks St. Andrews hotel, overlooking the Old Course's eighteenth hole. He came to the window with his one-year-old daughter, Poppy, in his arms. He jiggled her floppy arm to make a little wave, and on an outdoor deck one floor below, a big crowd of revelers cheered the charming scene. A few minutes later, another roar went up. It was down near the R&A clubhouse, where Smith had materialized to sign autographs. He, too, was carrying something in his arms: the Claret Jug.

In the days that followed, LIV Golf doubled its offer to Smith—to $100 million.

14.

THE NOTION OF RANKING THE BEST GOLFERS IN THE world has always been intertwined with the purpose of selling them. In the 1960s, the pioneering sports agent Mark McCormack began publishing his own ranking to help generate commercial interest in his Big Three of Arnold Palmer, Jack Nicklaus, and Gary Player. The idiosyncratic ranking was built on McCormack's personal feelings mixed with recent results. By the mid-1980s, golf was increasingly global, and McCormack's International Management Group represented a broad cross section of players, including Australia's Greg Norman. A new generation of Europeans was also asserting themselves in the Ryder Cup and at Augusta National. McCormack began pushing for a more formal and scientific system, but even then commerce loomed large: in a 1985 proposal to Panasonic to sponsor the nascent world ranking, he inserted a proposal for the electronics company to sponsor IMG client Curtis Strange at $150,000 a year, branding him as "Panasonic's pro."

Eventually, Sony signed on as the sponsor and the world ranking debuted on April 6, 1986. It sorted professional tournaments into four tiers, with Grade 1 being the major championships and Grade 4 consisting of the least prestigious events in the United States and Europe and events on minor-league circuits such as the Safari Tour. The results in each tier were assigned point values across a three-year period. The reigning Masters champ, Bernhard Langer of Germany, topped the inaugural weekly ranking, followed by Seve Ballesteros (Spain) and Sandy Lyle (Scotland). At number four, Tom

Watson was the only American in the top seven. IMG owned and operated the world ranking until McCormack's death in 2003, which led to suspicions that the books were being cooked. "The world ranking has always been corrupt," says Paul Casey. "Funny how IMG clients were always number one." After McCormack's death, an independent body formed and took ownership of the list, which was rechristened the Official World Golf Ranking (OWGR).

The mathematical formula underpinning the list would be tweaked relentlessly in the coming decades, but one of its uses remains commerce: virtually every player endorsement contract contains a bonus for reaching number one or, for less accomplished players, finishing a year in the top fifty or top one hundred. Still, over time the primary purpose of the OWGR became as a gatekeeping mechanism for the major championships. The Masters and Open Championship invite the top fifty, and the U.S. Open exempts the top sixty (each has a different cutoff date, whereas the PGA Championship does not explicitly cite the OWGR in its qualifying criteria but it influences its committee's decision making).

For the players jumping to LIV Golf, not earning world ranking points, and thus access to the majors, was one of the biggest risks. (To quote *Mad Men*'s Don Draper: that's what the money is for.) On July 6, 2022, LIV submitted its application to be recognized by the OWGR. Its fate would be decided by the governing board, which is made up of blue bloods of the establishment: Jay Monahan and Keith Pelley; European Tour COO Keith Waters, who represents the International Federation of PGA Tours (which consists of smaller circuits such as the Sunshine Tour, Japan Golf Tour, and Asian Tour); United States Golf Association CEO Mike Whan; Martin Slumbers, the CEO of the R&A, and his predecessor, Peter Dawson; PGA of America CEO Seth Waugh; and Augusta National Golf Club executive director Will Jones. No wonder Norman felt that the fix was in. In a parking lot chat at LIV Golf Portland, he called it a "farce" and a "sham" that Monahan and Pelley would be reviewing LIV's application, despite their glaring conflicts of interest. In a letter to his players, he wrote, "Without LIV's inclusion, the integrity and accuracy of the rankings themselves are severely compromised." It was a clever ploy: the world ranking needed LIV more than LIV needed it!

Norman and various LIV golfers are always quick to play the victim card, but they were not automatically entitled to ranking points just because they started a tour from scratch. The OWGR has a twelve-month review period for any tour that applies for recognition, and the governing board long ago set forth criteria that include: seventy-two-hole events with a thirty-six-hole cut; a field size that averages seventy-five or more across a full season; an annual qualifying tournament held before the start of each season. LIV had none of those, but, having staked out their victimhood, Norman and his players didn't want to get bogged down by niggling details. A group of LIV players sent a letter to Dawson, who chairs the governing board but does not have a vote. He is the quintessence of a sober, uptight, possibly constipated Brit; Tiger Woods says that when reflecting on his iconic chip-in at the sixteenth hole during the 2005 Masters, he always thinks of Dawson, the walking official in the group who had stood right behind him as he played the shot. Says Woods, "So everyone is screaming and yelling, and Peter is just as stoic as can be back there." Still, the LIV players tried to blow some sunshine up Dawson's ass, writing, "To maintain trust, we urge you—as one of the true statesmen of sports—to act appropriately to include, on a retroactive basis, the results of LIV Golf events in OWGR's ranking calculations. An OWGR without LIV would be incomplete and inaccurate, the equivalent of leaving the Big 10 or the SEC out of the U.S. college football rankings, or leaving Belgium, Argentina, and England out of the FIFA rankings." Dawson's fluency in college football remains unknown.

For decades, a seat on the governing board of the OWGR was a musty ceremonial position. The organization has a technical committee of math nerds who do the real work, running the numbers and every few years updating the formula (with the board's assent), inevitably infuriating players on different tours who believe that their careers are being messed with by an unknown algorithm. But now the stakes had been raised for the governing board. It met during the week of the Open Championship, as is the custom, though it was the first time anyone can remember lawyers being in the room. The whole gang was there, including Monahan, Pelley, and Waters; they would not recuse themselves until December under the urging of legal counsel, after having participated in two board meetings. Their tardiness in not recusing themselves immediately remains a baffling decision that tainted the process, or at least the public perception of it. "I don't have a good answer for why we didn't do it sooner," says Pelley. "Things were moving quickly at that time. I have a governance and fiduciary duty to do what is best for the ranking. I wasn't fussed either way—I felt that I could be impartial. But once the lawyers said we should recuse ourselves, I was okay with it. What is important to understand is that the major championships have the most influence on the OWGR. They have four out of the seven votes. So even if Jay and Keith [Waters] and I had not recused ourselves, and even if we somehow wanted to collude against LIV, which I can categorically say never happened, we wouldn't have had the votes to do that."

In St. Andrews, the feeling in the room was irritated resoluteness. Despite the pleadings of Norman and his players, the OWGR had zero intention of fast-tracking LIV's bid to get points. "We knew what Greg was saying and that it could get litigious," says a member of the governing board. "We kept saying, 'Let's follow the process, let's follow the process. Why do we need to change our process just because a new tour was being noisy and trying to put pressure on us?'"

Dawson's only public comment following the St. Andrews meeting was delivered in a tone drier than a week-old crumpet: "An examination of the application will commence."

Two weeks after the Open Championship, LIV rolled into Trump Bedminster. As had become customary, the run-up to the tournament featured a splashy player announcement; in this case, Henrik Stenson, 46. The 2016 Open Championship winner had not enjoyed a victory anywhere in the world in the preceding five years, but most of his value came from what he was giving up for LIV: the captaincy of the 2023 European Ryder Cup team, a giant middle finger to the golf establishment. Just hours before Stenson's acquisition was announced by LIV, Team Europe put out a statement that read, "In light of decisions made by Henrik in relation to his personal circumstances, it has become clear that he will not be able to fulfill certain contractual obligations to Ryder Cup Europe that he had committed to prior to his announcement as Captain on Tuesday March 15, 2022, and it is therefore not possible for him to continue in the role of Captain."

Stenson had long been linked to the PGL and then to LIV Golf. According to several LIV executives, he was always envisioned as one of three captains of a franchise along with his friends and contemporaries Lee Westwood and Ian Poulter. All of those rumors hung over his negotiations to be the Ryder Cup captain, what many decorated champions have called the biggest honor of their golfing lives. Knowing that Stenson was working both sides of the street, Team Europe sought ironclad assurance that he would not be going to LIV if he signed on as captain. "There were a number of conversations with Henrik," says Pelley, who was on the committee that chose Stenson as captain. "'Are you sure you want to do this?' He emphatically said yes. Because it was made very, very clear he could not join a tour in direct competition with the DP World Tour as long as he was captain. By the time we got to the vote, he had agreed to that verbally." Then Stenson signed a contract stating that he "will act as an ambassador exclusively for the Ryder Cup and DP World Tour." After he was announced as captain, Stenson participated in a press conference in Florida and flew to Rome to film are-you-not-entertained content in an empty Colosseum, Team Europe having called in numerous favors to get inside a half hour before the place was opened to the public.

Then Stenson cashed in with LIV. (It should be noted that in 2009 he had lost $8 million in Allen Stanford's Ponzi scheme.) He offered a long word salad on his social media channels in which he tried to paint himself as the victim: "I am hugely disappointed to not be allowed to continue in my role [as Ryder Cup captain] but wish you all the best in your ongoing preparations."

Says Pelley, "I have worked with athletes for the better part of thirty-five years across multiple sports, and I have never been more disappointed by an athlete than I was with Henrik. What he did was massively disrespectful to the Ryder Cup and to all the players and captains who came before him and to all of our staff who had worked tirelessly with him."

Asked for a response, Stenson says, "This is another side of the story that will come out someday, but today is not that day."

In the days before he hosted LIV at his Bedminster course, Donald Trump inevitably stirred the pot. In a post on Truth Social he wrote, "All of those golfers that remain 'loyal' to the very disloyal PGA, in all of its different forms, will pay a big price when the inevitable MERGER with LIV comes, and you get nothing but a big 'thank you' from PGA officials who are making Millions of Dollars a year. If you don't take the money now, you will get nothing after the merger takes place, and only say how smart the original signees were." If Trump could see the future, perhaps it is because he has a

messy past with breakaway leagues, having played a prominent role
in destroying the United States Football League (USFL), the would-
be competitor of the NFL.

In 1983, after the USFL had played one rollicking season, Trump,
37, bought the New Jersey Generals for just under $10 million. He
didn't really care about the USFL, what he called "small potatoes."
He wanted an NFL franchise—or, more precisely, the attention that
would come with owning one. At one of his first USFL league meetings, Trump waved a copy of the *New York Times* and said, "Look
at this! I build a skyscraper and nobody cares! I sign some obscure
defensive back and I get three paragraphs in the *Times*. That's why I
bought the Generals!"

The USFL's business model was predicated on playing in the
spring and not competing head-to-head with the NFL. Trump
thought that spring football was for losers. He began planting stories in the New York newspapers that the USFL would be moving
its games to the fall. The other owners were furious. John Bassett of
the Tampa Bay Bandits called Trump a "con man." He later mailed
a letter to Trump, reproduced in Jeff Pearlman's lively USFL history
Football for a Buck: The Crazy Rise and Crazier Demise of the USFL,
which included the line "You are bigger, younger and stronger than
I, which means I'll have no regrets whatsoever punching you right
in the mouth the next time an instance occurs where you personally
scorn me, or anyone else, who does not happen to salute and dance
to your tune."

Trump arranged a secret meeting with Pete Rozelle, the imperious commissioner of the NFL. He went in with a hard sell, but
Rozelle, wary of Trump's bombast and reputation as a charlatan, told
him, "Mr. Trump, as long as I or my heirs are involved in the NFL
you will *never* be a franchise owner in the league."

Undeterred, Trump kept pushing for a move to the fall, hoping
that his franchise would be absorbed into the NFL through a merger,
just as four ABA teams had joined the NBA in 1976. "He was not an

honorable man," says Jerry Argovitz, the owner of the USFL's Houston Gamblers. "The truth wasn't his thing. But I've always said one thing about Donald Trump: you don't ever underestimate him. He can charm you out of your pants. And he's like getting involved with a rainbow or tornado or a hurricane or a zombie—all at the same time, depending on his mood."

Trump eventually persuaded the USFL owners to vote on a move to the fall. The league commissioned a McKinsey report on the viability of competing head-to-head with the NFL, and the consultants concluded that it would be ruinous. Yet the USFL owners still voted to play their games in the fall. "It was Donald's sheer force of personality," says Bassett. "For good or bad, he was a leader of men."

The TV networks had minimal interest in televising the USFL in the fall. Teams that shared a city with established NFL franchises couldn't find a stadium to play in or vendors or employees to work the games. Rather than compete with the Steelers, the Pittsburgh Maulers simply shut down operations. The Chicago Blitz also folded instead of going head-to-head with the Bears. Other teams fled the fan bases they had worked so hard to build: The Boston Breakers moved to Portland (to get away from the Patriots), while the Washington Federals moved to Orlando (to avoid the Redskins).

A year later the USFL was dead, and for those on the inside, there's no question who had blood on his hands. Argovitz's postmortem could have served as a warning to LIV players and executives, if any of them were a student of history: "We had a great league and a great idea. But then everyone let Donald Trump take over. It was our death."

The pro-am at LIV Golf Bedminster was a rare occasion when Trump put his game on public display. He is surprisingly limber for a portly man of six foot two, and his good eye-hand coordination shows through in all aspects of his play, but especially in his ability to hole putts, which he does with a wristy, old-fashioned stroke that is nothing like the method preferred by the best players today. On the backswing of his full shots, he takes the club way inside and, impressively, gets his left shoulder well behind the ball. He then makes a lunging, down-the-line swing, with his feet dancing through the finish. It's not pretty, but it repeats, and it's a swing with rhythm and power. "He's a much better golfer than you think he'd be because he hits the ball a long way," says Phil Mickelson. "He has clubhead speed, and there's no substitute for that."

Trump added juice to LIV's pretournament party in Manhattan. The *Sun*, Rupert Murdoch's popular tabloid in the United Kingdom, carried a story under the headline "Inside Star-Studded LIV Golf Welcome Party as Donald Trump, Caitlyn Jenner and Nelly Meet Rebel Golfers and Their Wags."

The gorgeous and thirsty wives and girlfriends had already become an inextricable part of the LIV brand, their social media channels full of glamorous posts of them partying aboard yachts and private jets and lounging in their luxurious homes and cars. (Ashley Perez went so far as to crowdsource on Instagram which accessories she should buy to pimp out her new Rolls-Royce, and another post celebrated her four-year-old daughter doing bumps of caviar.) In the week before LIV Golf Bedminster, Page Six of the *New York Post* carried not one but two stories about Brooks Koepka's sudsy honeymoon aboard a yacht in the Mediterranean, including one with the memorable headline "Brooks Koepka Promoted to 'Instagram Husband' on Honeymoon with Jena Sims."

The WAGs flooded social media with posts from the LIV Golf Bedminster kickoff party in New York City and the *Post* covered the party extensively, including a story with the headline "Paulina Gretzky Parties with Dustin Johnson in NYC Ahead of LIV Golf Event." It included four photos of Paulina in a tiny leather dress that looked as though it had been borrowed from the wardrobe department of *The Matrix*. Another photo showed Samantha Maddox in a micro-miniskirt; the Barbie-esque fiancée of Dustin Johnson's brother-caddie Austin, Maddox has a large following on Instagram, where she routinely posts photos in bikinis that appear to be constructed of dental floss. (Part of the drudgery of the golf beat these days is monitoring social media to keep track of which wives are tanning which cheek on which boat.)

Three tournaments into the season, LIV Golf staffers were increasingly skewing young, female, and attractive. Reporter Dan Rapaport's first LIV event was at Bedminster, and after being on the grounds for a few minutes he blurted out, "Why are there so many babes here? Every woman working the tournament is a nine." Marty Hackel, the longtime fashion director at *Golf Digest*, is four decades older than Rapaport, but at his first LIV event he craned his neck after an Amazonian LIV social media staffer as she sashayed by. Said Hackel, "It appears part of the business model is to employ as many beautiful women as possible." Jane MacNeille is highly competent in her role as LIV's vice president of player communications; as it happens, her preferred work uniform is a short, tight miniskirt. One (happily married) sportswriter sighed, "The only reason I like covering these events is to get a hug from Jane."

While LIV strained to sell itself as sexy, glitzy fun, the artificial reality ended at the country club gates. That a former president was profiting from a Saudi-backed venture in the shadow of Ground Zero touched off a series of protests on the roads leading into Trump Bedminster. (Fifteen of the 9/11 hijackers hailed from Saudi Arabia, and evidence continues to be made public that Saudi government officials materially supported some of the terrorists.) Brett Eagleson of 9/11 Justice, the group that had protested at LIV Golf Portland, was part of the Bedminster protests, and on CNN he said of Trump, "He is choosing money over America. So much for America First. A sad day."

Trump was unmoved, saying, "Nobody's gotten to the bottom of 9/11"—an obfuscation that was outrageous even by his standards. He batted away questions about the demonstrators.

The golf had political overtones of another kind when Stenson stormed to a share of the first-round lead with a 65, alongside another lightning rod, Patrick Reed. David Feherty, making his debut as an announcer on LIV's YouTube live stream, hammered the theme of Stenson's victimhood during the first-round broadcast, calling Stenson's Ryder Cup demotion "a bitter and mean-spirited move."

During the second round, the golf was overshadowed by an impromptu Trump rally. Without giving anyone at LIV a heads-up, the former president hosted in his private box by the sixteenth tee two of the most polarizing figures in American public life: Georgia congresswoman Marjorie Taylor Greene and Fox News pundit Tucker Carlson, who earlier in the week had done long on-air interviews with DeChambeau and Norman, brokered by LIV consultant Ari Fleischer, a contributor to Fox News. Carlson's being so chummy with Trump sent a stir through the Republican electorate; he had seemed to be favoring Ron DeSantis in the 2024 presidential race, to the point that, in the weeks before the LIV event, Donald Trump, Jr., had journeyed to Carlson's summer home in rural Maine to woo him back. From the aerie by the sixteenth tee, Greene led the crowd in pro-Trump ("Four more years!") and anti-Biden ("Let's go, Brandon") chants while Carlson looked on approvingly. The LIV Golf–Trump nexis is easily explained: both have built their brands as oppressed underdogs, fueled by grievance, as they paradoxically rail against the elites. For LIV— populated by golf royalty, funded by actual royals, fronted by a man who had spent 331 weeks as the world number one—that means battling the staunch traditionalists at the PGA Tour and the old boys running the OWGR. Trump—born into great wealth, educated at expensive private schools, builder of hotels and high rises and private golf clubs that are strictly for the 1 percent—has convinced working-class folks that he is taking on the establishment that birthed him. Ideological inconsistencies aside, the LIV Golf–Trump connection at Bedminster was intense, and the impromptu MAGA rally led to heartburn among various LIV executives.

"We had to take a hard look in the mirror after that," says one. Quiet conversations ensued with Trump's people, and the former president would take a much lower profile at the ensuing event at his course in Miami, only playing in the pro-am and then departing the grounds. But by Saturday night in Bedminster, the damage was already done. Representative of the coverage was a scathing op-ed in *USA Today* by Dan Wolken:

> Last weekend at Bedminster, the ruse that LIV Golf isn't an expressly political organization fell apart like human skin under the teeth of a bone saw. And it should surprise absolutely no one that Donald J. Trump was right in the thick of it. Sorry, but you can't claim apolitical status when video clips emerge of the former president, owner of the golf course and perhaps a 2024 candidate for the presidency encouraging "Let's Go Brandon" chants while standing next to Congress' most well-known conspiracy theorist, Marjorie Taylor Greene. Dustin Johnson and the rest of the LIV bros can't seriously suggest they're not being used as political props when they're teeing off with "Trump 2024" banners in the background. . . . For an American audience, the overwhelming Trump factor makes it much clearer what LIV is all about: For those who attend it, for those who play it, for those who want it to crush the PGA [Tour], there isn't a single entity in all of sports as expressly political as LIV. This is now the MAGA Tour.

Stenson, befitting his old "Iceman" nickname, played through all the distractions and went on to win by 2 strokes over Johnson and Matthew Wolff. Like Charl Schwartzel at LIV London, Stenson was a long-in-the-tooth major champion who hadn't won anywhere in the world in the preceding half decade before moving to LIV. Did the change of scenery reawaken his old competitive instincts, or was the competition on LIV that weak? The golf world was still grappling with the significance of a LIV victory, but Stenson derived deep satisfaction from his win (to say nothing of $4 million). "I think there might have been a little bit of extra motivation in there this week," he said. "When we as players have that, I think we can bring out the good stuff. Yeah, I certainly did that this week."

The 4Aces won the team element again, despite Perez's second-round 77. Their early dominance helped sharpen the focus on the team competition. Page Six was certainly paying attention. At the end of a long, messy week, it brought its readers the news they craved. The headline said it all: "Dustin Johnson Kisses Paulina Gretzky After LIV Golf Team Win."

15.

THREE DAYS AFTER THE FINISH AT TRUMP BEDMINSTER, the first shots were fired in the inevitable legal battle between LIV Golf and the PGA Tour, as eleven LIV players sued the Tour for antitrust violations in federal court. Their complaint centered on their yearlong suspension by the Tour for teeing up in LIV tournaments without having been approved for a conflicting-event release. The plaintiffs included Phil Mickelson, Bryson DeChambeau, Ian Poulter, Abraham Ancer, Carlos Ortiz, Pat Perez, Jason Kokrak, and Peter Uihlein. Talor Gooch, Hudson Swafford, and Matt Jones were part of the larger lawsuit but also filed a separate request for a temporary restraining order (TRO) that would allow them to play in the PGA Tour's first FedEx Cup playoff event, to be contested the following week in Memphis, Tennessee. The rhetoric from both sides was predictably hyperbolic. According to the players' complaint, "The Tour has ventured to harm the careers and livelihoods of any golfers . . . who have the temerity to defy the Tour and play in tournaments sponsored by the new entrant. The Tour has done so in an intentional and relentless effort to crush nascent competition before it threatens the Tour's monopoly." In a subsequent press release, LIV added, "The players are right to have brought this action to challenge the PGA's anti-competitive rules and to vindicate their rights as independent contractors to play where and when they choose. Despite the PGA Tour's effort to stifle competition, we think golfers should be allowed to play golf."

The Tour fired back by leaking a letter that commissioner Jay

Monahan had sent to his players: "It's an attempt to use the Tour platform to promote themselves and to freeride on your benefits and efforts. To allow reentry into our events compromises the Tour and the competition, to the detriment of our organization, our players, our partners and our fans. This is your Tour, built on the foundation that we work together for the good and growth of the organization . . . and then you reap the rewards. It seems your former colleagues have forgotten one important aspect of that equation."

LIV's complaint would come to be identified by the name of the tour's chief muckraker: *Phil Mickelson et al. v. PGA Tour, Inc.* The stakes were massive. If LIV were to prevail, it would reshape the structure of professional golf, turning golfers into free agents who, theoretically, could float from tour to tour, unencumbered.

Six days after the LIV players filed the lawsuit, a hearing on the temporary restraining order was held at the Robert F. Peckham Federal Building in downtown San Jose, California, a squat concrete building that evokes postwar Soviet architecture. Things didn't get off to a promising start when the courtroom clerk called out the case name: "MIKE-elson versus the PGA Tour." Judge Beth Labson Freeman presided. A petite woman with a Bettie Page hairdo, Freeman had a no-nonsense vibe and a welcome literacy in golf despite carrying a 32.9 index at Peninsula Golf and Country Club in San Mateo, California. Representing LIV was Robert Walters, a silver-haired, silver-tongued smoothie. Despite his well-practiced gentility, Walters evoked strong emotions from in-the-know LIV folks; one still refers to him exclusively as "motherfucking Rob Walters." Walters works for Gibson Dunn, a global firm that employs more than 1,900 lawyers across twenty offices in eight countries, including the United Arab Emirates. LIV, and by extension the Public Investment Fund, was footing the bill for the lawyers, so the PIF handpicked the firm. Gibson Dunn has done a lot of business with the PIF over the years, particularly in mergers and acquisitions, which is very different from antitrust law.

In his long opening salvo, Walters nibbled on a couple of issues—notably that Tour rules spell out that all players are entitled to an appeal of disciplinary action and their penalties are to be stayed until an appeal is heard, meaning that Gooch and the others should be allowed to compete on the Tour until such an appeal is heard. But Walters's primary point, what he called "the real irreparable harm," was an eye roll to the more golf-savvy observers in the courtroom: that the players' careers were being destroyed by not being able to compete in the FedEx Cup and thus, as Walters said, "stamp themselves among the elite in golf. It's about more than the money. That's how the PGA [Tour] itself characterizes it: Winning the FedEx Cup puts you in the Jack Nicklaus, Greg Norman category of the elite golfers. By the description of the PGA Tour itself, this is their Super Bowl, this is their World Series."

Never mind that both Nicklaus and Norman had stopped playing full-time long before the FedEx Cup was invented. Despite the Tour's breathless promotion, no one outside Ponte Vedra Beach, Florida, thinks the FedEx Cup is a big deal. It's a moderately interesting way to end the season and for the players to get paid. That's it. Walters also talked a lot about the FedEx Cup money. "It is by a number of magnitudes the biggest prize in golf," he said. "As a financial matter, it overwhelms any other possible earnings—"

Judge Freeman cut him off archly: "Actually, I think the evidence would suggest that LIV overwhelms any other potential earnings."

She made the point that the LIV contracts were so extravagant precisely because they took into account lost Tour earnings. As the arbiter of the larger antitrust lawsuit, Freeman would have the power to award monetary damages. As she said, "If we're quantifying [the FedEx Cup] and showing how lucrative it is, then you're not going to get a TRO because at the end of the day I can compensate the players if they are successful with the appropriate amount of money." It was all over but the shouting, and after another hour-plus of wrangling, Freeman ruled in favor of the Tour and denied the temporary restraining order. There was rejoicing in the locker room at TPC Southwind, the site of the FedEx Cup tournament in Memphis, as Rory McIlroy and Jon Rahm, among other players, monitored the live feed of the hearing on an iPad.

I'm not a lawyer but I play one on Twitter, and it seemed obvious that Walters whiffed on the most compelling point, mentioning it only in passing: the irreparable harm had to be measured in points, not money. By denying the players access to the FedEx Cup, the Tour was using its quasi-monopolistic power to prevent them from earning crucial world ranking points that would help them qualify for the major championships: the real World Series and Super Bowls of golf. Judge Freeman can dispense dollars, but she does not have the power to grant OWGR points. Only a temporary restraining order could have given the players access to points.

Beyond the particular issue of the TRO, this first day in court served as a preview of the larger antitrust case, for which Freeman set a tentative trial date in September 2023. (It would later be bumped to January 2024, then to May 2024.) The Tour tipped its hand by arguing that it can't be a monopoly because LIV has already been so successful barging into the marketplace. A slide was presented showing the Player Impact Program results for 2021 and the fact that five of the top ten most impactful players by the Tour's own measurements had joined LIV: Mickelson, DeChambeau, Johnson, Koepka, and two-time Masters champ Bubba Watson, 43, who had signed with LIV ten days earlier. The Tour's lawyer, Elliot Peters, said with a touch of wistfulness, "The competition is fierce."

Yet the establishment prevailed in the first skirmish. When the TRO hearing ended, the lawyers for the PGA Tour slowly made their way out of the courtroom. They were a dozen strong. Many were rolling large wheeled briefcases, while one junior associate strained to control a dolly loaded with three crates of documents. Win, lose, or draw, the army of sharply dressed advocates sent a clear message: the Tour knew it was facing an existential threat to its survival, and every available resource would be mobilized.

Meanwhile, back in Memphis, Gooch and Swafford got the bad news on their phones. They had arrived that afternoon to be ready to play if the ruling on the TRO went their way. Swafford had been hoping to squeeze in some practice but the hearing kept dragging on, so he sat in a parked car near TPC Southwind. Gooch drove to Memphis from his home in Oklahoma City, a seven-hour haul, and settled into a hotel room. As soon as word came down, Swafford headed back to the airport and Gooch got into his car and started driving. For both players, it was a long, lonely journey home.

The TRO hearing was only the beginning of the LIV-related litigiousness; the Tour countersued, claiming that LIV had committed "tortious interference with contract" while seeking damages for lost profits, reputational and brand harm, punitive damages, and attorney fees. (As the stakes went up, players began withdrawing from the original antitrust lawsuit, ultimately leaving LIV Golf as the sole plaintiff.)

A week after the TRO decision came down, Patrick Reed went rogue and filed a civil lawsuit against Golf Channel and its star analyst, Brandel Chamblee, in the U.S. District Court for the Southern District of Texas. The complaint contended that Chamblee and Golf Channel had "conspired" with the PGA Tour and Commissioner Jay Monahan "to engage in a pattern and practice of defaming Mr. Reed, misreporting information with falsity and/or reckless disregard for the truth . . . purposely omitting pertinent key material facts to mislead the public, and actively targeting Mr. Reed since he was 23 years old to destroy his reputation, create hate, and a hostile work environment for him, and with the intention to discredit his name as a young, elite and world-class golfer." The suit also alleged that Golf Channel, Chamblee, and the PGA Tour were "defaming and smearing anyone associated with LIV . . . in order to try to maintain their monopolistic hold on professional golf." Reed sought a tidy $750 million in damages.

The lawsuit was withdrawn a month later, only for Reed to re-file an expanded version of the case in the U.S. District Court for the Middle District of Florida in Jacksonville. Along with Chamblee, he was now targeting Golf Channel broadcasters Shane Bacon and Damon Hack, as well as Golf Channel commentator Eamon Lynch, the magazine he writes for, *Golfweek*, and the magazine's parent company, Gannett. Then Reed brought *another* suit, against Associated Press golf writer Doug Ferguson and *Golf Digest*'s Shane Ryan and his book publisher, Hachette. The complaint claimed that Reed's move to LIV Golf "was primarily due to this mistreatment, where adequate security was not even provided at PGA Tour events, where hostile fans vilified and threatened Mr. Reed, his wife, caddie, and coach, thanks to the rank defamation and other alleged illegal acts of Defendants in these two recently filed lawsuits." It called the reporters "jackals who make their sorry and pathetic living spreading lies and false information."

The rash of lawsuits and their unhinged rhetoric were the work of one of America's most notorious lawyers, Larry Klayman, whom the Southern Poverty Law Center describes as "pathologically litigious," "thin-skinned and paranoid," and a "sanctimonious conspiracist." Among those Klayman has sued in his long and rancorous career: his own mother; Hillary Clinton; Iran's supreme leader; the FBI; George Soros; Mark Zuckerberg; OPEC; President Obama; and the Republic of China, for $20 trillion for the "creation and release" of covid-19. Naturally, there was a Trump connection. In 2021, Klayman's law license was suspended for eighteen months by the Washington, DC, Bar's Board on Professional Responsibility due to ethical violations related to his expressing romantic feelings toward a client. He claimed that unseen forces were "on a legal 'jihad' to attempt to remove pro-Trump, conservative and Republican lawyer advocates" from practicing. Then again, Klayman is an equal opportunity rabble-rouser: he has also sued Trump ally Roger Stone for defamation.

A lawyer who creates this much messiness was the perfect advocate for Reed, though the petitioner couches his legal offensive in the noblest terms. "It was about time I stand up not just for myself but also for my kids," Reed told me. "Windsor-Wells and Barrett have been bullied in school—one is eight, one is five. That's coming from the parents and the picture the media has created of me. It's not okay, it's not who I am. It's affecting me emotionally and financially and it's affecting my kids emotionally. When Windsor-Wells was in first grade, two kids who were also in first grade walked up to her and said, 'Oh, no one likes your daddy so no one likes you, boooo.' That's just not okay. There's too much bullying going on, of me and them." He says that if he collects any damages through the lawsuit, he will use them to fund anti-bullying initiatives.

Reed had long wanted to use the courts to try to clear his name but says he felt that powerful forces were aligned against him. "Let's be honest, the PGA Tour controls most of the media," he says cryptically. "If they're against you, you'll never be able to get your narrative out there the right way. People shouldn't have that much power."

Control is not the right word, but PGA Tour loyalists have undoubtedly sought to leverage long-standing relationships with reporters. Rob McNamara, Tiger Woods's day-to-day manager, got in the face of *Sports Illustrated*'s Bob Harig to scold him for having the temerity to cover LIV events. Never mind that Harig has written hundreds, perhaps thousands, of celebratory stories about Woods and made him the centerpiece of two books. At the 2023 Wells Fargo Championship, Jay Monahan made a snippy remark to ESPN's Mark Schlabach for wearing a hoodie with a Pumpkin Ridge logo. It was not a political statement by Schlabach; it had been unexpectedly chilly at LIV Portland, and he had ducked into the pro shop and bought the sweatshirt without giving it much thought.

During these tumultuous times, no member of the media has provoked stronger feelings than Chamblee, the Golf Channel analyst. "He has to take Rory's cock out of his mouth so he can suck off Tiger," says Claude Harmon III, swing coach to Brooks Koepka, Dustin Johnson, and Pat Perez. "And Jay Monahan is next in line."

Chamblee is paid to provide opinion, and he has been withering about LIV Golf. "I see this as very black and white," he said in an interview. "On one side there is a murderous regime that has repeatedly committed atrocities against its own people. And on that same side there is the narcissistic greed of Phil Mickelson and Greg Norman and the men who run LIV who are trying to destroy the PGA Tour. I don't see another side to this. I think the LIV players are in a morally indefensible position, with a willful blindness to the consequences of their action, making them complicit to the ongoing atrocities."

Chamblee's message has often been amplified by his friend and Golf Channel colleague Eamon Lynch, who has also regularly produced sneering columns about LIV for *Golfweek*. "They are state media," says Harmon. "Golf Channel would go out of business without their quote, unquote broadcast partner, the PGA Tour. So Brandel and Eamon just repeat over and over the party line that LIV is bad for the game. Really, it's just bad for the PGA Tour."

Says Chamblee, "I laugh when people say I am a stooge or puppet of the PGA Tour. I disagree with, and take issue with, the PGA Tour all the time. The PGA Tour holds no power over me. My feelings about LIV have nothing to do with Golf Channel's so-called alliance with the Tour and everything to do with human rights. In 2019, long before LIV, I spoke out when the European Tour added the Saudi International to the schedule. I felt they were making a very big mistake letting a snake into the garden, and I said that. My position has been consistent from the very beginning." He adds, "No one at the PGA Tour or Golf Channel has ever told me what to say. That's not the way it works. Never, ever, not even once have I worried about what the PGA Tour or Golf Channel thinks of my opinions."

Says Harmon, "The most ridiculous part is that Golf Channel masquerades as a news organization but it never tries to tell the other side. It's like Brandel's opinions are gospel. Don't they have an obligation to at least pretend to care about balance?"

Says Chamblee, "We've asked people from LIV to come on our set and provide balance. Every single one turns us down because they can't defend their position and they know it. Phil, Westwood, Poulter—every single one of them has said no. That's why you don't hear their voice: They won't fight for their side because deep down they know what they're doing is indefensible."

LIV has instead focused on planting interviews with Norman and select players on Fox News and other conservative media outlets. (Clay Travis, the founder of *OutKick the Coverage*, played in the Bedminster pro-am.) "We are not going to put our guys in situations that are hostile," says a LIV executive. "Unfortunately, the way it's played out, the more left-leaning outlets glom on to the Saudi/Khashoggi narrative. They're obsessed with that, and they don't even mention the actual golf. The conservative platforms are a more friendly audience, and they're willing to talk about golf and what we're trying to accomplish."

It was only after he arrived on LIV, with its antiestablishment pose, that Reed felt comfortable lashing out against the golf press. Did PGA Tour officials discourage him from filing lawsuits? "They discouraged me from doing a lot of things," he says. "There were a lot of things that were said and done that are just not kosher."

Another way of looking at it: the PGA Tour was trying to protect Reed from himself. One of his former Tour colleagues, Stewart Cink, says, "I like Patrick Reed. He's fun to play with. But when you start suing everyone on the golf beat, that's where I draw the line and say, 'C'mon, man. Really?'"

Adds Tour player Tom Hoge, "It's a weird strategy. When you're in the public light, there is always going to be scrutiny. Are you going to sue everybody who says or writes something you don't like? That creates a lot of bad energy. But he seems to thrive on that kind of attention."

One of the reporters whom Reed is suing says, "I think Patrick and his crazy lawyer know they can't win; they just want to make our lives uncomfortable. As bizarre as the lawsuits are, we still have to take them seriously. The point isn't to win, it's to create this chilling effect where people will temper their criticism of Reed's antics just because they don't want to get sued and have to hire lawyers to defend themselves."

The stress Reed has injected into the pressroom was evident when I bumped into Lynch at a tournament; actually we were at neighboring urinals, and to break the awkward silence I asked if there had been any new developments in the legal proceedings. Lynch shouted, "I am not going to answer any of your fucking questions about Patrick Reed!"

An unexpected twist to the LIV era was that legal briefs were coming as fast and furious as birdie putts. As the various cases dragged on—including the LIV players' action against the European Tour being heard in the United Kingdom—only two things were certain: the gentleman's game had reached unparalleled levels of acrimony, and the lawyers were getting paid.

16.

IT WAS THE MOST EXCITING THING TO HAPPEN IN DEL-
aware since Caesar Rodney's midnight ride in 1776: Tiger Woods
would be jetting in to rescue the PGA Tour! History will record that
Woods made landfall on the Tuesday of the BMW Championship
being played at Wilmington Country Club. Six weeks earlier, Woods
and Rory McIlroy had convened their players-only meeting at the
JP McManus Pro-Am. Since then they had been a part of numerous
phone calls with Colin Neville of Raine Capital, outlining their vision
and letting Neville figure out the details. Other advisers had chimed
in throughout the process, and everything was on the table, including the Tour renouncing its nonprofit status so it could bring in
heavy private equity money or other outside investors. Now Woods
and McIlroy had called another meeting with the biggest names on
the PGA Tour, for Neville to present all of their ideas and to foster discussion among the players. I had caught wind of the meeting
the day before and tweeted about it, and various sickos breathlessly
tracked Woods's 2008 Gulfstream V as it flew from Florida. Woods
wasn't playing in the BMW Championship, but his very presence
overshadowed anything else happening inside the ropes. TV cameras caught him stepping onto the tarmac, and he had a resolute air.
"He was excited," says Rickie Fowler, who flew with Woods. "You
could feel how much he cares and what the Tour means to him. It
was inspiring to all the guys, myself included."

"Tiger has realized that he needs the Tour as much as it needs
him," says Adam Scott. "As the game has been taken away from him

[as a competitor], he needs new roles to play. It's nice to see that evolution, to be perfectly honest. Having played against him for my entire career when he was this dominant force, you didn't know whether you'd get a hello out of the guy at times. You know what I mean? But what's nice to see is that Tiger obviously cares a lot about the PGA Tour and all of his fellow players. We've seen a more human side of the guy. That's kind of a relief because he was a machine for so long." We will never know what precipitated Woods's car crash—if it was a moment of madness, an attempt to end it all. Reshaping the Tour gave him a purpose and the human connection he needed on the road back.

The meeting was held in a conference room in the Hotel Du Pont; it was reserved under the name Adare Manor, as a nod to where the ideas had begun to germinate. Jay Monahan had been speaking regularly with Woods and McIlroy in the days before the Delaware meeting but hadn't been invited. Had he exerted any influence on which players would be in attendance? "That was a meeting that was called by Tiger and Rory," Monahan says. "I may have made suggestions, yeah. I mean, I understood who was going to be in the room."

How much did the commissioner consult ahead of time with the two de facto commissioners? "The reality is I had a lot of conversations with Tiger and Rory," he says. "So I had a general sense of what they were talking about, absolutely."

There were 68 players in the field in Wilmington, and two-thirds of them hadn't been invited to the meeting. The FOMO raged. "Other players were texting me and asking if I was in the meeting and whatnot, and I didn't even know what they were talking about," says Tom Hoge. "It was a weird deal. It was kind of like high school when the popular people throw a party and you're not invited."

"My ego definitely took a hit," says Keegan Bradley, the 2011 PGA Championship winner. "I was pretty bummed not to be there. It was like, Jeez, I want to be thought of as one of those guys. It pissed me off, honestly. That motivated me to work a lot harder and I won shortly thereafter, and I don't think that was a coincidence."

Daniel Berger, home in Jupiter, Florida, nursing a back injury, asked if he could call in. "It was like, Nah, we'll fill you in afterward," Fowler says with a laugh.

Woods, McIlroy, and Neville waited in the front of the room as the players filed in. A couple of days before, Will Zalatoris had won his first tournament, the FedEx Cup event in Memphis, despite an errant tee shot on the deciding hole during a playoff versus Sepp Straka. When he walked in, "Tiger asked me if I was aiming at the flag on number eleven, and I told him not only no but hell no," says Zalatoris. "He just rolled his eyes and said, 'I saw your lines, I know where you were aiming.' That was kind of cool." The players plopped down around a long rectangular table; seating was random. This collection of talented golfers respects McIlroy but reveres Woods, and the weight of Woods's presence was palpable. "Any time I see him I feel a little electricity," says Max Homa. "It's always weird to be in a room with Tiger Woods. I don't think I'll get over that one." In addition to Woods, McIlroy, Scott, Fowler, Zalatoris, and Homa, the "Delaware 23" consisted of Sam Burns, Patrick Cantlay, Tony Finau, Matt Fitzpatrick, Tyrrell Hatton, Billy Horschel, Viktor Hovland, Kevin Kisner, Shane Lowry, Collin Morikawa, Joaquin Niemann, Jon Rahm, Xander Schauffele, Scottie Scheffler, Jordan Spieth, Justin Thomas, and Cameron Young.

Woods and McIlroy each said a few words before ceding the floor to Neville. His presentation began with doom and gloom: falling TV ratings, an inconsistent product from week to week, and the vexing realization that elite players drive value but aren't compensated accordingly. What the PGL proposal had gotten right, and what LIV had copied, was the compulsory attendance of every player at every tournament, so fans, sponsors, and TV networks would know exactly what they were getting. That kind of mandate isn't possible with the PGA Tour's forty-eight-tournament schedule, but Neville proposed an elegant solution: a tour within the Tour of up to fifteen "elevated" events with $20 million purses and limited fields. But for the Tour to go all in, the top players would have to as well, committing to play in every one of the new megatournaments. Exactly which events would be designated had not yet been decided, but there were obvious choices in the three FedEx Cup stops and the three prestigious invitationals: the Arnold Palmer Invitational, the Memorial Tournament, and the Genesis Invitational at Riviera Country Club, the provinces of Arnie, Jack, and Tiger, respectively.

After the presentation ended, the conversation began. The room was animated, with a lot of back-and-forth but in the end little dissent. After decades with a monopoly on big-time golf, the beleaguered Tour desperately needed to reinvent itself, and here, at last, was a road map. Thorny questions remained: Would the elevated events have a cut? Would that rarified status rotate among tournaments each year? What would the field size be? But in a sterile conference room in Wilmington, Delaware, of all places, the PGA Tour was reborn. As the meeting drew to a close, Woods asked if the players were in agreement. There were whoops of assent, and then the players charged out the door into the future.

The week after the meeting in Delaware brought the season-ending Tour Championship at East Lake Golf Club in Atlanta. It is usually a sleepy thirty-player affair, but not this time. Rumors were rampant about which Tour players would leave for LIV the following week. More immediately, Monahan's annual Wednesday press conference was expected to bring the announcement of sweeping changes in the structure of the Tour. Around East Lake, the air crackled with anxiety, anticipation, excitement, uncertainty. In the eight days since the Delaware meeting, there had been numerous conversations between the Tour brass and top players. The ideas from Wilmington had been, says one player in the room, slightly "watered down" by

Tour leadership because, as McIlroy put it, they had been "self-serving," designed to create a closed shop so the players at the top of the money list could comfortably stay there. The compromise was to have fewer elevated events, slightly larger fields, and more opportunities for ascendant golfers to play their way in, all nods to pushback from the rank and file.

On that Wednesday afternoon at the Tour Championship, Monahan entered a press tent crowded with high-ranking Tour officials, television executives, and other interlopers who usually don't mix with the typing class. The commissioner's cheery mood matched his pink tie. After a long preamble, he said, "I mentioned at [Hartford two months earlier] that you could expect more changes. I think it's important to understand that this process represents a remarkable moment for the PGA Tour and showcases the essence of what being a membership organization is all about. With the best interests of the collective in mind, those players rallied together to strengthen the Tour platform, recognizing that if fans are going to invest in the PGA Tour, it means a hell of a lot more if they know the players are investing right back." He announced that beginning in 2023, a dozen (unnamed as yet) existing tournaments would be elevated to $20 million events. Then he came to what he called "the headline": that the top players (who have always loved to call themselves independent contractors) would commit to all dozen of the tournaments as well as the Players Championship and at least three other run-of-the-mill Tour events per season. "This is an extraordinary and unprecedented commitment, a testament to who these guys are and what they believe in," he said. He also made public that for 2022 the Player Impact Program—the commish's nebulous slush fund—would double to $100 million and expand to twenty players. And that the Tour, once sport's ultimate meritocracy, would continue sliding into socialism, as beginning in 2023, all Tour players would be advanced $500,000 against their earnings, which they would not have to pay back in the event of injury or poor play. Monahan and the Tour may have been slow to react to LIV's incursion, and the commissioner had helped poison professional golf with his we-are-at-war ethos, but the changes announced at the Tour Championship were the ultimate rebuttal. It had been only two months since LIV had conducted its first tournament, and the Tour—ordinarily a lumbering, unimaginative organization—had revamped itself on the fly and secured an unparalleled buy-in from its top players.

Monahan began taking questions—and shrapnel. I asked him why he had not made those moves sooner. LIV's primary selling point has always been unprecedented money; if the Tour had committed to funneling new riches to its top players in the winter of 2021, as LIV was still being thrown together, Monahan could have greatly reduced his players' incentive to join a rival league. The commissioner did not take ownership for the Tour's tardy response to the obvious threat to its business model. "We made the moves that we made," he said. "We made moves last year. We made moves at the [2022] Travelers Championship. To me, whether or not we were going to stop them from launching, they were going to move forward. I think that the moves that we're making right now are the right moves for this organization, and we're going to continue to make more of them. I don't think there's any scenario where they weren't launching."

Monahan was asked where all the new money would come from. He hemmed and hawed but ultimately gave it up: "Reserves." Phil was right! (Sort of.) But Monahan deserves some of the credit for all the money that had been socked away, as he had expertly guided the Tour through covid and closed the new TV deal that was providing so much cushion.

The newsbreaks didn't end with Monahan's press conference. McIlroy followed him to the stage along with Mike McCarley, the former president of golf at NBC Sports Group, to announce the formation of yet another breakaway tour, the TGL, short for Tech-Infused Golf League. The new concept had the full backing of the PGA Tour, which holds a minority equity interest in TGL; the TGL is also paying the Tour for a media release and has licensed intellectual property. The TGL would be a series of Monday-night, made-for-TV spectacles in which top Tour players would compete against one another on simulators in front of a live audience in a ministadium in Orlando. The TGL may or may not engage the coveted, nearly mythical youth demographic, but that doesn't really matter in the context of battling LIV. It was another way for players loyal to the Tour to get paid. And it's co-owned by Woods and McIlroy, further intertwining their business interests with each other and the Tour.

McIlroy dusted Woods at the 2012 Honda Classic to reach world number one for the first time, at twenty-two, and they have circled each other ever since. Rory is now Woods's peer in every way, but even he is not immune to Tiger's cult of personality. When I asked McIlroy in the press conference how it felt to be collaborating with Woods, he said, "It's funny, I never in a million years thought that I would be in this position in particular, and in this position doing this stuff with Tiger Woods. I said to him the other day, I remember the first golf shot I ever saw him hit live [when I was fifteen]. It was the fifteenth hole at [the 2004 World Golf Championship at] Mount Juliet with my dad, and I watched him hit a drive off the fifth tee and a long iron into the middle of the green, a par five. Tiger was my idol ever since I watched him play the 1996 U.S. Amateur. He has been an idol and a hero of mine over the years, and I feel pretty lucky that I've gotten to know him more intimately than some. And he is so passionate about what we're doing. He realizes that the PGA Tour gave him a platform to build his brand and let him be who he is, and he has tremendous respect for the people that have come before us. Having his influence and having his counsel, not just myself but all of the players on the PGA Tour, he's a great advocate to have, and it's awesome to be doing these things with him. I have to pinch myself pretty much every day that I'm in this position."

As Rory and Tiger have further emerged as the faces and voices of the Tour, they have evoked the activism of Jack and Arnie when the Tour was born of rebellion in 1968 as the players broke away from the rigid bureaucracy of the PGA of America. There is more than a passing resemblance between these linked pairs of legends. Nicklaus and Palmer were born a decade apart, whereas Woods is thirteen years McIlroy's senior. On the golf course, Jack was tactical and Arnie daring, just as Tiger is a plodding strategist compared to the freewheeling Rory. The personable Palmer connected intensely with the fans in the same way McIlroy does, whereas Nicklaus and Woods have always been more remote figures. The friendly alliance between Woods and McIlroy is a stark contrast to Tiger's inability to forge a lasting business relationship with his contemporary Phil Mickelson. (Anyone remember Lefty and Woods's now-fizzled made-for-TV franchise of mano-a-mano matches?) Tiger and Rory had spent the preceding two years putting together TGL. Cofounder McCarley observed them closely and says this about the dynamic: "There is a mutual respect there. Tiger values Rory, and he listens to him. He certainly doesn't treat him like a little brother. Maybe a nephew."

Yet Woods needs McIlroy, and he knows it. Tiger is rarely on Tour these days, and the younger players barely know him. Rory is more accessible to his peers and more personable. (There is also a subset of people in the game who will never forgive Woods for his scandals and transgressions; meanwhile, the squeaky clean McIlroy is universally respected.) It was McIlroy's position on the Tour's board of directors that helped facilitate their shared vision for the revamped Tour.

Once the Tour Championship began, McIlroy further elevated his standing by roaring to a victory (and an $18 million payday) that felt like destiny. The first congratulatory text, as always, came from

Woods. McIlroy's peers at East Lake were wowed by his level of play despite the burden of being the Tour's chief spokesman and boardroom warrior.

"I had dinner with him," says Adam Scott, "and asked how he was playing so well with these distractions, and he said all the controversy is motivating him to play his best. He feels like he has put his reputation on the line and the most effective way to defend himself is to win golf tournaments."

"I think it is a huge testament to Rory," says Max Homa. "What is he, thirty-five? [Actually, he was thirty-three at the time.] He's got a young kid. He's got a lot better things to probably do with his time, but he's fighting so hard to make the PGA Tour as good as it can possibly be. Watching the guys you look up to, who aren't that much older than you, doing these big endeavors is pretty impressive in my opinion. I think Tiger could do okay on this on his own, but I would say having Rory on your side is not exactly a bad thing. Everybody could use a Rory in their life."

Of course, around LIV the mere mention of McIlroy's name provokes violent eye-rolling. "Fuck Rory," says one of his former Ryder Cup teammates. "I'm so sick of hearing about how he's some kind of hero who is saving golf. He's bought and paid for like everybody else, it's just that his money is coming from the other side. Did you know that when Whoop [the personal fitness device] wanted to do a deal with the PGA Tour, the Tour insisted that Rory be one of the endorsers? He was given a $10 million equity stake that is now worth $200 million. How do you think he got his own deal with NBC [in Golf-Pass+, a $99 annual subscription that delivers exclusive McIlroy-centric content]? The Tour brokered that, too. The Tour is so reliant on Rory now they've given him his own league [the TGL], even though it will compete with the Tour for viewers and advertisers. Rory's fighting so hard for the Tour because he wants to preserve his revenue streams, not because he cares about the Tour itself. That he is being held up as some kind of savior on Twitter and by all the fanboys with their shitty podcasts tells you how little people really understand what's going on."

Asked to fact-check the assertions above, McIlroy's manager, Sean O'Flaherty, would say only, "Has the Ryder Cup teammate been drinking?" (No, at least not during the practice round when those words were uttered.) O'Flaherty asked for the identity of the person quoted, but I couldn't reveal it because the player had agreed to speak only on the condition of anonymity. "Coward," O'Flaherty said, shaking his head. "They're cowards." McIlroy had once seemed as jolly as the Keebler leprechaun, but in 2022 he became the most politicized golfer since, well, Greg Norman three decades earlier. Now their legacies were inextricably linked.

For the PGA Tour, the good vibes from East Lake lasted all of two days. As soon as he collected his $640,000 for finishing twentieth at the Tour Championship, Cameron Smith signed his $100 million LIV deal. He was the headliner in the announcement of a big slate of new players. In 2022, he had already won the crown jewel of the sport (an Open Championship at St. Andrews), the PGA Tour's flagship event (the Players Championship), and one of the Tour's other most exclusive gatherings (the Tournament of Champions in Kapalua, Maui). Joining him on LIV was Joaquín Niemann, 23, the nineteenth-ranked player in the world, who earlier in the year had won another of the Tour's premier tournaments, the Los Angeles Open, at which Woods had served as the host. (Niemann was the tenth GSE Worldwide client to sign with LIV.) His switching sides was intensely personal for those loyal to the PGA Tour because Niemann had been in the inner sanctum in Delaware. "He's dead to me now," says one of the other players. Also going to LIV was Harold Varner III, one of the few Black golfers at the highest level and a fan favorite with his easy laugh and swaggy Air Jordan apparel. If, as was often said, LIV is where all the assholes went to play, the tour got some much needed nice guys in Marc Leishman, an amiable Aussie beloved by his peers, and Cameron Tringale and Anirban Lahiri, two unflashy and noncontroversial veterans who would make good teammates. (One of the most likable guys in golf, Charles Howell III, had joined the tour a month earlier.)

That would be LIV's last batch of in-season signings, but one name loomed large in absentia: Hideki Matsuyama. Even before LIV officially launched, Norman had confided that Matsuyama, the 2021 Masters champ, was his number one target. The thinking went: if we get Matsuyama, the entire Asian market will follow. "We knew that a franchise fronted by Hideki with all Asian players would easily be the most valuable," says a LIV executive. "It would be the quickest to attract blue-chip sponsors. If we signed him, we would have played a tournament in Japan every year. He's not the sexiest player, but economically it would have been massive." LIV's offer kept climbing and ultimately dwarfed the contracts of Mickelson and Johnson. At the Open Championship at St. Andrews, Matsuyama's manager/translator, Bob Turner, told a few Tour players, "He's gone." That it didn't happen is a testament to, among other things, the recruiting prowess of Woods and McIlroy, both of whom made strong pitches for him to stay on the Tour. (Of course, Rory had called Cam Smith a couple of days after the Open to give him a sales pitch and that hadn't exactly worked out.)

Smith, Niemann, and the other newbies made their debut a couple of days after the press releases dropped, at LIV Boston. Varner had put out a long, impassioned statement to his fans on his social media channels and in Boston was asked what the reception had been like. "It sucked," he said. "Who likes to be hated? It's terrible. I hate being hated. I'd rather not even be known than be hated. So yeah, it was terrible." Three months into the LIV era, passions were still clearly inflamed.

Varner, 32, has zero career PGA Tour victories, but in February 2022 he holed a ninety-foot eagle putt on the seventy-second hole to nab the Saudi International. That will go down as one of the most lucrative putts of all time. Varner had already been in negotiations with LIV for what one of its executives calls a "modest" deal. Then he won the Saudi International and charmed everyone at Golf Saudi with his ebullient personality. A long courtship began. "His agent [Preston Lyon] played that situation like a world-class musician," says the LIV executive. Varner wound up signing for $27 million plus $3 million more for the HV3 Foundation. A self-described "ordinary kid from rural Gastonia, North Carolina," Varner said that his baby boy and "future Varners" would have a life that "I could have only dreamt about growing up." That financial security was worth the slings and arrows on social media and even the possibility that he wouldn't get to play the major championships; at forty-sixth in the world ranking, he was likely to fall out of the all-important top fifty as long as LIV events were not earning OWGR points. "This is my first year playing in every major, so it was cool," he said. "But I think it's way cooler making sure my kid doesn't have to worry about anything. That's about it." His rawness and realness did a lot to blunt the hate—how can you fault a guy who grew up with nothing wanting to take care of his family?

Of course, Dustin Johnson had offered the same rationale for jumping to LIV, even though he had left the PGA Tour third on the all-time money list with $74.9 million (not counting endorsements!), behind only Woods and Mickelson; it's safe to say that his family was already well taken care of. Johnson had contended in each of his first three LIV events, finishing eighth or better, but at Boston he finally delivered a signature moment the tour badly needed from its O.G. headliner, banging in a long eagle putt to win a sudden-death playoff over Niemann and Lahiri. It capped a dizzying series of events, from Delaware to East Lake to a rowdy scene in Boston. But golf's long, hot summer was far from over.

The week after LIV Boston brought the flagship event on the European Tour, the BMW PGA Championship at the Wentworth Club outside of London. LIV golfers were still allowed to compete as their legal case made its way through the arbitration process in the United Kingdom, and fourteen of them turned up. McIlroy set the tone for the latest commingling of the warring tribes, saying at the Tour Championship, "It's going to be hard for me to stomach going to Wentworth in a couple of weeks' time and seeing them there. I hate it. I really do." LIV's Martin Kaymer promptly withdrew from the tournament, saying, "Of course, there will be friction there, that's why I'm not going. I don't need to go to a place where, feel-wise, you're not that welcome." By order of Keith Pelley, the LIV golfers were dropped from the Wentworth pro-am and banished from the TV coverage.

Florida's own Billy Horschel, who had been making cameos in Europe for years, was the defending champion. He was not happy to see his former PGA Tour colleagues suddenly develop an interest in the European Tour. "I don't think those guys should be here," he said. "The Abraham Ancers, the Talor Gooches, the Jason Kokraks, you've never played this tournament, you've never supported this tour. Why are you here? You're here for one reason only, and that's to try and gain world ranking points because you don't have that." Horschel and Ian Poulter later became embroiled in a heated conversation on the practice putting green. Poulter, an Englishman playing on his home soil, a Ryder Cup hero who had flown the flag for Europe for the entirety of his long career, was actually booed on the first tee in the first round.

Things only got spicier when Sergio García withdrew after the first round without explanation. Much of the resentment toward the LIV golfers from their peers at Wentworth stemmed from their bumping out of the field loyal European Tour players, some of whom were fighting for their jobs. The first alternate was García's countryman Alfredo Garcia-Heredia, who sat 134th on the Race to Dubai rankings, needing to crack the top 121 by season's end to secure his spot on the Tour in 2023. He never got a chance to tee it up. Two days after García's hasty departure from Wentworth, he lit up social media with a very public appearance at a University of Texas football game. (His father-in-law, Marty Akins, had been an All-America quarterback for the Longhorns.) García's obtuse selfishness helped make him public enemy number one on the European Tour, though he had company in Poulter and Lee Westwood, heretofore exalted Ryder Cup stars. None of their colleagues was particularly rankled that they had taken the money; fellow pros understand that it's a business. But it was their litigiousness and lippiness—in the locker room, in press conferences, and on social media—that rankled. The same held true on the PGA Tour. No one was mad at the Dustin Johnsons or Louis Oosthuizens; they kept their mouth shut, didn't participate in the lawsuits, and played only the LIV events plus the majors. It was the Mickelsons and DeChambeaus and Gooches who created so much angst by slurping up the LIV money and then turning around and suing their former colleagues, talking trash all the while.

At Wentworth, Gooch continued his emergence as one of professional golf's most noteworthy players, summoning a gritty performance to finish fourth, nabbing crucial world ranking points in his bid to secure exemptions into 2023's major championships. But McIlroy and his close friend Shane Lowry decided the tournament with a spirited Sunday shootout. Lowry prevailed by one stroke when McIlroy's seventy-second-hole eagle try expired one inch short.

"I wanted to go out and win this tournament for myself, first and foremost, but I think for this tour and everyone that has stayed loyal to this tour," Lowry said afterward. "I really feel like this is one for the good guys."

The next day, the PGA Tour began its annual tournament in the Napa Valley, the Fortinet Championship. Xander Schauffele, Patrick Cantlay, and their significant others went wine tasting, and Cantlay's fiancée posted on Instagram a photo of all of them posing stiffly for the camera. Golf.com deemed that worthy of a story, and in the comments Ashley (Mrs. Pat) Perez wrote, "I'm sorry. That doesn't look like fun. . . . at all," adding a snoring emoji for effect. Over in the United Kingdom, the *Daily Mirror* picked up on the cattiness and wrote an article about it under the headline "LIV Wag Takes Aim at Partners of PGA Tour Stars as Golf Civil War Spills Over."

You can't make this stuff up.

17.

ASKED TO DESCRIBE HIS FRIEND AND COUNTRYMAN Cam Smith, Adam Scott lets loose a little giggle and comes up with one word: "Bogan." That's Aussie slang for "redneck." Smith's luxuriant mullet is a giveaway, but Scott fleshes out the meaning a bit more, saying, "Just a good, down-to-earth, simple bloke."

Yet Smith also possesses an otherworldly golfing skill and heavy mettle: his first three PGA Tour wins came by way of sudden-death playoffs. Then at Kapalua to start the 2022 season, he went a mind-bending 35 under par to outduel Jon Rahm. He made ten birdies in the final round to nab the Players Championship and a $3.6 million payday. "This won't change him," Jack Wilkosz, Smith's best friend, said during the trophy ceremony, swallowing tears. "That's what makes him so great as a friend, person, countryman, and player." Smith said that he might use the money to splurge on new fishing gear. A month later, he nearly stole the Masters. (In 2020, he became the first man to post four rounds in the 60s around Augusta National.) A back-nine 30 to crush Rory McIlroy and win the Open Championship at St. Andrews cemented Smith as a player for the ages. Then LIV came calling.

Before Smith, it was easy to come up with a justification for practically every player who defected to LIV: Brooks and Bryson were hurt and their futures uncertain; Phil needed vindication (and perhaps to pay off some debts); DJ wanted to play less; Reed and Sergio had worn out their welcome on the PGA Tour; a bunch of others were old and looking for a final payday. But Smith's renunciation of the Tour provoked real anguish. He was twenty-nine and entering the prime of his career. Mark Rolfing, the NBC announcer, founded the PGA Tour event at Kapalua and, thinking about his defending champion not showing up in 2023, said, "I'm sad that we may never know how good Cam Smith could have been. He could have been the next Tom Watson, but who knows if he'll keep chasing that potential on LIV."

That was one of LIV's primary marketing challenges: exploding the notion that the golfers who had left the Tour for guaranteed money would lose their hunger and see their skills and competitive instincts diminish. Of course, the critique doesn't make sense in the context of the larger sports world. The best and most decorated athletes in team sports tend to be the highest paid. Michael Jordan had an enormous guaranteed contract. So did Tom Brady and Derek Jeter. Did all that money make them stop caring about winning? Of course not. Killers remain killers, regardless of the paycheck. Claude Harmon III, Koepka's swing coach, brought it all home when he told reporter Dan Rapaport, "Brooks is finally getting paid like a Super Bowl–winning quarterback, which is what he is worth."

All of that was in the air when LIV Golf arrived in the Chicago suburbs in September 2022. Yes, the vibes on LIV can be different—during a practice round, Koepka's wife, Jena, was bopping around in a cart with the couple's black Labrador retriever, and the fan village featured a barber giving fans mullets to match Smith's. (LIV donated $1,000 to a local charity for each spectator who took the plunge.) But Smith radiated real desire in storming to a three-stroke victory. "I think I had to prove to myself and some other people that I'm still a great player," he said. "I'm still out here to win golf tournaments." He admitted that he had been trying a little too hard during his mediocre LIV debut in Boston two weeks earlier. "I think probably that first event was the most pressure I've been under all year inside of an event," he said. "I feel as though I needed to prove to myself, and probably more so to other people, that just because I've changed tours doesn't mean I'm a worse player for it."

Dustin Johnson's 4Aces won their fourth consecutive team title and another $3 million to split, a helpful bit of dominance as LIV labored to get golf fans to pay attention to the team element. Johnson's teammate Talor Gooch, suddenly LIV's leading keyboard warrior, posted a photo on Instagram and looked to Shane Lowry at Wentworth for inspiration on the caption: "Another win for the good guys."

As its first miniseason rolled on, LIV continued to fight battles in the legal system and the court of public opinion. A couple of days after LIV Chicago, Greg Norman went to Capitol Hill to try to win hearts and minds. Throughout the summer, the U.S. Justice Department had been sniffing around players, agents, and PGA Tour bureaucrats, requesting phone records and beginning to compile an antitrust case much like the one it had launched against the Tour in 1994. The Justice Department seemed to lose interest once the LIV golfers filed their antitrust lawsuit; with the courts weighing in, an investigation would potentially be redundant. But Norman still wanted to plead his case in Washington. Or at least, LIV consultant Andrew McKenna wanted him to do so. McKenna's eponymous consulting firm is a longtime client of the NRA, and he is a quintessential DC character; around LIV, he is referred to as "the red tie guy" because at tournaments he always wears the same costume—blue slacks, white oxford cloth shirt, red tie. He arranged for Norman to spend two long days pressing flesh with senators and representatives from both parties, including members of the House of Representatives' Republican Study Committee, House Congressional Golf Caucus, House leadership, and House Judiciary Committee. The reaction was mixed at best. In quotes that would be recycled on seemingly every golf website, Representative Tim Burchett, a Republican from Tennessee, told the *Washington Post*, "They wanted to talk about antitrust, and I could care less. It's not Congress's job. We're a country of laws; take it up to the courts. That's where it needs to be, not in the halls of Congress. How in the hell are we wasting any time talking about a bunch of millionaires and a golf game? This is all just Saudi propaganda." He added, "It just ticked me off. Everybody's assumption of Congress is a bunch of country clubbers out there playing golf with millionaires. By bringing Greg Norman in here, they've just perpetuated that myth even more."

Representative Chip Roy, a Republican from Texas, offered an equally harsh assessment, telling reporters, "Don't come in here and act like you're doing some great thing while you're pimping a billion dollars of Saudi Arabian money and the Kingdom of Saudi Arabia in the United States." Norman took the blowback personally. Says one LIV executive, "He thought all the meetings went really well. In the moment, he was very high on it, very excited, and then it got spun into a circus. Greg was upset about it."

Less public, but just as ineffectual, were Norman's back-channel lobbying efforts with the Official World Golf Ranking. So in October, LIV pulled one of the more audacious stunts in a season full of she-nanigans, announcing a partnership with the MENA [Middle East and North Africa] Tour. MENA is a micro-minitour with a dozen or so tournaments a year, each carrying a $75,000 purse. Owing to covid and financial difficulties, it had not held a tournament in more than two years at the time of the LIV announcement. In minitour circles, MENA was known for having stiffed numerous players by failing to pay the prize money they had earned. The dodgy, dormant tour's only value to LIV was the OWGR accreditation it had earned in 2016. Suddenly, MENA announced a 2022–23 schedule with twenty tournaments—sixteen of which were LIV events. A press release from MENA stated, "The final field for LIV Golf Thailand, the opening event of the 2022/23 MENA Tour season, will be submitted to OWGR by the MENA Tour ahead of play commencing on Friday when the final field rating and winners' points are expected to be confirmed." Put simply, LIV was trying to buy world ranking points with a groan-inducing end-around. The OWGR stewards were not impressed. A press release was swiftly released stating that no points would be awarded for any of the LIV events under the MENA imprimatur because an alliance with another tour doesn't automatically transfer OWGR approval and, further, a radical change in format and qualifying criteria can trigger potential decertification of any tour that merges with another. The OWGR governors gathered the week after the MENA announcement for a previously scheduled board meeting, but LIV's latest antics were not discussed. One member of the governing board says, "There was no need to talk about it because the whole thing was so preposterous."

In a matter of a few months, LIV had suffered a high-profile defeat in federal court, been repudiated at the European Tour's flagship tournament, laughed off Capitol Hill, and rejected yet again by the OWGR. No one said that being a disruptor would be easy, but did it have to be so embarrassing?

LIV Thailand came and went without world ranking points, but it did feature one important development: the long-hitting Eugenio Chacarra earned his first professional victory. The twenty-two-year-old Spaniard by way of Oklahoma State had dropped out of school to join LIV, leading to angst among college coaches, who visit every corner of the globe recruiting talent. But after securing the $4 million winner's check in Thailand, Chacarra said, "I'm still dreaming." His playing partner Richard Bland, recognized a very mature talent, saying, "He hardly missed a shot. He's only twenty-two but played like he's been out here for twenty years."

Chacarra's win had far-reaching implications. To get off the ground, LIV spent big on fading stars and thirtysomethings in their primes, but if it was going to have a self-sustaining future, it would need to produce homegrown stars. Chacarra's victory may or may not launch a big career, but it served as a useful recruiting tool for other young talent. After his win, Chacarra talked about the tension of having to choose between joining LIV and trying to make it on the PGA Tour, saying, "It wasn't easy, but I feel this was best for me and for my future, and what LIV is doing is something unbelievable. The PGA Tour University doesn't give you much; it can just give you six events, and then if you don't play good—one of my best friends Austin Eckroat was playing [cutthroat] Monday qualifying all year."

PGA Tour University is a system that began in 2020 in which college seniors accrue points based on their performance to help them earn a spot in the PGA Tour ecosystem. In August 2022, responding to the LIV threat, PGA Tour University expanded its exemptions, granting the top points earner a season-long exemption to the Tour, while numbers two to five would become full members of the Korn Ferry Tour and be exempt into the final stage of the PGA Tour Q-School. Those finishing sixth through tenth were to be granted conditional KFT status, while numbers eleven to twenty would attain full status on the minor-league PGA Tour Americas and be exempt into the second stage of Q-School. As Chacarra suggested, none of these routes offers anything like the job security of his three-year guaranteed LIV Golf contract. LIV's alliance with the Asian Tour is also a key component in the battle for talent, as LIV can guarantee young players spots in the Asian Tour's International Series, a tour within a tour that boasts purses of up to $2.5 million, more than double what is typically offered on the KFT. (Each Asian Tour event has two dozen sponsor's exemptions at its disposal for LIV-aligned players.)

In the war between tours, in which young players now face hard decisions about which road to travel, Andy Ogletree became an unlikely protagonist. Injuries, poor play, and covid-related cancellations of minitour opportunities had left the 2019 U.S. Amateur champion running out of options—and money. He accepted a one-off invitation to LIV Golf London, even though he was still recovering from hip and elbow injuries. "I needed somewhere to play golf, that's the bottom line," he says. "For me it was a no-brainer.

That week of London there was no GProTour (minitour) event, no Korn Ferry Tour event, no PGA Tour Monday qualifier. There was nowhere else for me to play." He finished dead last in London, 31 strokes behind Charl Schwartzel, but the $120,000 he was paid enabled him to keep funding his career.

Even though Ogletree was not a PGA Tour member and had only conditional KFT status, the Tour vindictively suspended him for the rest of 2022. So he lit out for the Asian Tour. A month after Chacarra's breakthrough, the now-healthy Ogletree dropped a final-round 62 to win the International Series Egypt by four shots over LIV golfer Bernd Wiesberger, a 2021 Ryder Cupper. The victory, worth $270,000, provided sweet vindication for Ogletree, who had taken plenty of abuse on social media for playing in London. "I didn't like that I was grouped into this category of these guys that kind of rebelled against the Tour or chose a different path," he says. "I didn't choose a different path; I just chose to play in a golf tournament." Yet he had become an unwitting trailblazer. Four months after Egypt, he won again, at the International Series Qatar, claiming $450,000, a massive sum for a developmental circuit. With his Tour suspension over, he could have pursued opportunities in the United States in 2023 but chose instead to focus on the International Series, as the leading money winner is guaranteed a spot on LIV in 2024. The KFT is brutally competitive, and it's easy to go broke out there. LIV's investment in the Asian Tour has created a viable new career path, and Ogletree's success has captured the attention of his contemporaries. "I definitely get a lot of questions from other players," he says. "I think people are beginning to realize there is a lot of good golf being played around the world. And good money to be made."

Following Thailand, the LIV world tour rolled into Saudi Arabia for the penultimate tournament of the season. The dramatic tension came by way of Phil Mickelson's first visit to the kingdom since he had been quoted calling its people "scary motherfuckers." He channeled all of that anxiety into a relentless charm offensive. A fellow LIV golfer says, "If you think Phil is a bullshit artist normally, this was another level. You've never seen anyone kiss so much ass with that kind of enthusiasm and skill. He was 'on' from the second he got off the plane and never broke character. I'm pretty sure by the end of the week he could have been elected mayor of King Abdullah City, if they actually held elections over there." Mickelson had finally found a spark late in the season, tying for eighth in Chicago and fifteenth in Bangkok, but he never got it going in Saudi Arabia, finishing a distant thirty-fifth.

The tournament was decided by the resurgent Brooks Koepka and the upstart Peter Uihlein. A decade earlier, they had shared a house in Florida and innumerable hotel rooms in Europe as each was trying to launch his pro career. Uihlein won the 2010 U.S. Amateur and turned pro a year later. After bombing out of the PGA Tour Q-School in 2011, he came to the first of a few crossroads. His father, Wally, offered a bit of advice by way of Ralph Waldo Emerson: "Do not go where the path may lead, go instead where there is no path and leave a trail." Peter lit out for the Challenge Tour, earned a promotion to the European Tour, and wound up as the 2013 Sir Henry Cotton Rookie of the Year. But for most of the next decade he was a man without a country, bouncing among the European Tour, the PGA Tour, and the Korn Ferry Tour, with minimal success. He improved his fitness, made a series of swing changes in 2020 and '21, and felt his game go to another level, but he wasn't getting enough starts to showcase the improvement. When the LIV folks began recruiting players, *he* pitched *them*, selling his credentials as a global player who had teed it up in more than three dozen countries. They were impressed and for the London tournament made Uihlein team captain of the Crushers, in part because he intimately knew pretty much every player in the eclectic field. At the team draft party, he called out as one of his picks the name of Scott Vincent, a young

Zimbabwean who had won the week before on the Asian Tour, but the MC somehow misunderstood and instead announced Hideto Tanihara, a seventeen-time winner on the Japan Tour. Uihlein tried to clear up the misunderstanding, but, not wanting to make a fuss, he welcomed Tanihara to the team. After the draft ended, he was able to trade Tanihara for Richard Bland, and Bland's final-round 67 was crucial as the Crushers finished second, with each player claiming $375,000 in team winnings. That alone was the second biggest check in the long career of the forty-nine-year-old Bland. The lords of LIV giveth and taketh away.

After a decade as a golfing vagabond, Uihlein finally felt at home on LIV. "I'm a lot happier out here than I have been the last five years playing the [PGA] Tour," he says. "The team aspect of it I like. I was never really a fan of the lone-wolf type of thing that we had to do. But being part of a team, practicing, hanging out kind of like college—it resonates with me and really sticks with me." A bomber with soft hands, he finally turned into the player he was always supposed to be, finishing fourth in London and second in Chicago, carrying his team to a pair of podium finishes. (That team was the Smash, as rosters continued to shift as new players joined LIV.)

As for what Uihlein's old man thinks, a cell number for Wally was finally procured. The former big cheese at Titleist/FootJoy said that he has no enduring love for Peter's former place of business based on decades of equipment-related governance issues. "My dealings with the PGA Tour were not that harmonious," says Wally. "I incurred the heel of the boot from Mr. Finchem and Mr. Beman. I felt the Tour was pretty imperious and inflexible." As for how his old-school golf friends have reacted to his support of LIV, he says, "I am not a 'conservative thinker' or however else I have been maligned. I have always had a global perspective on the game. When I explain why this has made sense for Peter, people get it."

Back in Saudi Arabia, Peter was two strokes behind Koepka on the back nine on Sunday but mounted a rally that included a birdie on the final hole. Koepka matched that birdie to force sudden death and then vanquished Uihlein on the third extra hole. It was an important milestone in Koepka's comeback and also deeply meaningful for LIV; the circuit's only hope of attracting a wider audience is if its antiheroes are consistently atop the leaderboard. "The last two years haven't been fun—it's been a long road," said Koepka, 32. "I didn't know if my career was over for half a second, so it's nice to be able to come back and be able to win."

Koepka talked movingly about the humble start to his career and how Uihlein had been his inspiration to play the minor leagues in Europe when he had had no other options. "Watching him do it made it easier, knowing somebody that was over there," Koepka said. "I still think it's probably the most fun I've had playing golf, 2012 to 2014 playing in Europe. Got to travel the world, and to get to do it for a living, I think it's pretty cool."

The Koepka-Uihlein bromance produced one of the feel-good stories of LIV's stormy first season. But as always with LIV, decadence became an inescapable part of the story. Koepka and Uihlein's Smash team won the team title in Saudi Arabia, with each player bagging $750,000. The squad also featured Koepka's kid brother, Chase. Said Brooks, "I told my brother I'd buy him a Lambo if we won the team thing, so now I've got to buy one." Chase had initially wanted the supercar in lime green but ultimately went with white. More understated, ya know?

18.

LONG AFTER THE DEFEATED BRYSON DECHAMBEAU barricaded himself in his hotel room to pout about his team's struggles and Harold Varner III dropped a few F-bombs on his teammates for not playing with enough intensity; in the wake of Cam Smith vanquishing Phil Mickelson in an epic singles match and Brooks Koepka downing Ian Poulter in another soap opera between the ropes; well after Pat Perez saved his reputation (and the team title!) with the most important 70 of his life and Dustin Johnson became golf's $35 million man; after the last drop of champagne had been sprayed and the last MAGA-hatted fan had departed Trump Doral, the LIV players and staff gathered for an end-of-the-season party, both exhilarated and exhausted. None of them could have imagined the excess of controversy, hyperbole, bitchiness, and invective that would come their way in the preceding months (to say nothing of the fabulous riches). It had left everyone at LIV battle-hardened and trauma-bonded. One of the tour's keynote players, Talor Gooch, floated around the party passing out hats he had created for the occasion, emblazoned with FEA. That was LIV's unofficial motto: Fuck 'Em All.

If Gooch and his colleagues were feeling themselves a little more than usual, it's partly because LIV Miami, which had ended the day before Halloween, had easily been the most compelling tournament of the beta test season, owing to a cool and inventive match play format that had simultaneously pitted players against players and teams against teams. A big-time golf course set up with plenty of teeth also elevated the event. A whopping $50 million was on the line in the team competition, and in the final round all four scores counted. (Throughout the season, only the three best individual scores per round were applied to the team tally.) There was another $30 million pot for the season-long points race for the three top-performing individuals, but Johnson's relentless excellence enabled him to clinch the $18 million bonus before the tournament even began; his 2022 winnings on LIV would come to $35.6 million, in addition to his monster signing bonus. Not bad for five months of work. (Branden Grace finished second and Peter Uihlein third in the individual points race, claiming bonuses of $8 million and $4 million, respectively.)

DJ's fine play at Doral put the 4Aces in position for a fifth win of the season. All eyes were on one particular teammate down the stretch. Perez's struggles had been well chronicled by the snarkier elements of golf Twitter: an 80 in Portland, a 77 in Bedminster, a 76 in Chicago, a 77 in Jeddah. But he birdied two of his final three holes and made a monumental six-footer to save par on his final hole, shooting a 70 that was bettered by only two players on a tough day. That set the stage for Captain Johnson, playing in the final group with a red-hot Smith, who would run through the tape with a 65. The most hyperbolic screenwriter could not have come up with a better scenario for LIV than a future Hall of Famer going head-to-head with the Champion Golfer of the Year for all the marbles. In the end, Johnson gutted a four-footer on the final hole to propel the 4Aces to a one-stroke victory that was good for $4 million apiece; Smith's all-Aussie Punch came in second while the Smash, featuring Uihlein and the Koepka brothers (and Jason Kokrak), finished third. For the season, Perez earned more than $8 million even though his best individual finish was fifteenth at Boston, the only time all year he cracked the top thirty. In victory he displayed typical humility, saying, "I get a lot of grief, people saying I never show up, so I did today. So everybody can shut up."

LIV's us-against-the-world chippiness can get tiresome, but as the curtain dropped on its debut season, it had to be considered a smashing success, from a particular point of view. After years of the Premier Golf League knocking around with little traction, seemingly overnight LIV had corralled a roster of Hall of Famers, major championship winners, and Ryder Cup stars. It had created a thriving feeder system through its alliance with the Asian Tour and locked up a handful of emerging talents. It had also dominated the sports world's discourse in a previously unimaginable way for a new product in a niche sport, from obsessive coverage on the front page of the *Wall Street Journal* to the endless jousting of everyday folks on social media. In a *Sports Business Journal* poll of the top stories of 2022, LIV would dominate the voting.

But a worldwide golf tour cannot subsist on buzz alone. For all the noise around LIV, it failed to attract the interest—or, worse yet, provoked the distaste—of large swaths of golf fans. The tour was never going to land a TV deal in 2022 with so much swirling uncertainty, and the (free!) streaming on YouTube attracted meager numbers: rarely more than 100,000 viewers at any given time and usually significantly less than that. In its first season, LIV blew through $794 million, almost $200 million over budget. Any start-up is going to spend more than it makes initially, but LIV's outlay was astonishing, with no clear path to profitability. In its recruitment efforts, sweet-talking LIV folks (to say nothing of Phil Mickelson) had repeatedly assured the players that any bans by the existing tours would not hold up in court and that LIV tournaments would be granted OWGR points. Both of those promises remained in doubt as the season came to a close, compromising efforts to woo more talent and leading to restlessness among the players already under contract. But those were all concerns for another day. On Sunday night in Miami the party raged on, and, inspired by the new headwear, a rallying cry occasionally rang out among the loyalists whose lives had changed thanks to LIV: "Fuck 'em all!"

Exactly one day into LIV's off-season, heads began to roll, as it was announced that chief operating officer Atul Khosla had left the organization. Officially, he resigned, but the man known as AK—universally liked and respected by LIV staffers—was the first casualty in a larger power struggle. "There are golf guys, and there are PIF [Public Investment Fund] guys," says a LIV executive. "The golf guys are laser-focused on the product. Greg's a golf guy, Majed's a golf guy. AK was a bridge between the golf guys and the business side but he wasn't a PIF guy, so he was never going to last. The PIF guys, they're laser focused on the numbers. They are very smart and very disciplined. Everyone says the Saudis have unlimited money, but that's because they have made one clever move after another to grow the PIF into what it is. Despite the narrative, they don't burn up money recklessly. There is always a larger plan, and they will not stop until that plan is executed." Yet to launch LIV Golf—to turn every tournament into a splashy event and to pamper the players so they wouldn't immediately have buyer's remorse—no expense was spared. LIV spent $3 million to rent the venue for its kickoff party in London, and throughout the season, pricey musical acts were flown in for the postround concerts: Diplo, Jason Derulo, Nelly, Afrojack, Jessie J, the Chainsmokers. Every player was given free hotel rooms and airplane tickets to spread among their family, caddie, swing coaches, and assorted hangers-on, and during tournament weeks they were provided with a driver and a luxury SUV. The free breakfast, lunch, and dinner spreads were fit for King Louis XIV.

His Excellency Yasir Al-Rumayyan is the boss of both the golf honks and the PIF bean counters and often has to referee disputes. He started the season as an unabashed golf guy, having the time of his life playing in every pro-am and hosting every party. But he became increasingly influenced by the PIF guys as the spending became more profligate; LIV chartered a deluxe Boeing 747 to ferry players from Portland to the JP McManus Pro-Am in Ireland, and Al-Rumayyan was incensed when social media posts made the plane's cabin look like a debauched frat party. He is hardly a prude, as he has westernized attitudes and appetites; in the MBS biography *Blood and Oil*, Al-Rumayyan is described as having "a taste for fine cigars and after-hours bars in Dubai frequented by long-legged, short-skirted Russian women." The images from the plane to Ireland grated not for their rowdiness but because they suggested a more elemental sin: wastefulness.

LIV had some nice momentum coming out of Miami, but it dissipated during the awkward silence of the long off-season as the PIF guys battled the golf guys for supremacy. The schedule announcement was delayed, and then delayed again. No new player signings were made public. LIV rang in 2023 with . . . nothing. (Though Rory McIlroy did receive a holiday treat when, relaxing at home on Christmas Eve, he was served a subpoena by Patrick Reed's mad-dog lawyer Larry Klayman, who had filed a class action lawsuit against the OWGR for denying ranking points to LIV.) Norman and his motley crew of scallywags had turned everyone in the golf world into news junkies with their nonstop hullabaloo. Following all of the headlines, controversies, lawsuits, and mudslinging was exhausting but addictive. LIV Golf going dark for almost three months was the most unexpected plot twist of all.

But in this quiet period of contemplation, a momentous shift occurred: Al-Rumayyan decided it was time to reach out to the PGA Tour. One of his closest friends in golf is Pascal Grizot, the president of the French Golf Federation. They began discussing ways to open lines of communication with Monahan. "In our game we have too many governing bodies and too many tours," says Grizot. "Nobody makes decisions in the general interest; they look after their own

interest. Who is thinking of what's best for the game? I am Mr. Nobody, only a small French guy. But I love the game and I want to see
it come back together. The only way that can happen is with H.E.
and Jay Monahan sitting around a table, talking. No Greg Norman,
no players who are fighting with each other. To get H.E. and Monahan together will not be easy, but someone has to try." Grizot is not
giving himself enough credit—no one ever imagined a Ryder Cup in
France until he made it happen. Grizot met with the French sports
minister, who in turn extracted a commitment from President Em-
manuel Macron to host a secret golf summit between LIV and the
PGA Tour. But Grizot could not get Monahan to engage.

Al-Rumayyan sought help from another well-connected friend,
Roger Devlin, a British businessman and the chair of Sunningdale
Golf Club outside of London (and recently retired member of the
R&A's board of directors). In November, at the DP World Tour
Championship in Dubai, Devlin had brokered a conversation be-
tween Al-Rumayyan and Rory McIlroy, an important olive branch.
Recognizing that the PGA Tour's sleek new $75 million headquar-
ters is as impenetrable as the Kremlin, Devlin tried a side door. On
December 8, he sent an email to Jimmy Dunne, who a month earlier had become a member of the PGA Tour's board of directors in
what he called a "wartime deal." It was a shrewd choice by Devlin, as
Dunne carried none of the baggage or siege mentality of the incum-
bent directors who had walked the Tour into an intractable battle
with the Saudis.

"Dear Mr Dunne," the email began. "I am writing to you in the
strictest confidence." In an attempt to build trust, Devlin noted golf's
version of the secret handshake: "our mutual membership of the
R&A." He went on to say that Al-Rumayyan "has been frustrated by
his inability to engage constructively with the PGA [Tour]." Devlin
noted that H.E. recognized "the need for compromise to benefit all
the game's stakeholders." He mentioned the meeting between Al-
Rumayyan and McIlroy and their discussions about reviving the

nations-based World Cup of Golf and creating a new Aramco Series of co-sanctioned PGA Tour events. Then came the guts of the letter: "His Excellency recognises the merits of compensating those PGA players who have remained loyal to the Tour and he would undertake to establish a substantial Equalisation Fund for their benefit. Equally arrangement would have to be made for LIV players to be admitted to PGA tournaments and recover World Ranking points. . . . His Excellency appreciates that the situation has not been helped by the approach adopted by certain individuals"—better start getting your affairs in order, Shark!—"and would be happy to explore a combined management structure whereby LIV and the PGA might work in partnership especially in respect of media rights."

Dunne did not immediately respond, and, like a needy lover, Devlin re-sent the email the next day. Dunne continued to ghost him. In his very successful golf and business lives, Dunne has always emphasized personal connection. Finally, after three days of silence, he responded in his folksy way: "Roger—I would like to have a cup of coffee first—just like to visit with you not to discuss anything specific just like to know you a little before anything else if you are up for that—Jimmy." Devlin parried that London to Florida is a helluva long way to go for a cappuccino. Dunne suggested they get together after New Year's, and on January 3, Devlin wrote again: "Happy New Year! I hope it will be a more peaceful one in the golf world. I do detect that since I first corresponded with you a month ago the Saudi position is hardening as they are confident LIV will prevail over the long term if only because of almost limitless financial resources." He added that an unspecified "we" were happy to fly to Florida for further discussions. Dunne's cold-blooded reply: "Probably not at this time." The correspondence fizzled.

Dunne later said that Monahan did not want to come to the table until he was in "a position of strength." The various legal questions remained unsettled, and the Tour had yet to unveil the new product that Monahan had staked the future on: the huge-money, "elevated" events. Al-Rumayyan's desire to negotiate would remain unrequited, for now.

History will show that a new era on the PGA Tour was ushered in by, of all people, Adam Svensson. On a perfect January morning on Maui, Svensson, a twenty-eight-year-old Canadian with one career win, smoked a towering draw down the first fairway of the Plantation Course at the Kapalua Resort, kicking off the Tournament of Champions. The mood wasn't exactly *elevated*; maybe a hundred fans were on hand, and Svensson didn't even have a playing partner, as he went out alone in a thirty-nine-man field that was otherwise playing in twosomes. But don't let the sleepy start fool you, as Kapalua began a grand experiment that helped define the future of professional golf. "Being here always feels like the start of *something*," said Adam Scott, playing for the eighth time at Kapalua. "I guess this time it is the start of something big."

Indeed, seventeen of the top twenty players in the (now semi-) Official World Golf Ranking crossed an ocean to support a tournament that had routinely been skipped by Tiger Woods and Phil Mickelson in their heydays. It helped that the Tournament of Champions is no longer that; the field had always been strictly for tournament winners in the preceding season, but beginning in 2023, winless players who otherwise made it to the season-ending Tour Championship, including Scott, were invited. That was one of many compromises the Tour made to appease its high-value members, who had become voracious with the arrival of LIV Golf. In 2022, the purse at Kapalua was $8.2 million; now, befitting its status as one of the thirteen newly elevated events, the payout was $15 million. (The Players Championship was bumped to $25 million, and the other elevated events, with bigger fields than the Tournament of Champions, had $20 million purses.) The runner-up at Kapalua earned $1.5 million, more than the $1.48 million that 2022 champ

Cam Smith had collected. No wonder Justin Thomas went to bed at nine o'clock on New Year's Eve and the whole vibe around the Plantation Course was different this time around. With that much money at stake, the revitalized Kapalua could no longer be treated as a working vacation.

Yet there was an inescapable sense of paradise lost. Smith's empty locker (with his winning score on the nameplate) served as a tangible sign of what had been taken away from the Tour; thirteen players who had teed it up at the 2022 Tournament of Champions had defected to LIV, including Dustin Johnson, a two-time champ at Kapalua. "DJ grew up with this tournament," says tournament founder Mark Rolfing. "It became part of the fabric of his life." Indeed, the pool at the Ritz-Carlton was the site of the public unveiling of Johnson's romance with Paulina Gretzky, now his wife. (Previously, it was where his fling with LPGA starlet Natalie Gulbis had become public.) Johnson remains a legend around the Ritz for his New Year's Eve partying, including the time he borrowed Rolfing's truck and then abandoned it at the wrong hotel, touching off a multiday scavenger hunt. As for Smith, his record-shattering performance (258 strokes for four rounds!) began his ascent as the best player in the world, no matter what the increasingly outdated world ranking showed at that moment. "I'm sad about this whole thing," Rolfing said. "I just saw a picture of me and Phil [Mickelson] from last year's tournament, and it stopped me in my tracks how much things have changed in one year."

Even with the missing star power—Rory McIlroy caused some heartburn at Tour headquarters by skipping the event—Kapalua's new status certainly energized the coverage of the tournament. The year before, Doug Ferguson of the Associated Press had been the only writer in the pressroom. "It got kind of lonely," he says. This time around, the Fire Pit Collective, *Sports Illustrated*, *Golf Digest*, *Golfweek*, *Golf Magazine*, and Global Golf Post provided daily coverage, as did a strong contingent of Japanese media outlets.

Representatives of *No Laying Up*, Barstool Sports's *ForePlay*, and GolfWRX were on site early in the week to pump out content. "Why does F1 work?" asked Will Zalatoris, making his first appearance at the Tournament of Champions. "Well, you know Lewis Hamilton's going to be there at every single race. So is Max Verstappen. So now when you have these elevated events, you know that the top guys are going to be there. If you're sick of the top guys playing events against each other, then maybe go watch something else? Like, you know what I mean?"

The Tour had bet its future on that model, but it was hardly a sure thing. Adam Scott went full Milton Friedman, saying, "What's now going to happen is the market is going to decide what the Tour should look like. Certainly, having forty-seven, forty-eight events a year doesn't seem to offer the most premium product. This is a step to probably test the waters to see if the top guys come together more often, what kind of impact does that have all the way through? What is the response from the viewers, from television, from sponsors? But yeah, if I was a player not getting into these elevated events, I would definitely be a little apprehensive about the future."

Such jitters had swept through the Tour ever since Tiger and Rory's cool-kids-only Delaware meeting. That twenty-three of the richest and most successful players were now setting policy for the entire PGA Tour was deeply unsettling for many of their less accomplished colleagues, whose livelihoods would be profoundly affected. The bitterness (and perhaps envy) spiked when the 2022 Player Impact Program results came down: Tiger Woods predictably won again ($15 million), even though he had played only three major championships and no actual PGA Tour events; McIlroy was rewarded for his advocacy with second-place money ($12 million); and Jordan Spieth finished third ($9 million). More vexing to the Tour's rank and file was that, in addition to paying out $100 million to the top twenty players as had been previously announced, the Tour added three more handouts just for the heck of it, at $2 million apiece: to Hideki Matsuyama, a long-standing LIV lust object; the young stud Sam Burns, one of the few GSE Worldwide clients not to go to LIV; and Cameron Young, 26, who had become a star in waiting in 2022. Officially, the Tour granted the players their bonus because, applying the tweaked 2023 criteria, they would have finished in the top twenty. Tour veteran James Hahn may or may not be a Dire Straits fan, but he accurately summarized the situation: "They're giving away money for doing nothing."

Peter Malnati effectively tapped into this sentiment while running for the Tour policy board, which is usually reserved for esteemed veterans with lengthy résumés. Malnati's only win had come in 2015 at the B-list Sanderson Farms Championship in Jackson, Mississippi, but he got himself elected for 2023 as a Bernie Sanders–like protest candidate railing against the ruling class and promising to represent the proletariat. Okay, that's a stretch, but Malnati did say in January 2023, "Are players concerned? I mean, honestly, that was the platform that got me elected to the board. My job is to make sure that, going forward, policy change goes through the governance process the way it is supposed to. Last year, yes, we were in extraordinary times, but the changes that were implemented, if they went through the governance process, they rushed through it. I want to make sure as I'm in that room that changes go through the proper process and channels before they're just implemented. I feel like some of the changes that got rushed through are really going to drastically change what we've done for the last thirty or forty years. My fear is that by almost creating this bifurcated tour, with so much focus on the top level, we're going to destroy some of the smaller events on Tour."

Malnati took the spot on the board vacated by the expiring term of Hahn, who says he was asked to serve on the Players Advisory Council but declined in protest. "The problem is that we as a collective whole are made up of a lot of individuals who will not stand up for the greater good," Hahn says. He is particularly troubled by what he calls "the obvious greed" of the Delaware 23. "They want free money," he says. "They want money for being popular. They want money as payback for turning down LIV, right? They want money that they feel like they're entitled to, but they don't want to play for it—they want it handed to them."

Hahn, 41, believes it is time for the Tour's middle class to union-ize, which athletes in the team sports did decades ago. "You can't have a Tour for thirty guys," he says. "You just can't. It's changing our whole business. But if I say [that we need a union], I will get a call from someone at the Tour and they will probably threaten legal action or suspension or fine me. And so that's why I haven't. But fuck it, I've only got a few years left out here, and someone has to say these things. I know for a fact a lot of guys agree with me but they won't speak up because they're afraid of losing sponsors or what the Tour will do in retaliation."

Kapalua was supposed to be the start of an exciting new era on the Tour, but for all the fanfare, the tension below the surface was very real. "It has become so hostile between the commissioner, the top players, and everybody else," says Hahn. "Rory said in a board meeting, 'Nobody pays money to come watch Peter Malnati play.' If he said that about me to my face, I'll see you in the parking lot, man. I will fuck you up in the parking lot. If someone wants to disrespect me like that, I will fuck you up."

Thank goodness for Jon Rahm. The regal, dignified Spaniard prevailed at Kapalua with a stellar Sunday 63, reinserting himself into the conversation about who is the game's best player. After the trophy ceremony and champion's press conference, he was ushered upstairs in the Kapalua clubhouse for a private gathering with the host sponsor, Sentry. A nosy reporter who sneaked in found an un-obtrusive spot in the back of the room, near the tables of food. (The sashimi was to die for.) Nursing a piña colada, Rahm took questions from perennially embattled PGA Tour commissioner Jay Mona-han, who is not exactly an expert interrogator. (Almost every query began, "Talk about . . .") In his courtly English, Rahm talked about his dedication to his wife, Kelley, and their two young sons and his desire to be the best person he can be. It sounds corny, but the adoring crowd spooned it up, and Monahan beamed with an almost paternal pride, cooing, "How good is that?"

Rahm was the right winner at the right time for a tour in transition. The disgruntled journeymen can make a lot of noise, but it is the stars who drive the show, same as it ever was. After the leaders teed off for the final round at Kapalua, Monahan deigned to have a rare gathering with reporters. I asked him about the Tour's ongoing efforts to remake itself in response to the LIV threat. "I think you've heard me say a bunch of times that we're focusing on what we control," he said. "We're at a point now where it's product versus product. And we have our schedule, we've laid it out, we're going to keep getting better and better and better. What they have is very different from what we have. We're going down our path, and they're going down theirs."

A week after Kapalua, LIV finally emerged from its public slumber, announcing that it had, at long last, secured a broadcast and streaming deal. That was always going to be a crucial development for the long-term health of the tour, and so, with much fanfare, LIV trumpeted its pact with . . . the CW Network?! That provoked much confusion and plenty of derision. CW had previously been known for teen-centric fare such as *Gossip Girl*, *Veronica Mars*, and *Gilmore Girls*. It was not an obvious landing spot for a controversial global golf circuit that caters to a demographic more in line with the dads of the network's typical viewers. But in October 2022, CW had been purchased by Nexstar Media Group, a behemoth company with an industry-leading 200 affiliates in 116 U.S. markets. Its ambitious CEO, Perry Sook, had grand plans to transform the network— already the fifth largest in the United States, reaching 120 million homes—with live sports being one of the keys. By becoming CW's first sports property, LIV could potentially benefit greatly from the network's evolution. At least, that was the optimistic view. The devil is always in the details, and it turned out that CW would not be televising the first round of any LIV tournament, streaming it only on the CW app. (A secondary streaming platform, LIV Golf Plus, would later be introduced.) In some markets, the tournaments would not be available in high definition, setting back the coverage a few decades in look and feel. Whereas the PGA Tour collects $700 million a year in rights fees, CW pays LIV nothing upfront; the network and the tour split any ad revenue, while LIV has to cover all of the production costs, which are more than $10 million a tournament, including the on-air talent salaries. On social media the reaction to the deal was so scornful that *USA Today* published a story about it under the headline "Golf Fans Roasted LIV Broadcasting on the CW with So Many Jokes."

But realistically, what more could LIV have done? CBS and NBC are longtime partners of the PGA Tour. So is ESPN, which is under the same corporate umbrella as ABC. After its disastrous run televising the U.S. Open—in which Greg Norman was a notable flop—Fox walked away from golf coverage in 2020. There had been discussions between LIV and Fox; according to a LIV exec, "They were mildly interested. The problem was that we wouldn't have a home. Some tournaments were going to be on FS1, some on FS2, some would start there but then have the final round on big Fox. It's been hard enough to get viewers to seek us out, and that would have made it worse."

Univision made a respectable bid, but no one at LIV thought a Spanish-speaking network made sense. So CW turned out to be the best available option. The dismissive reaction to the deal was reflective of the damned-if-you-do-damned-if-you-don't coverage that LIV often receives. When the tournaments were streamed on YouTube during the beta test season, it was often presented as embarrassing evidence that LIV was too small-time to attract a TV deal. As soon as the CW announcement dropped, the YouTube nostalgia began. D. J. Piehowski of *No Laying Up* tweeted, "I know the numbers weren't great when it was publicly available to anyone on earth for free on the most popular app in the world, but this could change everything." Of course, LIV's lawyers didn't help matters when they later referred to CW as a "secondary network" in a court filing. That had the ring of truth, undercutting all the fancy press releases.

Four days after the CW announcement, LIV released its fourteen-tournament schedule for 2023. There were some wins. LIV had poached from the PGA Tour schedule El Camaleón Mayakoba Golf Course, a lively Greg Norman design near Cancún, where Viktor Hovland had claimed his second and third career wins. (Pat Perez and Graeme McDowell have also won there.) LIV also snagged Real Club Valderrama in southern Spain, the site of the 1997 Ryder Cup and numerous European Tour events, with a roll call of winners that includes Tiger Woods, Nick Faldo, Bernhard Langer, Sergio García, and Colin Montgomerie. Sentosa Golf Club has hosted the Singapore Open more than two dozen times, with past champions including García, Ángel Cabrera, and Adam Scott. The Gallery Golf Club outside Tucson, Arizona, comes with the prestige of having hosted two WGC Match Play Championships, won by Woods and Henrik Stenson, just as the Greenbrier's Old White Course was elevated by being a PGA Tour venue from 2010 to 2019. But there were some dogs on the schedule, too, notably the Crooked Cat at Orange County National Golf Center in Orlando, a flat, nondescript, overplayed muni, and Broken Arrow Golf Club outside Tulsa, Oklahoma; thanks to local resident and Twitter wit @BunkiePerkins, Broken Arrow came to be widely known as the "fifth best course in Tulsa."

Despite the forty-fifth president's mounting legal woes, LIV doubled down on Trump courses, adding a third one to the schedule, outside Washington, DC. That had been negotiated the year before as part of the long-term partnership. LIV was learning the

ALAN SHIPNUCK

hard way that aligning itself with Trump came at a steep cost in the marketplace. Says a LIV executive, "Brands don't want any political affiliation; they want whoever they align themselves with to be Switzerland so they don't scare off any customers. Monica Fee"—LIV's global head of partnerships—"has been saying since the beginning that having Trump involved was creating strong headwinds for getting any corporate deals done."

The wonky cadence of the schedule reflected continued growing pains: LIV would conduct only three tournaments in the three months ahead of the Masters but cram in three events in the five weeks between Augusta and the PGA Championship, including sojourns to Singapore and Australia. At the height of summer, back-to-back events in London and Spain would lead directly into the Open Championship, meaning a long three weeks overseas. (Remember when joining LIV was supposed to mean more time at home?) Internally, by far the most controversial change was moving the season-ending team extravaganza from Miami to Jeddah, Saudi Arabia. Instead of a celebrated golf course in a lively city, LIV's Super Bowl would be played in front of almost no fans while the rest of the world was sleeping. But the PIF guys wanted the tournament on home soil, extracting a little more ROI by bringing LIV's biggest event of the year to the kingdom.

The simmering internal strife between the golf guys and the PIF guys went public on the same day the schedule was released when word got out that Majed Al-Sorour had been relieved of his day-to-day duties. Bob Harig of *Sports Illustrated* had caught wind of what happened and was working on a story, compelling LIV to preemptively release a short statement: "As the business transitions into its first full season with a new broadcast partnership in place, the time is right for the Managing Director role to transition and for Majed to focus efforts and attention on other interests." Translation: Al-Sorour was the fall guy for LIV's reckless spending. (That evoked the famous quote by Washington Redskins president Edward Williams in explaining why he had fired coach George Allen: "I gave him an unlimited budget and he exceeded it.") That extreme measure reflected Yasir Al-Rumayyan's concern about the underpinnings of LIV's business because Al-Sorour is a close friend and at one time was responsible for overseeing security for His Excellency's family. With the impetuous, freewheeling Al-Sorour gone, "PIF has put a strict delegation of authority in place," says a LIV exec. "There are different boards of approval that things have to go through now. There are a lot of checks and balances. It's no longer one person with complete, unfettered power—that's the biggest difference with Majed out. Just a lot more governance."

Al-Sorour's ouster was a political victory for Greg Norman when he badly needed one. The war of words targeting Norman had only intensified in the preceding months. At the European Tour's season-ending Tour Championship, where he secretly met with Al-Rumayyan, McIlroy said, "I think Greg needs to go. I think he just needs to exit stage left. He's made his mark, but I think now is the right time to sort of say, 'Look, you've got this thing off the ground, but no one is going to talk unless there's an adult in the room that can actually try to mend fences.'" Two weeks later, at the Hero World Challenge, Tiger Woods was asked a similar question about what it would take to reunify the game. "Greg has to go, first of all," he responded. (The word choice made it feel as though Tiger and Rory had been workshopping their answers together.) But now Norman had outlasted a formidable rival. "Greg and Majed hated each other," says a LIV executive. "It was always World War III with those two." A second LIV exec says, "It's more complicated than that. It was more like love-hate. I think they actually enjoyed each other's company, but it was two huge egos always battling to be the loudest voice. Greg had the title of CEO and commissioner, but the buck always stopped with Majed. Majed could override any decision."

LIV 2.0 debuted in February 2023 at Mayakoba. Asked what he liked about the course, Pat Perez said, "I love it because we are here and the Tour is not. End quote." The tournament had the usual LIV trappings, with loud reggaeton music amplified throughout the course, but something looked very different: the golfers. They were kitted out in matching team uniforms, owing to a momentous off-season decision to go all in on every aspect of the teams. Around LIV, 2023 is referred to as Season 1. The team element was not supposed to be fully baked out until the second season, but during the tumultuous off-season it had been decided to fast-track LIV's biggest differentiator from the PGA Tour. That affected the personnel; unlike the constant onboarding of new players throughout 2022 and the corresponding tweaking of team rosters, LIV committed to locking in its forty-eight players for 2023 before the first ball was struck in anger. They included the underwhelming crop of new recruits: Thomas Pieters, Brendan Steele, Danny Lee, Mito Pereira, Sebastián Muñoz, and Dean Burmester. Pieters, 31, sat thirty-fourth in the world ranking and had been in a pretty good position to make the European Ryder Cup team. Steele, 39, has won three Tour events. Pereira, 27, had contended to the bitter end at the 2022 PGA Championship. But none of them is anywhere close to being a needle mover.

At Mayakoba, the teams played practice rounds together, hit balls on the range next to each other, and ate lunch together, always in matching polos with oversized team logos. "It kind of feels like I'm in college again," said Charles Howell III, everybody's All-American at Oklahoma State. Players with existing apparel deals were allowed to honor their contracts, so they wore the same color polo as their teammates but the logos were different; once a clothing deal expires, the player is compelled to wear the team uniform. At Mayakoba the juicy news broke that Dustin Johnson had parted ways with Adidas after fifteen years as a high-profile ambassador; DJ wanted the company to sponsor his 4Aces teammates, too, including the lippy Perez and Patrick Reed, one of the tour's bad boys. It didn't happen.

The Crushers (Howell, Paul Casey, Anirban Lahiri) sported matching Rolexes in the team colors of gold and blue, a gift from captain Bryson DeChambeau. Nobody was reveling in the newfound team spirit more than DeChambeau, who finally had some friends, even if the other guys were being forced into it. "He thrives with that social environment around him, which maybe doesn't come naturally to him," Lahiri says. "But in this case, it's not a matter of choice. The social element is very good for him. He enjoys the company, he enjoys the hang."

Says DeChambeau, "They're wise individuals—a lot wiser than me. They've taught me how to play certain shots, how to think through certain situations, little tricks on the greens. Nuances I never knew about. We're able to talk about things freely and openly because we're all in it to win together. I've learned so much from them."

"Yeah, we've been telling him to stop trying to find a girlfriend on Instagram," says one of DeChambeau's teammates.

Beneath the good cheer there was the discord that is inevitable with LIV. In the ongoing effort to reshape the tour into a semiviable business, the PIF guys had ordained that LIV stop paying for all of the player travel and offload the expenses to the individual teams. It was also unilaterally decided by the PIF guys that the $5 million from the team competition would no longer be paid directly to the players but instead go into team coffers. Each player is now given an annual salary by his team, and at year's end bonuses and/ or profit sharing is a possibility. But that depends on how much the team earns and how much it spends, which suddenly brought class wars to LIV. Each team has to decide what it will cover for players, families, and caddies. One golfer said at Mayakoba, "There is already tension. This week some caddies flew economy and are staying at a motor inn, while [the loopers from Brooks Koepka's Smash] flew business class and are staying at the [swank] Rosewood." The Smash is giving team members a set amount that can be spent however they want for travel, but if a player burns through this allowance, he is on the hook for his expenses for the rest of the season.

Meanwhile, the 4Aces continued to live large, especially Johnson and Perez, whose wives love to flaunt their conspicuous consumption on their Instagrams. Last year, the 4Aces won the team component five times, including the season-ending $50 million tournament at Trump Doral. But one member of the squad, Talor Gooch, had become a part of Bubba Watson's rebranded RangeGoats. I asked Johnson if Gooch had been fired or traded. "All of the above," he said. Peter Uihlein came aboard, which he likened to being drafted by the Yankees; it was said with just enough of a knowing smile not to be patently absurd. Asked if his team would be more thrifty now that LIV was no longer footing all the bills, Perez offered a hard no. "I mean, I traveled on my own for twenty-five years and I did it one way, and I don't see it changing with the way it's going," he said. In fact, each of the 4Aces flew a private jet to Mayakoba. Separately. There had been talk about trying to rendezvous and coordinate the jet(s), but Collin Yost, the 4Aces' team manager says, "I don't think there's a plane big enough. Do you know how much luggage these guys travel with?" Throw in the various entourages, and, Yost says, "We'd need a plane for forty people."

In addition to managers, social media staffers, and attorneys to hammer out all the details, each team has a "principal," a term cribbed from F1. "I have the same responsibilities as a team president in the NFL," says David Cornwell, the 4Aces' principal. One of his mandates is to generate revenue, but individual endorsement deals are no longer a thing on LIV; going forward, all deals will be collective, covering four players, with the money going to the team. Making the teams profitable is a big part of the LIV business model, as it owns 75 percent of each franchise; the rest of the equity goes to the captain and perhaps another key player. The goal is to sell each franchise to a bored billionaire or a multinational company, generating a windfall for the tour (and the captains). The plan was for the teams to go up for sale in 2024, once the P&L statements look more sound. The powers that be at LIV were hoping to shift more of the total purse toward the team. "It would maximize the team values," says one executive, "because their valuations are based on revenue. From a pure business point of view, it would have made more sense from the very beginning to put all of the purse toward the teams [as happens in the season-ending team tournament]. But that would have been a vast departure from what the world of golf has known forever, and we wouldn't have been able to sign all the players. In time we may move in that direction—we're fluid on that."

All that fluidity, mandated from on high, had created a deep angst among many of the LIV players. "They're just making stuff up as they go," one said of both the golf and PIF guys. In Mayakoba, the twelve captains met to try to better understand their new fiscal responsibilities with the teams and to bring their concerns to LIV with a unified voice. A mandatory meeting with LIV leadership and all the players was set for the ensuing tournament in Tucson. In the meantime, Howell, 43, won at Mayakoba, only his second victory anywhere in the preceding sixteen years. DeChambeau finished nineteenth, continuing his woeful play; he had yet to finish as high as ninth in any tournament. But the Crushers brought home the team title, putting $3 million into their bank account and validating all of Captain DeChambeau's hokey team building. Said Howell, "I'm not sure I've ever seen Bryson happier."

It is always fascinating to observe professional golfers in their non-native environment, and on the eve of LIV Tucson, the Dove Mountain Ritz-Carlton provided ample material for the curious anthropologist. Parked out front was Paul Casey's black Porsche 911

GT3 RS with gold wheels and a customized Arizona State license plate; the Scottsdale resident had driven from home, presumably at 180 miles per hour. In the hotel lobby, Jason Kokrak made the scene in a plaid flannel shirt like a roadie for Soundgarden, circa 1993. In his jeans, puffer vest, and oxford cloth shirt, the graying Howell looked like a visiting lecturer at a community college. Numerous players milled around, showing off a variety of Air Jordans and flip-flops, backward baseball caps and receding hairlines. The lobby was also alive with khaki-clad agents, with their telltale leather-encased notebooks, and a phalanx of hot blondes, including Paulina Gretzky in a skin-tight minidress. Cam Smith and Jediah Morgan were tossing around a rugby league ball. Harold Varner III approached a random kid and tickled him without breaking stride. Pat Perez strolled by a couple of dour cops and said, "At ease, gentlemen. At ease."

The players had gathered in a ballroom for a mandatory meeting led by commissioner Greg Norman and interim chief operating officer Gary Davidson, who, along with his fellow Performance54 consultant Jed Moore, had assumed a greater role in the wake of Al-Sorour's departure. Among the topics addressed were the coming drug-testing procedures and a new pace-of-play policy, of which one player said, in a tone as dry as the Sonoran Desert, "It's basically modeled on the [PGA] Tour's, so expect it to be just as effective." But the primary topic of the night was the ongoing evolution of the LIV business model. With only the top three teams being paid at each tournament, struggling squads such as the Majesticks and the Cleeks could easily be in the red at year's end. At the players meeting, LIV leadership introduced the notion of spreading out the $5 million team purse to the top five finishers. Casey, sitting at the back of the room, generated some laughs when he raised his hand and asked, "Is that retroactive?" It's not; his Crushers would not have to spread the wealth from their team win at Mayakoba.

LIV's accelerated timeline is the root of the consternation. The original plan called for ten tournaments in the first full season and fourteen in year two. Having now crammed fourteen events into year one had left the schedule at odds with some players' expectations. "Some guys thought their contracts for this year are for ten tournaments, not fourteen," one player said in Tucson. "But even with more tournaments there is no bump in the guaranteed money they signed for. Last year the players kept their share of the team winnings"—Perez famously won more than $8 million on the season despite an average individual finish of thirty-second—"but now that money goes back to the team. I heard one guy say, 'Why are we standing on a podium spraying each other with champagne when we don't get the money?' So that's interesting. And now there is talk that [LIV leadership] wants to put more of the total purse toward the team component. But, again, guys have it in their contract they would be playing for twenty million dollars on their own. So you can imagine there is a lot of conversation right now."

It is often said that LIV has unlimited resources, so shouldn't all of this be easily solvable with more barrels of money? LIV could simply add $10 million for the team component to each purse and everyone would be happy, right? One LIV executive counters that its financial forecasting extends for ten years, so a purse increase of only $2 million per tournament quickly becomes a $250 million expense that has to go into the model.

"Jay Monahan himself said this is an arms race the PGA Tour can't win, so let's win the arms race," says the player. "But that isn't the climate out here anymore."

Indeed, one barometer is the pressroom lunch: the 2022 tournaments featured decadent buffets with hot entrees and a cornucopia of desserts, but in Tucson it was the same cold sandwiches and prepackaged cookies day after day. "Every expense is double- and triple-checked now," says one player.

Kevin Na, the captain of the Iron Heads, provided some needed perspective when he described the bubbling discord as "first-world problems." He was unbothered by any proposed changes to how the money is doled out, saying he's not even sure what is specified in his contract. "It's a long contract!" he says. "I'll have to ask my agent." In the perfect coda to that moment in professional golf, he added, "There is a shit ton of money out here, and I already got a shit ton. If you play well, you're gonna win a shit ton more. I'm not worrying about the details."

19.

WHEN THOMAS PIETERS SIGNED WITH LIV IN FEBRUARY 2023, he made a certain kind of history, becoming the first Excel Sports Management client to take the plunge. Pieters flew to Mexico for the first tournament of the season and upon arriving was greeted by a text message from an Excel representative terminating the relationship. According to Pieters, Tiger Woods made a phone call to Mark Steinberg, and that was the end of Pieters being an Excel client. "Weirdest thing ever," Pieters said about Steinberg firing him and the coldhearted delivery of the news. "He's just gone." Asked specifically about the role Woods played in ousting Pieters, Steinberg offered a shit-eating grin and said, "My comment is, 'It was chilly this morning but turned into a beautiful afternoon.'" Pieters continued wearing Nike Tiger Woods 13 shoes but, as an act of protest, used a Sharpie to black out the logos.

In early 2023, professional golf's bitchiness simply wouldn't quit. On the same day as Ian Poulter's forty-seventh birthday, the Ryder Cup Europe Twitter account posted a highlight of a lovely Francesco Molinari pitch with the caption "Incredible touch." Poulter's non sequitur reply: "What's really an 'incredible touch' is the Players that helped build the @RyderCupEurope Brand with other players as well. You just can't bring yourself to say a simple Happy Birthday." To repeat: that came from a forty-seven-year-old man.

At the European Tour event in Dubai, Rory McIlroy surged into contention and Phil Mickelson offered a masterfully understated troll job on Twitter: "What a great -7 3rd round by @McIlroyRory in

DUBAI to open up a 3 shot lead. See if he can finish it off. Watch live final round action from the Middle East on the golf channel."

Golf Channel commentators Brandel Chamblee and Eamon Lynch have been relentlessly critical of LIV as a sportswashing exercise for MBS and Saudi Arabia, and McIlroy has certainly been spicy on the topic, too. Mickelson was calling out how unbothered all of them appeared to be about supporting a tournament in the United Arab Emirates, which, according to a United Nations report, engages in "a pattern of torture and ill-treatment against human rights defenders and persons accused of offences against state security." At least twenty-six Emirati prisoners remained behind bars because of their peaceful political criticism, and the UAE Civil Code's Article 184 allows the government to imprison, for up to five years, "anyone who mocks, insults, or damages the reputation, prestige or standing of the state." But the show must go on, and McIlroy defeated Patrick Reed in a riveting back-nine duel that stirred memories of their epic Ryder Cup singles match seven years earlier. The Dubai tournament week had been already enlivened by a juicy/ridiculous controversy when Reed approached McIlroy on the driving range to exchange pleasantries and Rory pointedly ignored him. Just to be a brat, Reed flicked a 4Aces-logoed tee in McIlroy's direction while walking away. "Patrick came up to say hello and I didn't really want him to," Rory said. ". . . I was subpoenaed by his lawyer on Christmas Eve. Trying to have a nice time with my family and someone shows up on your doorstep and delivers that, you're not going to take that well. I'm living in reality, I don't know where he's living. If I were in his shoes, I wouldn't expect a hello or a handshake."

Reed shot back, "Funny how a small little flick has turned into basically me stabbing him. It's unfortunate because we've always had a good relationship. But it is one of those things, if you're going to act like an immature little child then you might as well be treated like one."

You could practically hear the facepalms.

As for McIlroy, five months after his Tour Championship triumph, he was clearly still fired up for a worldwide revenge tour. But with player poaching on hold and the various lawsuits grinding along out of sight, the new golf season was increasingly about product versus product, to borrow Jay Monahan's phrasing. In February, the PGA Tour conducted three elevated events in the span of four weeks, and that put a charge into the golf world as all of the best (non-LIV) players gathered. At the Phoenix Open, Scottie Scheffler roared to victory to return to number one in the world ranking. (Irony alert: Pretty much everyone in golf professes to love the raucous party atmosphere in Phoenix, but LIV is often criticized for trying to foster the same vibe at its tournaments.) At the Genesis Invitational in Los Angeles, Jon Rahm outdueled local favorite Max Homa, snatching the number one ranking back from Scheffler. Then Kurt Kitayama produced a Cinderella story at the Arnold Palmer Invitational, surviving a dogfight with McIlroy, Scheffler, Jordan Spieth, and others to earn a life-changing first Tour victory. Each of those wins was worth $3.6 million, and then, two weeks after Bay Hill, Scheffler claimed the $4.5 million first-place check at the Players Championship, which carried a $25 million purse. (Where have we heard that number before?)

The fans were clearly tuned in to the Tour's improved product, as the TV ratings were up for each of those events, especially the Genesis Invitational (a 30.8 percent increase) and the Players Championship (42.3 percent), even though defending champ Cam Smith wasn't in the field at the latter and the PGA Tour gleefully removed his reserved parking spot at TPC Sawgrass. The elevated events were a home run for the Tour's top players. "It's exciting getting so many tournaments where I'm getting to play against the best players in the world," said Scheffler. "The elevated events for us have been a ton of fun and we've had some good battles and had a lot of great champions. So it's been a fun stretch for us." They were suddenly playing for ungodly amounts of money that would have been unfathomable even a year earlier. Rahm, who had remained an even-keeled voice of reason throughout all the controversy, wasn't afraid to admit as much. "I think on this side of things we should be thankful that LIV happened," he said. "I don't know if [the elevated events] would have happened if LIV wasn't in the picture. So to an extent, yeah, we should be thankful."

Of course, not everyone in the PGA Tour ecosystem was rejoicing. With the top players loading up on elevated events, the other tournaments were suffering with starless fields and plunging TV ratings. A sampling of final-round telecast numbers from early 2023: the Pebble Beach Pro-Am down by 26 percent; the Farmers Insurance Open at Torrey Pines down by 18 percent; the Honda Classic down by 17 percent; the Valero Texas Open down by 22 percent. The news that both Honda and Dell Computers were walking away from long-standing title sponsorships sent shudders through the Tour. In March, a tournament director at an old, proud event called me to vent. "With all the changes happening at the Tour, there is one side to the story that is not being told: ours," he said. "Monahan, Tiger, Rory, all the other top players—they seem to have forgotten their biggest customer, which is the title sponsors of the tournaments. If the Tour keeps losing big sponsors, none of this other stuff matters because the business model is going to collapse. Those of us at the tournament level, we're on the front lines right now, trying to hold everything together." He continued, "Nobody knows what the future will look like. There are still so many unanswered questions. The most frustrating part is that the Tour has done so little to engage with the title sponsors and the tournaments. The communication has been clunky and minimal at best. It's almost like a form of avoidance. They do the absolute minimum, and that has led to a lot of animosity between the Tour and the sponsors, which is unbelievable to me. You would think they would be working overtime to make their corporate partners feel valued and get them to buy into this new vision they are trying to create. None of this feels like a well-laid-out plan. From the very beginning, the Tour has been reactionary all the way across the board. They're just making this stuff up by the seat of their pants."

Behind closed doors, Monahan was struggling to piece together the 2024 schedule. In the hastily thrown together, transitional 2023 season, the Tour offset most of the costs of the elevated purses. If an event previously had an $8 million purse that was now being bumped to $20 million, the Tour asked the title sponsor to kick in half the difference: $6 million. Some corporations pushed back and negotiated a lower number, while some refused to put in any additional money at all. With no leverage, the Tour was forced to burn up nearly $100 million of its reserves to cover the purse increases. For the 2024 season, the Tour was demanding that the sponsors cover the entire $20 million purse, leading to widespread mutiny; it was hard enough for a publicly traded company to justify the outlay at the old price. "Despite what Jay is saying publicly, a number of sponsors are on the verge of walking away," a member of the Player Advisory Council said in March 2023.

The Tour was facing another money crunch, as its legal bills had begun to run into the tens of millions of dollars. In the endless wrangling related to the antitrust lawsuit and countersuit, a pair of rulings from February 2023 loomed the largest. In one, a California magistrate judge denied His Excellency Yasir Al-Rumayyan's claim that he and the Public Investment Fund were exempt from having to participate in discovery because he enjoyed the privileges of sovereign immunity. The judge ruled that, when it comes to LIV, Al-Rumayyan's role had been that of a businessman, not a diplomat, writing, "It is plain that PIF is not a mere investor in LIV; it is the moving force behind the founding, funding, oversight and operation of LIV. PIF's actions are indisputably the type of actions by which a private party engages in trade and traffic or commerce." LIV appealed the ruling to the Ninth Circuit Court of Appeals, and it was ready to take the issue before the Supreme Court, a process that would take years to play out. A separate but related ruling allowed the PGA Tour to add Al-Rumayyan and the PIF to its countersuit. That introduced the possibility that Tour lawyers would get to glee-fully grill a top member of the Saudi government and comb through the financial statements of his all-powerful but intensely secretive fund. Every development in both lawsuits was fiercely contested by an army of lawyers, each charging up to $2,000 an hour. The start date of the all-important antitrust trial was bumped from September 2023 to January 2024 and then to May 2024, with further delays a distinct possibility. "It feels like they're trying to bleed us dry," Peter Malnati, a Tour board member, said of LIV's legal strategy. Monahan had promised his players fabulous new riches, but it was increas-ingly looking as though he had written checks he wouldn't be able to cash.

LIV Golf was enduring its own growing pains. Its third tourna-ment of the 2023 season was held in Orlando, and it was a disaster. Orange County National Golf Center's Crooked Cat course was a pushover with scruffy conditions that looked terrible on TV sets and other screens. (Orange County's other course was open for pub-lic play, leading to the discordant sight of weekend hackers sharing the driving range with the pros.) The few fans who bothered to show up never felt engaged; why should they, with the PGA Tour having just played four tournaments in the state? LIV did not report view-ership numbers for the tournament on CW, the beginning of a new policy; that's how bad the ratings were. The only good news was that Brooks Koepka won again, establishing himself as LIV's most dom-inant player. But how much does a LIV win mean? It remained an open question that the ensuing week's Masters Tournament would help settle.

During the topsy-turvy summer of 2022, the U.S. Open and Open Championship waved into the field every qualified player with minimal public discussion. But in the long months between St. Andrews and Augusta, it became an annoyingly persistent question, particularly on social media: Would the major championships change their criteria to keep out LIV golfers? It was a stupid debate, and not just because any such move would figure prominently in the pending antitrust litigation. Each major championship gets the spotlight for only one week, and its leadership's mandate is to put on the best show possible. Whatever the personal feelings of the lords of the Masters, they had zero interest in besmirching their tournament by barring (previously?) beloved past champions and some of the other best players in the world. But Augusta National, in particular, had naked self-interest in not picking a moralistic fight with LIV. What had ultimately forced the club to accept women members in 2012—more than three decades after Sandra Day O'Connor had become the first female Supreme Court justice—was the intense criticism and pressure applied to the old-boy members who were CEOs of publicly traded corporations. Did Augusta National really want to touch off a bruising public discussion about the pervasiveness and influence of Saudi Arabian money? "On my first trip to play in Saudi, the very first person I ran into at the airport was John Carr," says a LIV golfer about one of Augusta National's prominent members. "I said, 'John, what the hell are you doing here?' He said, 'Just a little business, like you.' How many Augusta members have made money in Saudi—half of them? Two-thirds? They don't want that smoke."

Just before Christmas 2022, Augusta National chairman Fred Ridley released a pithy statement affirming the obvious: "We will invite those eligible under our current criteria to compete in the 2023 Masters Tournament. Regrettably, recent actions have divided men's professional golf by diminishing the virtues of the game and the meaningful legacies of those who built it. Although we are disappointed in these developments, our focus is to honor the tradition of bringing together a preeminent field of golfers this coming April."

Come Masters week, Augusta National's rigidly enforced gentility carried the day, as players from both tours strained to be polite. Phil Mickelson sat glumly through the Tuesday-night champions' dinner, barely uttering a peep lest he get wound up and offend half the room. But even Augusta National can't keep the outside world entirely at bay. The week before the Masters, Donald Trump had been indicted on thirty-four criminal charges related to paying hush money to cover up his affair with the porn actress Stormy Daniels and reporting it as legal fees on his company's tax returns. Under the famous oak tree behind the Augusta National clubhouse, golf gadflies whispered to each other about whether LIV could break its contract for the three upcoming tournaments at Trump courses, to avoid further guilt by association. At the Masters, I asked Jack Nicklaus if he would still support Trump in the 2024 presidential election. "Well, depends on who is running, doesn't it?" he said. "We'll have to see what happens. You know, I've always supported who I thought was the best candidate. I thought Donald Trump was the last time. Whether Donald will be this time or not, I don't know. We'll wait and see. I don't like to brand myself as a Republican. I like to sort of brand myself as being able to think freely, and I have voted for a lot of Democrats through the years as well as Republicans, and I tried to pick the person I think would do the best job for our country." That was a sensible answer, but, given Nicklaus's previous unreserved enthusiasm for Trump, it could also be read as his distancing himself from his longtime golf buddy.

The members of the OWGR's governing board were at the Masters in various capacities, and there were numerous quiet conversations about the LIV predicament. I bumped into Seth Waugh, the CEO of the PGA of America, under the tree and asked if he could share a world ranking update. Without breaking stride he sighed, "All I can say is, it's the gift that keeps on giving." But the real thunderbolt came on the morning of Masters Tuesday, when word leaked out that the European Tour had prevailed in the arbitration case in which LIV golfers were challenging their tour suspensions and

£100,000 fines for having competed in LIV tournaments without obtaining conflicting event releases. The full ruling was released on the morning of the first round, and once again LIV had suffered a resounding loss in the legal system. The arbitrators found that the LIV rebels had committed "serious breaches" of the tour's rules and that their actions had "increased the likelihood that commercial partners would be tempted to terminate or limit relationships with the tour." Noting "the scale and importance of the potential harm" to the tour, the panel declared that Keith Pelley, the European Tour's CEO, had "acted entirely reasonably" when he had denied the players' requests to appear at LIV events.

"Individual players have to accept some limitation on their freedoms inherent in tour membership," the panel wrote. ". . . It is not part of competition law to require incumbents to offer no resistance—they are entitled to react and retaliate, even if dominant." The ruling focused on the narrow issue of whether the European Tour could impose rules on its membership, but it had sweeping ramifications: if LIV Golf had prevailed, it could have blown up the structure of professional golf, allowing players to jump from tour to tour with minimal restrictions. More immediately, it put pressure on the LIV players to formally cut ties with the European Tour, which had made clear that it would retroactively add additional hefty fines for every LIV start a player had made. Tour membership is a requirement to play on, or captain, a Ryder Cup team. Sergio García, 42, is Europe's all-time Ryder Cup points leader and in a vacuum would have been a contender for a team that looks likely to have a bevy of untested players. Would he pay millions of pounds in fines just for the chance to be a captain's pick? Bernd Wiesberger had played on the 2021 European squad, and Thomas Pieters would have been a strong contender this time around, but both had cast their lot with LIV. Like García, they would resign their tour membership in the weeks after the Masters to avoid having to pay any additional fines. (And even though LIV would reimburse him, García refused to pay the initial £100,000 fine mandated in the arbitration ruling, saying with a shrug, "I have always played multiple tours. Since I have done nothing wrong, I don't think the tour should be collecting any money.") The European Tour was damaging its immediate Ryder Cup chances but deemed that a small price to pay to affirm the rule of law. The arbitration ruling touched off jubilation among the ruling class under the tree, though, with a nod to the court case's intrusion on Augusta National's meticulously curated artificial reality, one green jacket called the timing of the decision "a skunk in a garden party."

But the Masters is the Masters, and attention eventually turned to the action inside the ropes, though the LIV subplot remained prominent when Koepka shared the first-round lead with a sizzling 65. He followed with a 67 and then a 73 to forge a 2-stroke lead heading into the final round. For those who enjoy controversy— which is to say, almost every member of the media—a LIV player fighting for the green jacket was yet another gift from the content gods. "This is beautiful," said the English reporter Kevin Garside. "We have a term for this sort of stuff: shithousery. This would be perfect golf shithousery. All we need is Norman tweeting his congratulations from Mar-a-Lago to make it better." Koepka would play alongside Rahm in a blockbuster final pairing on Sunday the twenty-eight-year-old Spaniard had already won three times in the season's first three months. Given Tiger Woods's continued decline, no other players in golf today can match the intensity of these brooding, big-boned ball bashers.

Koepka didn't have his best stuff on Sunday. As he faltered, an unlikely pursuer emerged on the back nine: Phil! Mickelson started the day 10 shots off the lead but raced up the leaderboard with a burst of birdies. He had missed the 2022 Masters while still in exile, and for most of Masters week the crowd treated his return with ambivalence. But as Phil the Thrill birdied his way through the back nine, he whipped the gallery into a frenzy. "It felt very, very like eight, nine, ten years ago," said his playing partner, Jordan Spieth, referring to peak Mickelson and when he was the most popular player around Augusta National this side of Arnie.

Mickelson ran out of holes and tied for second alongside Koepka as Rahm produced a commanding four-shot victory. Afterward, Mickelson was openly emotional. His life had been turned upside down in the preceding year. Straining for reinvention, he had dropped twenty-five pounds in the off-season with a strict diet. He had been putting in long hours working on his game even though his results on LIV didn't show it. But in the run-up to Augusta, Mickelson credited LIV teammate Brendan Steele with helping him improve his driving and another HyFlyer, Cameron Tringale, with straightening out his putting. All Mickelson needed was a spark, and the three-time Masters champ found it on a course his former swing coach Butch Harmon had once called "Phil's playground." By the time he uncorked a lusty fist pump on the eighteenth green after a final birdie, Mickelson's recent siege mentality and media-trained stiffness had melted away and he looked like his old, jaunty self. His 65 was the low round of the day and matched the low round of the tournament. Asked if returning to the Masters had been therapeutic, he said, "I would use the word *spiritual*, because if you love golf, when you come here, it's more of a spiritual experience, where you feel this appreciation for this great game and the gratitude that you have."

It surely helped that Amy had been by his side, the first time I had spotted her at one of Phil's tournaments since he had been a vice captain at the 2021 Ryder Cup. (Not for nothing, in the weeks before the Masters he had restored "husband" to his Twitter bio.) After his thrilling final round, he retreated to the lounge outside the champions' locker room on the second floor of the Augusta National clubhouse. He was seated at a table with his college sweetheart, and they were holding hands and cooing at each other, their smiling faces no more than a foot apart. Danny Willett, the 2016 Masters champion, was at a neighboring table, acting like a lad with some of his boys, but Phil and Amy were in their own little world. The intimacy of the moment was breathtaking.

Rahm snatched the green jacket, but LIV golfers shared second place and tied for fourth, thanks to Patrick Reed's closing 68. It was a very satisfying showing for a tour still struggling for credibility. Said Harold Varner III, "I guess we don't suck."

20.

TWO WEEKS AFTER THE MASTERS, LIV BLEW INTO ADE-
laide for its first tournament in Australia. Vibe check?

"Sick," said Jed Morgan.

"Epic," said Cam Smith.

"Unbelievable," said Marc Leishman.

LIV Golf Adelaide accommodated 25,000 fans a day, and the anticipation was such that tickets sold out months in advance. The all-Aussie Ripper team of Smith, Morgan, Leishman, and Matt Jones was the focus of the week. Of his opening tee shot, Smith said, "Yeah, that first fairway looked pretty narrow this morning—it seemed like everyone was on the edge of the fairway."

The Grange Golf Club featured a Phoenix Open–style party hole, encasing the par-3 twelfth hole with five thousand fans. The beer—including Leishman Lager, a "dry, crisp malt with notes of lime zest," according to one web review—flowed like a river, leading to the nickname "the Watering Hole." Players strutted to the tee with booming walk-up music. Dustin Johnson chose AC/DC's "Back in Black," and Phil Mickelson went with Eminem's "Lose Yourself," a couple of classic bangers. Brooks Koepka's selecting Meek Mill's "Dreams and Nightmares" added some context as to why he had bought his brother, Chase, a Lamborghini after their team win in Jeddah, as the song includes a memorable paean to a "Lambo." Chase produced a highlight that went around the world when he aced the Watering Hole during the final round, touching off a wild celebration with the sodden fans showering the players, and one another, with various beverages. "I smelled like beer for the rest of the round," he said.

Talor Gooch wowed the crowd by opening with rounds of 62–62 to forge a stunning 10-stroke lead. "This is what gets you up in the morning, to play in front of crowds like this with energy like this," he said. The tightly bunched team leaderboard provided needed final-round drama, as the 4Aces eked out a one-stroke win over Gooch's RangeGoats. Gooch labored to a closing 73, winning the individual title by three strokes. His teammates—Bubba Watson, Harold Varner III, and Thomas Pieters—mobbed him on the final green, but the champ apologized to his fellow Goats for not playing better and helping the squad get a win. That buy-in on the team component, along with the raucous crowds, led Gooch to say, "I think they're just now starting to get a feel for what LIV is."

Indeed, the success of LIV Golf Adelaide left LIV commissioner Greg Norman in a triumphant mood. He had been treated by his fellow Aussies as a conquering hero upon returning to the town where he had won his first professional tournament, in 1976. Given Norman's penchant for gaffes, he had not been part of a press conference since LIV had launched, but he finally sat for one in Adelaide, alongside the premier of South Australia, Peter Malinauskas. "We are not coming in here just flashing and burning and disappearing," Norman said. "It's a partnership with the state. It's a partnership with the country, but it's a partnership for the game of golf. Forgetting all the white noise that everybody writes about and talks about, this is all about what's good for the game of golf and what's good for the local region. From my perspective, having the ability to be able to move the needle in that direction and to be involved with the South Australian government or any other country around the world is very, very powerful and poignant. Trust me, this morning my phone is ringing off the hook, but it's not just Australia, it's the rest of the world, too." (We don't trust you, Greg, but okay.)

Australia is a proud golfing nation that has largely been abandoned by the highest levels of the professional game. The reception at the Adelaide event drove home that LIV can be most meaningful playing around the world in markets that rarely see big-name players. "You could see how this LIV thing is just really exploding," said Pat Perez. "I think when we go more worldwide, you're going to see this kind of stuff. I think that's what we should stay with, myself."

Of course, the Australian national character embraces the rebellious and the antiestablishment, making for a perfect match with the image that LIV, and Norman, have cultivated. (Aussie golf fans also blame the PGA Tour's increasingly year-round schedule for preventing many players from supporting historic tournaments Down Under.) Sky Sports commentator Jamie Weir had been a biting critic of LIV, putting him on the front lines of various social media battles. Of the LIV supporters, he tweeted, "They come in all shapes and sizes, but there definitely seems to be two MAIN groups who are the staunchest pro-LIV, anti-established Tours and OWGR, the angriest, most vocal and easily-irked on Twitter: The MAGA/Trump contingent and . . . Australians."

At his press conference, Malinauskas brushed aside questions about being an enabler of sportswashing with a clear-eyed perspective. "We sell extraordinary amounts of barley, beef, lamb, amongst other things to Saudi Arabia," he said. "It's a $3 billion trading partnership between Australia and Saudi Arabia. There are $4 billion worth of active investments in Australia alone. So we choose as a country to actively trade with Saudi Arabia, the largest economy within the Middle East, and we do that knowingly, without at any step of the way compromising what we collectively believe in as a country."

After a slow start, Smith rallied to tie for third, delighting the home crowd. He admitted he chose LIV in part because of the promise to be able to play in front of his loved ones and countrymen; owing to covid travel restrictions, he didn't see his family for three years. At the end of a satisfying week in Adelaide, the Champion

Golfer of the Year said, "I think it's a massive boost. I think it gives the tour a lot of confidence and momentum. I think it's going to be the benchmark for LIV Golf going forward."

Less than a year into the LIV era, the battle between the tours was turning into a war of attrition. Jordan Spieth made a spirited run at the Masters, shooting a final-round 66 to tie for fourth, but afterward lamented that his chances at victory were torpedoed by a "tremendous amount of mental mistakes." The Masters was Spieth's seventh tournament in the span of nine weeks, a very heavy workload for a top player, especially one with a young child. "I think I played way too much golf," he concluded glumly. "I came in mentally fatigued." But the revamped PGA Tour schedule was relentless, and he felt the need to tee it up again the week after Augusta at Hilton Head for the next elevated event. As always, follow the money: for players to collect the final 25 percent of their 2022 Player Impact Program cut—in Spieth's case, $2.25 million—the Tour compelled them to play in every elevated event. At least, that was the original plan that Jay Monahan had announced at the Tour Championship the previous August. Player pushback led to the rule being amended, allowing one elevated tournament to be skipped. Rory McIlroy was disdainful of his fellow pros' complaining about having to play for previously unimaginable riches. "I said, 'If I'm willing to do this, so should you.' I said to these guys, 'No other athletes in the world get to choose where and when they play.' We have all just got a little bit soft."

But McIlroy wasted no time in using his get-out-of-the-Ritz-free card to skip the season opener, the Tournament of Champions at Kapalua. He sent a jolt through the Tour when he withdrew from the RBC Heritage on Hilton Head Island, too. In the golf press it was trumpeted as a $3 million vacation for McIlroy, who had suffered a crushing missed cut at the Masters after putting on a stripe show during the practice rounds. He received little sympathy from his weary colleagues who showed up for work at Hilton Head. "Rules are rules," said Xander Schauffele. "For the most part, a lot of what he wanted is what's happening. And the irony is that he's not here."

Monahan affirmed that McIlroy would be forfeiting the $3 million that was still owed to him from the Player Impact Program, but then McIlroy turned up at the Wells Fargo Championship at Quail Hollow—yet another elevated event, three weeks after Hilton Head—and smartly couched his withdrawal as an issue of "mental and emotional well-being." When it comes to doling out the PIP money, Monahan has absolute power, though he phrases it slightly differently, saying, "I have discretion, okay? I'll work with our team, I'll understand the situation, and we'll make a decision." Translation: McIlroy would get his $3 million one way or another.

For the Tour's most strident advocate, the post-Masters funk was a moment of clarity. "I wasn't gassed because of the golf, I was gassed because of everything that we've had to deal with in the golf world over the past twelve months and being right in the middle of it and being in that decision-making process," he said. "I've always thought I've had a good handle and perspective of things and where golf fits within my life, but I think over the last twelve months I'd lost sight of that, lost sight of the fact that there's more to life than the golf world and this silly little squabble that's going on between tours."

The PGA Tour had reached an inflection point. In the battle for golf's soul, Monahan had pushed all of his chips to the middle of the table, because what else could he do? But it was becoming increasingly obvious that the Tour was on a financially unsustainable path. Its most important players were already being ground up by the new schedule. LIV golfers had put a huge charge into the Masters and were clearly going to remain relevant on the biggest stages, undercutting the Tour backers' wishful thinking that Koepka et al. would just fade away. And the energy around LIV Adelaide resonated all the way to Ponte Vedra Beach.

Hockey Jay, Monahan's alter ego, had made a rash decision to take on the Saudis even as he knew, and would later admit publicly, that it was a battle the Tour couldn't win, dollar for dollar. It took more analytical business and legal minds to help lead him out of the morass. Monahan had been increasingly looking for counsel from the chairman of the Tour's board of directors, Ed Herlihy, a mergers and acquisitions specialist at perhaps the most renowned law firm in the United States, Wachtell, Lipton, Rosen & Katz, where he is cochairman. Herlihy had started his legal career as a staff attorney for the Securities and Exchange Commission. He played a crucial role in solving the 2008 financial crisis, overseeing Bank of America's $44.7 billion acquisition of Merrill Lynch and Wells Fargo's buyout of Wachovia. Monahan was also under the sway of the Tour's newest board member, Jimmy Dunne, one of the leading investment bankers in the world as a cofounder of Sandler O'Neill + Partners. Dunne is a quintessential insider, reputed to be the first man to become a member of all four leading private golf clubs in the United States: Augusta National, Cypress Point, Seminole, and Pine Valley. Dunne is a good enough stick to have once shot 63 at Shinnecock Hills (where he is also a member), and golf probably saved his life. On September 11, 2001, he was attempting to qualify for the U.S. Mid-Amateur Championship instead of sitting in his office on the 104th floor of the South Tower of the World Trade Center. Sandler O'Neill lost sixty-six of its eighty-three New York City employees that dark day. Dunne insisted that the company pay ten years of salary to the family of each victim and cover the college tuition of the seventy-six children who had been left behind. Decades later, he was still known to weep when discussing 9/11 with friends. Both Dunne and Herlihy could see clearly what Monahan was too prideful to say out loud and what LIV's Pat Perez diagnosed in his inimitable way:

"Their whole model is fucked because it is dependent on squeezing more and more money out of corporations that are already tired of getting squeezed. We don't have to worry about that out here. Our money comes out of the ground."

Yet the meager crowds and TV ratings for LIV Golf events in Tucson and Orlando made it clear that the U.S. market remained indifferent, even hostile, to the product. As both sides became more entrenched, it was going to become increasingly hard for LIV to lure new talent, including the next generation of would-be stars, after the Tour again sweetened its PGA Tour University program by adding an extra year to the exemption for the player who finishes atop the standings and granting the top twenty players exemptions onto the Korn Ferry Tour. So the Tour locked up the most exciting prospect in years, Ludvig Åberg, a Swede by way of Texas Tech who became exempt through the end of the 2024 season. LIV had a potent recruiting advantage when it was offering $25 million per tournament and PGA Tour purses were hovering around $9 million. Now that the players were regularly teeing it up for $20 million on Tour, with $3.6 million going to the winner, the incentive to jump was greatly diminished. Would the PIF approve another huge outlay, bumping the purses to $35 million or $40 million? Putting that much more money into the product would make it impossible for LIV ever to break even, even if the team franchises could be sold. Of a massive purse increase, one LIV executive said, "That's something that we are looking at and will continue to evaluate." But to what end? Say that LIV could snag Patrick Cantlay, Xander Schauffele, or Matt Fitzpatrick, if not all of them; it wouldn't really change anything. They're nice players but are not going to send the masses running to the CW telecast. Said the PGA Tour's Billy Horschel, "I don't know how the current situation is sustainable for either side."

And then there was the Department of Justice's looming anti-trust investigation. With the lawyers for LIV and the Tour fighting tooth and nail over an endless number of procedural matters, casting doubt on the trial beginning as scheduled on May 17, 2024, DOJ became reengaged, interviewing players, agents, and executives from both tours. The feds went particularly deep with Phil Mickelson, Bryson DeChambeau, and Sergio García. PGA of America CEO Seth Waugh was deposed for twelve hours regarding potential collusion to deny world ranking points to LIV events. Key protagonists had to surrender their phone so evidence could be extracted. "You give them all your passwords, and they take the phone for five or six hours," says LIV golfer Carlos Ortiz, who was one of the original plaintiffs in the antitrust lawsuit before dropping out. "Then they know everything you've ever said to anyone. And they tell you not to delete anything because they will find that, too. It's fine, I have nothing to hide. But I know other people were nervous." That included Monahan, who had used all of his political capital to thwart LIV. Surely the DOJ knew that Endeavor—the parent company of International Management Group and the William Morris Agency, with Spieth and Cantlay among its clients—had been considering a $1 billion investment in LIV but scuttled the deal under pressure from Monahan. "We're all connected in golf," Ari Emanuel, Endeavor's CEO, would say on the *Freakonomics* podcast. "And [the PGA Tour] said, 'Please don't do it.' So we stopped. I'm friends with Jay. We have a lot of business with Jay. I don't want to hurt Jay." Was that merely hard-nosed business or illegal antitrust bullying? The clues to this, and many other instances of potential malfeasance, were buried in the phones of Monahan and his lieutenants, and the government investigators had access to everything.

On the legal front, LIV's cause had been severely weakened by its defeat in the UK arbitration case, and everyone at the PIF was unsettled by the prospect of Al-Rumayyan being deposed about his game-changing fund's unseen dealings. "The PIF guys will withdraw the lawsuit before they'll open up their books," predicted a LIV executive. "There is zero chance they will let Jay Monahan stick a finger up their ass and feel around." The Tour brass may have been fretting about being able to pay its legal bills, but it had clearly seized the upper hand in the legal battles.

With all of this as a backdrop, perhaps the most momentous text message in golf history was sent on the morning of April 18, a few days after the Hilton Head tournament concluded: "Yasir—my name is Jimmy Dunne I am a member of the tour policy board I would like the opportunity for a call and then hopefully a visit best Jimmy."

21.

ON THE MORNING OF THE FIRST ROUND OF THE PGA Championship, Brandel Chamblee talked expansively in a phone interview about why LIV golfers were inexorably sliding toward irrelevancy. "They have some good players, but their games will decay," he said. "They're not playing under the most competitive environment. They're just not. The bottom half of their field is very weak. Who are they beating? How are these courses set up? You look at how low the scores are, it's ridiculous. Where is the data? There are no advanced stats to tell us how each of them are really playing. I just don't see Cam Smith staying on the same trajectory. I don't think Brooks and DJ and Patrick Reed are going to remain the players they were."

But didn't LIV's strong showing at the Masters a month earlier repudiate this line of thinking?

"I don't think one week vindicates them at all," parried Chamblee. "For all of its appeal, the Masters has the smallest field and the weakest field in major championship golf. It's the most predictable tournament in terms of knowing who's going to play well. LIV has bought several of the best players in the world—it's not inconceivable they would play good golf on a course where they've previously had success. But one tournament is not a large amount of data."

The oddsmakers agreed with Chamblee. The week after his dominant win in Australia, Talor Gooch roared to another victory at LIV Singapore, becoming the circuit's first back-to-back champion. But the online bookmaker Bovada didn't list him among its top fifty contenders at the PGA Championship, deeming him less of a threat than Emiliano Grillo, who had been winless on the PGA Tour since 2015. The week before the PGA Championship, Dustin Johnson earned his second win (and ninth top ten) since joining LIV, at the tournament in Tulsa. Yet for the PGA Championship, among the players the gambling site FanDuel had at shorter odds than Johnson were Cameron Young (winless in forty career PGA Tour starts) and Collin Morikawa (zero victories in nearly two years, including a blown 6-shot lead on Sunday at Kapalua).

The week of the PGA Championship was when professional golf stopped making sense. With the PGA of America as the host organization, there was much talk about the looming Ryder Cup. By decree, a player must be a member of the PGA of America to compete for the U.S. team; being a member of the PGA Tour automatically confers membership on the PGA of America. Every LIV player, including those who resigned from the Tour, remains eligible for the Ryder Cup because the PGA of America extended them a "grace period" through June 2024. That bureaucratic sleight of hand can roughly be translated as, "Here, Zach, you deal with this shit."

U.S. captain Zach Johnson met the transatlantic press at the PGA Championship and displayed an impressive amount of point-missing. Six players will qualify for the team based on a points system pegged to their on-course results and six more by way of Johnson's captain's picks. Asked if he considered Dustin Johnson, who had gone 5–0 at the 2021 Ryder Cup, to be one of the twelve best Americans, Captain Zach said, "Really difficult for me to judge that. Again, I don't know the golf courses they're playing. Never seen them. It's not fair for me to guess his true form or anybody's true form that I can't witness." This is nonsensical; two venues on which LIV had already conducted tournaments in 2023—El Camaleón Mayakoba in Mexico, and the Gallery Golf Club in Tucson—had hosted PGA Tour events. Various Americans have competed in the Singapore Open at Sentosa Golf Club, which hosted the LIV event; in fact, Johnson's Sea Island neighbor Matt Kuchar had won there in 2020. And nothing was stopping Johnson from firing up CW to watch a little golf. If he had no clue about a LIV player's form or the caliber of the playing fields, it's because he was choosing to be ignorant.

The Ryder Cup dates to 1927, half a century before the European Tour formed. The mission of this goodwill exhibition is simple: to bring together the best players from Europe and the United States to play for pride and their flag. But the European Tour attached itself to the Ryder Cup like a parasite, sucking enough money out of it to float its entire operation. To protect its interests, the European Tour established convoluted membership rules and qualifying criteria. By forcing LIV golfers to resign their memberships under the threat of continued fines, the European Tour banished an entire generation of Ryder Cup heroes: Lee Westwood, Ian Poulter, Martin Kaymer, and Graeme McDowell were all no-brainers as future captains, and some if not all of them would have served as vice captains to Henrik Stenson in 2023. Sergio García, after going 3–0 in partner play with Jon Rahm in 2021, would have been a contender to play on Europe's underdog squad in Rome. Rahm was not happy that turf wars unrelated to the Ryder Cup had cost him his *compadre*. "I have a hard time to believe that the best player Europe has ever had, the most successful player Europe has had on the Ryder Cup, isn't fit to be on the team," he said. "It's a little sad to me that politics have gotten in the way of such a beautiful event. . . . Again, it's the best Europeans against the best Americans. Period. And who is playing LIV and who is not playing LIV to me shouldn't matter."

The run-up to the PGA Championship was also dominated by talk of the world ranking quagmire. In the seven months leading into the PGA, Koepka had two wins and three other top ten finishes on LIV and nearly stole the Masters, yet he arrived at Oak Hill for the PGA Championship a distant forty-fourth in the world ranking, behind K. H. Lee and Sepp Straka, among others. The OWGR had made itself worse than irrelevant; it was now approaching farcical. Reporters and other observers were increasingly citing other rankings that incorporated LIV players, including the Data Golf Rankings and the Universal Golf Rankings. But the major championships continued to cling to the OWGR as a criteria for qualifying, making it impossible to ignore. Talor Gooch, seemingly always in the middle of everything, became ensnared in the messiness. He earned an exemption into the 2023 U.S. Open by virtue of achieving enough FedEx Cup points to qualify for the 2022 Tour Championship, even though he had left for LIV before the PGA Tour season was complete. But in February 2023, the USGA tweaked the wording of its Tour Championship exemption, adding that a player had not only to qualify but also to be "eligible"; Gooch had forfeited his eligibility to play in the Tour Championship by joining LIV. He was the only player affected by that arbitrary change to the language. USGA CEO Mike Whan did not help matters when he said haughtily, "I'm not concerned about not having the greatest players in the world [at the U.S. Open]. Anytime we make changes to our criteria going forward it impacts somebody and that stinks, but we can only look forward."

Gooch's colleague Phil Mickelson took to Twitter to blast Whan and the USGA: "Hey Mike, what about changing a rule and making it retroactive to exclude someone who has already qualified? How can Talor Gooch not take that personal? It's a direct attack on him and his career. How does it benefit the usga or US open? It doesn't. Just a d!*k move." In another tweet, Mickelson wrote, "This doesn't make the US open better in any way but does help collude with the Tour." Surprisingly, he didn't tag the Department of Justice. The 2023 U.S. Open exempted into its field the top sixty in the world ranking as of May 22, the day after the PGA Championship. Gooch arrived at Oak Hill ranked sixty-third, so the PGA would be his last opportunity to rack up enough points to be exempt for the Open.

With Jay Monahan, Keith Pelley, and European Tour COO Keith Waters having (finally) recused themselves from the OWGR's governing board, only four voters remained to determine whether LIV events would be granted points. Whan is one of them, and his sanctioning the rule change that penalized Gooch is a window into his belief system. Seth Waugh, the CEO of the PGA of America, is another member of the OWGR's governing board, and the week before he played host at Oak Hill, he disparaged LIV in an interview with the *Times* of London, saying, "I don't see they are accomplishing much." He added, divisively, "I don't think division is good for the game. Hopefully, it's good for those individuals that have made whatever decisions they have, but the game has moved on. It's amplified those who have stayed, and the ones who have left have largely disappeared from the landscape—in terms of an exposure perspective." *Disappeared?* LIV golfers made the Masters must-see TV, helping to drive its highest Sunday ratings in five years.

At Waugh's annual pretournament press conference at the PGA Championship, I asked him if those comments had been appropriate given that he is supposed to be a neutral arbiter in the OWGR process. "When asked, I tend to try to say what I believe," he said. "That's not being a neutral body. I think being a neutral body is always acting in the best interest of the game, and that's what we'll always do and that's what I'll always do."

But which interests was Waugh trying to protect? He loves to reference his career as the CEO of Deutsche Bank, saying, "As a former businessman, I think disruption is a good thing. I think good things have happened from that." Yet he had been a gatekeeper in maintaining professional golf's status quo; granting OWGR points to LIV would be a huge boost to a tour that he openly denigrated. Waugh is an active member at Seminole Golf Club in Juno Beach, Florida, where the golf world is run out of the grillroom, with Jimmy Dunne, the longtime club president, riding herd. The Seminole cabal includes two other PGA Tour board members, Ed Herlihy and Mark Flaherty, as well as Fred Perpall, the USGA president; Mike Davis, a former CEO of the USGA; and Pete Bevacqua, Waugh's predecessor at the PGA of America. Dunne invited Rory McIlroy's father, Gerry, a former bartender, to join the inner sanctum, bringing Rory further into the fold and giving Dunne more access to the Tour's leading spokesman. Dunne counseled McIlroy throughout the various stages of the tour wars and did not hesitate to make known his disdain for the LIV golfers, pointedly excluding them from the 2023 Seminole Pro-Member, a one-day tournament that is the quintessence of the clubby, insider circle jerk. Says LIV's Peter Uihlein, "The Seminole guys, the Augusta National guys, they're used to having all the power in the golf world. They don't like to be challenged. They're not used to it."

Had Greg Norman given the Seminole and Augusta National guys ample reason to hate him? Definitely. Were the LIV players and leadership being presumptuous and entitled in assuming that they would immediately be awarded OWGR points? Certainly. Had Norman and Mickelson, among others, been obnoxious in advocating in the press and on social media for world ranking recognition? Without a doubt. But by slow-playing the OWGR process, Waugh, Whan, and their comrades from Augusta National and the R&A created, at the very least, the appearance of collusion, to say nothing of obstinance. Around the time of the PGA Championship, Whan said, "I'm proud of the fact that the world ranking, we're not just rushing to figure this out, because it is different." Since when is bureaucratic inefficiency something to celebrate? The twelve-month waiting period that the OWGR bakes into its review process has traditionally been done to ensure that fledgling developmental tours will remain in business; LIV clearly has the resources to last forever. When I asked Waugh why the OWGR was being so strident about a twelve-month review process, he cut me off, saying, "That's a total mischaracterization." But he then said, "There is no magic to twelve months. It's just most of these, certainly since I've been around, have taken more time than I think was assumed early on. This is not us versus them."

One of the stated reasons for the OWGR to deny recognition to LIV has been its lack of a thirty-six-hole cut, touted by PGA Tour loyalists as a fundamental aspect of competitive golf at the highest level. But for the Tour's revamped 2024 schedule, eight of the elevated events will not have cuts as the Tour product continues to mirror LIV's. (For the new season, the elevated tournaments have been rebranded as "signature" events.) In laboring to sell the Tour's sudden embrace of no-cut events, McIlroy offered a pragmatic rationale: "It keeps the stars there for four days. You ask Mastercard or whoever it is to pay twenty million dollars for a golf event, they want to see the stars on the weekend. They want a guarantee that the stars are there. So if that's what needs to happen, then that's what happens." Naturally, LIV golfers were quick to point out the irony/hypocrisy in all of this. As Westwood tweeted, "I've spent the last year reading how good full fields and cuts are!"

Poulter saw a through line with both the OWGR and Ryder Cup seeking to disenfranchise LIV golfers. "The so-called leaders of this sport are making decisions based on emotion," he said. "They are fighting so hard to protect their narrow interests without thinking of the good of the game, so they are making irrational decisions. If you don't like competition in business, then you are not ready for it. And when you're not ready for it, you're going to get caught out."

The on-course action at the PGA Championship continued to roil the golf world as Bryson DeChambeau grabbed the first-round lead with a 66. His reemergence was wholly unexpected as he had been a nonfactor on LIV while he changed his body and his swing. In the summer of 2022, he went on a radical diet that precluded dairy products, corn, wheat, and gluten—"pretty much everything I liked," he says. He lost eighteen pounds in twenty-four days. Just like that, gone were the dizziness, lethargy, inflammation, and volcanic bowel movements that had dogged him since the spring of 2020, when he had begun eating like Joey Chestnut in an effort to bulk up and increase his driving distance. At Oak Hill, he looked healthy, happy, and spry, just the latest reinvention for a onetime boy wonder on the cusp of turning thirty. The mad scientist who obsessed over *The Golf Machine* and prattled on like a physics professor on trucker-speed had finally figured out his swing and was seeking only to keep on keeping on. "I just want to be stable now," he says. "I'm tired of changing, trying different things."

Brooks Koepka, who arrived at Oak Hill still smarting from his shaky Sunday at Augusta National, was straining for his own return to form, back to when he was golf's most ruthless big-game hunter. During the second round of the PGA Championship, he shot the low round of the day with a 66 that propelled him to a tie for sixth. (Gooch missed the cut to miss out on the U.S. Open, meaning that he would have to go through final qualifying if he wanted to play in the U.S. Open; he elected not to try, in part as a protest against the USGA's rule change.) DeChambeau, with a 71, slipped into a tie for third, and on Saturday these leading men of LIV were paired together. Earlier in the week, Waugh had hailed the Masters for "returning civility to the game" by inviting all of the LIV players and forcing everyone to get along at the point of a bayonet. But the Noo Yawkers crowding Oak Hill's first tee on Saturday were not shy about weighing in on the LIV-Tour divide, lustily booing Koepka and DeChambeau. "Not a warm welcome," Jim Nantz said on the CBS telecast, barely disguising his glee; one of the more amusing developments in golf was that the genteel Nantz had turned into a low-key LIV troll. "I've never heard [boos], for that matter, at any point back to last summer."

Koepka's frame of reference is team sports, and he took the fans' invective as a compliment. Then he dropped another 66 to claim the fifty-four-hole lead. On a wet, wild weather day, he looked eerily calm. "Major championship golf is like the kill zone on Everest," says his swing coach, Claude Harmon III. "A lot of guys are comfortable at Camp IV—they can see the peak from there, but they don't want to suffer to get to the top. They're not willing to step over the dead bodies just for the chance to get to the summit. Brooks is comfortable in the chaos. Some guys are, some aren't. Tiger was, Phil was. Certain guys live for the chaos. Most are afraid of it."

Koepka overwhelmed the final round with his demeanor and physicality as much as his macho ball striking and silky putting. There have been a lot of great golfers through the years, but only a select few have had *presence*. Hogan had it. Arnie. Jack. Seve. Ray Floyd. Faldo. Tiger, obviously. Golf skill is a big part of it, but the presence is metaphysical. It is a distillation of will, want, grind, grit, confidence, belief . . . badassery. On Sunday at the PGA, Koepka flushed iron shots on holes two, three, and four to set up birdies that pushed his lead from 1 to 3 strokes. He looked as though he were ten feet tall and the fairways at Oak Hill were barely wide enough to contain his puissance. "In the north of England we say, 'He has a lot of twat in him,'" says Koepka's short-game coach, Pete Cowen, "which means, 'I'm the man. Bring it on.' Brooks is afraid of nothing. He's a gun for hire. Bang, you're dead."

Koepka birdied the twelfth hole to push his lead to 2 strokes, but the key sequence came at thirteen, an unreachable (on that day) par 5. With the game Viktor Hovland, his playing partner, already in with a birdie, Koepka faced a terrifying ten-footer for par straight down a vertiginous hill. Making a putt like that, under such conditions, has little to do with technical proficiency; it is an X-ray of the soul. Koepka gutted the putt and then swaggered off the green. On the long par-4 sixteenth, after Hovland had a misadventure in a fairway bunker, Koepka nearly knocked over the flagstick from 157 yards, making another birdie to stretch the lead to 4 strokes. *Bang, you're dead.*

"Seeing how much he was hurting after the Masters, I knew he'd win the PGA Championship," Harmon said after Koepka had closed out the victory. "People love to say Brooks doesn't care anymore because he took the LIV money. If that's the case, why does he have such a big team around him to help him get better?" That squad includes a swing coach, a short-game coach, a putting coach, two trainers, a chef, and sundry others. But on Sunday at Oak Hill, he was alone in the arena. There is no lonelier feeling than having the fifty-four-hole lead at a major championship; Koepka is now four for five at converting those leads into victories. With his five major championship victories, he broke a tie with McIlroy to become the most decorated champion of the post-Tiger/Phil era. He is now tied with three all-time geniuses on the career majors list: Seve Balles-teros, "Lord" Byron Nelson, and Peter Thomson. Up next, at six, are the legends Mickelson, Lee Trevino, and Nick Faldo. Of course, a couple of years ago, Koepka said that his goal was to win fifteen, Woods's total. "In my mind, I'm going to catch him on majors," he said. "I believe that. I don't see any reason that can stop me."

"Listen, he's a generational talent," says Harmon. "He's not like everyone else. Brooks is Aaron Rodgers, right? He's one of those guys. He's a franchise quarterback in the NFL. He's a starting pitcher who just threw another no-hitter, won another World Series and an-other Cy Young Award. He's Kevin Durant."

Koepka's win had a larger meaning, giving LIV Golf a massive boost as it continued to try to carve out an identity. Ahead of the Masters, Norman had made another in a series of preposterous pro-nouncements, saying that if a LIV player prevailed, all of his col-leagues would mob him on the eighteenth green. After Koepka's win, DeChambeau was the only LIV golfer who lingered to offer congratulations. Bryson radiated a fraternal pride. "It validates ev-erything that we've said from the beginning: That we're competing at the highest level [on LIV]," said DeChambeau, who tied for fourth. "I really hope people can see the light now."

Noting that Cam Smith had also cracked the top ten at Oak Hill, Harmon woofed, "Someone needs to do a health and wellness check on Jay Monahan."

Only hours after his text message to Yasir Al-Rumayyan, Jimmy Dunne received an enthusiastic response from H.E. saying he'd love to have a conversation. (It had been two years and a day since Majed Al-Sorour had typed out his letter to Monahan inquiring about a partnership, which the commissioner had militantly ignored.) Less than a week later, Dunne landed in London with his fellow Augusta National member Ed Herlihy as his wingman. "I believe in getting to the right person," Dunne said. "I had said to Jay, 'At some point, we need to do that. Let's really understand what's important to them. What are they trying to do? And is there a path between what they want to do with the game of golf, and what we want to do? Could we possibly work this out?' That [was] the entire master plan." The collegial tone was set in advance when both sides dismissed the notion of an NDA.

The Americans rendezvoused with Al-Rumayyan for an afternoon of conversation, which bled into dinner and then cigars. A deal was never going to get done on that visit; it was the first step toward détente, with each side appraising the other's motives, sincerity, and desperation. Dunne, with his many glittering club memberships, was a walking embodiment of everything Al-Rummayan craved and hoped to achieve through golf: acceptance, access, validation, status. Oil money can buy yachts and planes and even golfers and politicians, but pretty much the only thing not for sale is a locker at Seminole, Augusta National, Cypress Point, or Pine Valley. At least, not directly.

Despite the shadow of 9/11 that still haunts him and his newcomer status on the Tour's board of directors, Dunne was always destined to take the lead in negotiating with the Saudis because forging such an armistice would require unique interpersonal skills. Dunne could have any job he wants at Augusta National, including being chairman of the club, but during Masters week this son of a tailor prefers to oversee the caddie shack, where he busts the balls of Hall of Fame golfers and scruffy caddies with equal aplomb. (And if he overhears a looper say how much he would love to play Augusta National, he has been known to make it happen.) "There are lots of rich guys who belong to fancy golf clubs, but there is only one Jimmy Dunne," says one of his close friends. "He is an incredibly beloved and respected figure everywhere he goes. He has a unique mix of charm, intelligence, and integrity in how he's lived his life and the way he treats people."

Dunne wears his power comfortably and doesn't suffer fools gladly. He employs a cobbler to make gorgeous, unique golf shoes in an array of colors, and on the Masters driving range there's always much conversation about his footwear. One year he was paid a visit by Billy Payne, the imperious, uptight, killjoy chairman. "Jimmy, there's been a lot of talk about your golf shoes," Payne said. "This week we prefer the focus to be on the Masters golf tournament."

"Sure, Chairman. Whatever you say."

The fancy shoes stayed in the closet. Eventually the winds of change blew through Augusta National, and Dunne began wearing his flashy footwear again. Payne came by for another scolding. "Jimmy, I thought we had a conversation about your shoes."

"We did."

Pause.

"When you were chairman."

On the American emissaries' second day in London, golf was played. Al-Rumayyan and Herlihy beat Dunne and Brian Gillespie, the general counsel to the Public Investment Fund, in a spirited match at Beaverbrook Golf Club in Surrey. Before heading to the airport, Herlihy made a heartfelt appeal to Al-Rumayyan: professional golf was suffering, and reunifying the game would be in the best interests of the Tour, LIV Golf, the Public Investment Fund, and every other stakeholder in the game.

Al-Rumayyan had been coy about his intentions to that point, but, responding to Herlihy, he signaled his openness to a truce, saying, "Let's see how that would work."

Dunne and Herlihy were impressed with Al-Rumayyan and returned home with a simple message for Monahan: *It's time to swallow your pride and come to the table.*

Both Monahan and Al-Rumayyan wanted to meet on neutral

ground. (A wayward photograph of the commissioner of the PGA
Tour in Riyadh would have blown up the delicate diplomacy.) In
mid-May, the week before the PGA Championship, Al-Rumayyan
and his family were in Venice for the wedding of the daughter of
Lawrence Stroll, the Formula One racing tycoon. Monahan flew in
furtively. On his first afternoon in town he met with H.E. for their
initial discussion. It's easy to imagine the moment being as fraught as
Robert De Niro and Al Pacino meeting in the diner in *Heat*, but the
conversation flowed easily because the two very different fifty-three-
year-olds—a Beantown brawler and a banker from an ancient culture on the other side of the world—knew they needed each other.
Monahan was desperate for LIV's lawyers to stand down and to get
his hands on the Public Investment Fund's cash so the PGA Tour
could fulfill the promises it had made to the top players who had
stayed home. Al-Rumayyan craved the legitimacy that would come
with partnering with the Tour, and leveraging Monahan's distribu-
tion channels and corporate partners could potentially lead LIV Golf
out of the wilderness. "We just sat down, him and I in Venice for
about two hours, trying to understand each other," Al-Rumayyan
said. "He talked about his aspirations, his life. I did the same thing."
On Monahan's second afternoon in Venice, he joined Al-Rumayyan
and his family for lunch, a sign of their growing trust and intimacy.
That was the same day as the final round of LIV Tulsa. A weather
delay pushed the tournament finish outside CW's broadcast window. Affiliates across the country switched to regularly scheduled
reruns just as a juicy playoff among Dustin Johnson, Cam Smith,
and Branden Grace was about to begin. That meant *Magnum, P.I.*
in Philadelphia; *Family Feud* in Boston; *Penn & Teller: Fool Us* in
Brooklyn; *The Goldbergs* in Miami; *S.W.A.T.* in Phoenix; a Nutrisys-
tem infomercial in Palm Beach County; a mattress infomercial in
San Francisco. It was a graphic reminder to Al-Rumayyan that his
pet project still had a very long way to go before it would be taken
seriously by the masses.

The talks in Venice were pivotal in tearing down the wall between the commish and His Excellency and their respective organizations. But what would a deal between the Tour and the PIF look like? There were a dizzying number of questions and concerns. The latter half of May featured numerous phone calls and video conferences involving Monahan, Dunne, Herlihy, Al-Rumayyan, and his advisers Amanda Staveley, the CEO of PCP Capital Partners, who sits alongside H.E. on the board of Newcastle United, and the high-profile banker Michael Klein, formerly of Credit Suisse, who every year brings together sundry billionaires at a conference he hosts in Sun Valley, Idaho. Over Memorial Day weekend, the Tour contingent flew to San Francisco to rendezvous with Al-Rumayyan, who was in town for unrelated PIF business. (Monahan had previously been wounded by a *Wall Street Journal* story that had chronicled in detail his indulgent use of the Tour's Cessna Citation X jet; he must have gotten heartburn when the *New York Times* reported that on a stopover during the flight from New York to meet H.E., the Tour contingent had grabbed takeout hamburgers in Omaha.)

On the evening of May 29, at the Four Seasons in San Francisco, both sides drilled down on the details. Midnight came and went. Finally, at long last, the framework of a deal was agreed upon. Glasses were raised to a cease-fire and the endless possibilities of the future. A new world order had arrived for professional golf, and maybe a dozen people on the planet knew it.

22.

ON JUNE 6, 2023—362 DAYS AFTER LIV PLAYED THE FIRST round of its inaugural tournament—golf's fever dream reached a climax with the most confounding sight imaginable: Jay Monahan and Yasir Al-Rumayyan sitting elbow to elbow on CNBC as they announced that the war was over and the PGA Tour, the Public Investment Fund, and the European Tour would be collaborating to create an as-yet-unnamed entity to reunify the game. LIV Golf's lawsuit against the Tour, and vice versa, would be terminated immediately. Only a handful of top players and key sponsors were alerted to the breaking news in the minutes before Monahan and Al-Rumayyan went on air. Every other stakeholder on both sides of golf's great divide found out in real time.

"I turned on CNBC and saw Jay and Yasir, and it was like, Did I accidentally take an edible?" says one LIV executive.

Reached in the frenzied aftermath of the announcement, PGA Tour board member Peter Malnati was all but speechless, saying, "I'm too stunned to opine."

Monahan and Al-Rumayyan offered many words but provided few specifics during their twenty-five minutes on *Squawk Box*. Their body language told the real story. His Excellency was perched on the edge of his seat, relaxed, all smiles, and ready to take on the world. The slumped Monahan looked weary, wary, and defeated. When Al-Rumayyan spoke, he projected restraint and not a hint of bravado; he didn't need to take a victory lap, as the magnitude of the triumph was self-evident. Monahan did most of the talking, because he had so much explaining to do. He had been anointed the CEO of the new company ("NewCo" for the time being) with Al-Rumayyan installed as chairman of the board of the directors, meaning that Monahan would report to him. The commish was deferential to his new boss, saying, "I give Yasir great credit for coming to the table, coming to discussions with an open heart and an open mind."

The airwaves and interwebs immediately lit up with talk of a PGA Tour–LIV Golf "merger," but that did not capture the reality of the new arrangement, which was merely a framework agreement, as it would take months of painstaking negotiations to try to hammer out all of the specifics. If the deal is consummated, the Tour, and its allied circuit in Europe, will have forged an alliance with the Public Investment Fund, not with LIV Golf. The PIF will become the investor in the for-profit NewCo and float the old, proud tours on both sides of the Atlantic while looking for new ways to extend, and monetize, the reach of the tours. For the rest of 2023, LIV Golf will continue operating independently, untouched in its day-to-day doings. "We will have both LIV and PGA Tour in addition to all of our assets, and we will be investing in the growth of the game of golf," Al-Rumayyan said. Later in the CNBC interview, he added, "The idea is to keep everything independent, but strategically they're all aligned. So the idea that we have, instead of competing, we're going to be complemented and to look for additional venues, and that's where the PIF capital investments will kick in. So we'll be either creating or acquiring and doing some new things to grow the game of golf."

When *Squawk Box* host David Faber asked if the PIF was ready to commit billions of dollars, Al-Rumayyan replied, "So whatever it takes, that is how much is the commitment." Monahan laid out some of the potential new revenue streams, including sports betting, "our data business, our proprietary data . . . the real estate and club business."

"It makes financial sense to us," Al-Rumayyan said. "And that's the only way going forward. We don't like to subsidize things, but we would like to have it sustainable, and the only way—"

Faber cut him off: "So you think the billions that you'll be investing in this new entity are going to generate a significant return?"

"That's the whole idea."

But that's boring business stuff. The real intrigue surrounded the long-term future of LIV, the freighted question of how players will flow back and forth between the tours, the scale and mechanism for reparations, and the related human costs of all of this. After leaving the CNBC studios, Monahan jumped into the PGA Tour jet and flew to the Canadian Open for a meeting with his players. This was Daniel being led into the lion's den without any providential oversight. Monahan knew he was going to get pounded because many Tour members had already weighed in on social media. Wesley Bryan tweeted, "I feel betrayed, and will not not [sic] be able to trust anyone within the corporate structure of the PGA Tour for a very long time." Dylan Wu also went off on Twitter, "Tell me why Jay Monahan basically got a promotion to CEO of all golf in the world by going back on everything he said the past 2 years. The hypocrisy. . . . I guess money always wins." He tagged the PGA Tour account, then added another dagger: "Can I also say that I love @PhilMickelson and everything he's said the past two years has been spot on. He went up in flames in the media cuz of his brutal honesty and now everyone's finally realizing he was right and the PGA Tour does whatever they feel like." Mickelson showed heroic restraint, dashing off only one tweet that said, "Awesome day today." But Bryson DeChambeau went on CNN and said, "I do feel bad for the PGA Tour players because they were told one thing and something else happened. On our side we were told one thing and it's come to fruition. . . . It does stink a little bit from my perspective that the PGA Tour players are not necessarily winning. I hope that they can find a way to make sure that they are valued in the same way that we are over at LIV."

With emotions running so raw, the last thing any PGA Tour folks could stomach was LIV Golf players talking trash; that it came from DeChambeau made the gloating all the more grating.

Monahan arrived at the players' meeting in his rumpled gray suit. For three years running he had been in a meat grinder, guiding the Tour through covid, fending off the Premier Golf League, battling a relentless and much better capitalized foe in the Saudis, and now, finally, being forced to capitulate. Whatever his missteps, he loves the PGA Tour and at every step had fought for its players. From a certain point of view, he had just cut the best deal in golf history, tapping into an unlimited source of money to secure the Tour's long-term future without having to give up anything—except his reputation and maybe his soul. That could be hailed as the most selfless kind of leadership, but that was not the prevailing mood in the conference room in Toronto, where more than a hundred of his players had gathered. "The boys came into the room ready to string him up," says one attendee.

Monahan plowed through his talking points but, as on CNBC, could offer few specifics. His restless players had come to be heard, not talked at. More than two dozen spoke up, and they were not shy about ripping the commissioner to his face. "The voices got very loud at times," says U.S. Open champion Geoff Ogilvy.

Grayson Murray, a twenty-nine-year-old with one career victory, became an unlikely central character. Murray might be the least popular player on the Tour, a good ol' boy from North Carolina who has been an outcast ever since openly flirting with a teenager on Twitter. ("I hate the fact you are in high school. You are pretty.") He subsequently blamed his wide-ranging bad behavior on a drinking problem, writing in a social media post that he "hate(s) everything that has to do with the PGA Tour Life." He continued, "The PGA Tour didn't force me to drink but the PGA Tour never gave me help. In my 5 years of experience of being on tour not once have I ever had a request been acknowledged by the commissioner or the [Player Advisory Council] other than 'we will get back to you.'"

Now Murray released some of that bottled-up angst, shouting at Monahan, "We don't trust you, Jay! You should resign right now! You lied to our face!"

Rory McIlroy, the tournament's two-time defending champ, had heard enough. He shot back, "Just play better, Grayson." That did not go over well with the Tour's middle class crowding the room. Played the week before the U.S. Open, the Canadian Open struggled to attract most of the top players, its field being filled by kids trying to find their way onto the Tour and journeymen clawing to stay there. The exodus to LIV had opened up jobs for those grinders, but the reshaped schedule had marginalized the lesser players and imperiled the tournaments where they ply their trade, including the Canadian Open. Now cataclysmic change was coming again, and the collective jitters were distilled into the two words Murray offered McIlroy in rebuttal: "Fuck off!"

The room exploded into applause when a second player called for a change to Tour leadership, but count journeyman Johnson Wagner among the players impressed by how Monahan handled himself in the crucible. "If it's possible, I gained even more respect for Jay because he was taking it from every single angle," he said. "Players were mad, players are calling for his resignation, and Jay sat there and took it like a champ."

The hits kept coming for Monahan, who then hosted a video press conference. The Tour media people strained to stage-manage the event, handpicking the reporters who could ask questions—funny, they didn't call on me—and cutting it absurdly short for such a momentous event, but not before Monahan offered a mournful coda: "I recognize that people are going to call me a hypocrite. Anytime I said anything, I said it with the information that I had at that moment, and I said it based on someone that's trying to compete for the PGA Tour and our players. I accept those criticisms. But circumstances do change."

The folks at 9/11 Families United, the advocacy group that had spent the preceding year praising Monahan for his strong stance against the Saudi money, were particularly incensed at having been used and abandoned. Terry Strada, the organization's chair, released a withering statement that said, "Jay Monahan co-opted the 9/11 community last year in the PGA's unequivocal agreement that the Saudi LIV project was nothing more than sportswashing of Saudi Arabia's reputation. But now the PGA and Monahan appear to have become just more paid Saudi shills, taking billions of dollars to cleanse the Saudi reputation so that Americans and the world will forget how the Kingdom spent their billions of dollars before 9/11 to fund terrorism, spread their vitriolic hatred of Americans, and finance al Qaeda and the murder of our loved ones. Make no mistake—we will never forget."

The next day, McIlroy held his previously scheduled press conference, what he would call "the most uncomfortable I've felt in the last twelve months." He handled himself with admirable grace considering that his friend Jimmy Dunne and Monahan had ripped open his chest cavity, torn out his heart, and stomped on it with metal spikes. McIlroy allowed that he felt like a "sacrificial lamb" but said, "Ultimately, when I try to remove myself from the situation and I look at the bigger picture and I look at ten years down the line, I think this is going to be good for the game of professional golf. I think it unifies it and it secures its financial future. All I've wanted to do is to protect the future of the PGA Tour and protect the aspirational nature of what the PGA Tour stands for."

As for the Saudis' encroaching influence in professional golf, he said, "I've come to terms with it. I see what's happened in other sports. I see what's happened in other businesses. And, honestly, I've just resigned myself to the fact that this is what's going to happen. It's very hard to keep up with people that have more money than anyone else. And, again, if they want to put that money into the game of golf, then why don't we partner with them and make sure that it's done in the right way? And that's sort of where my head's at. . . . Whether you like it or not, the PIF and the Saudis want to spend money in the game of golf. And they weren't going to stop."

McIlroy's measured diplomacy faltered only when he was pressed on one topic. "I hate LIV," he said. "Like, I hope it goes away. And I would fully expect that it does."

On the morning after everything changed, the two hundred–plus employees of LIV Golf received an email alert to join an all-call with CEO and Commissioner Greg Norman. "My first thought was *Greg is saying goodbye*," says one LIV executive.

It was a logical assumption. Norman has been the polarizing face and voice of LIV ever since its inception. But just like everyone else in the game (except for a few all-powerful shot callers), Norman had been kept in the dark as the future of professional golf was hashed out in a series of far-flung secret meetings. In all the fanfare surrounding the announcement of NewCo, Norman was glaringly absent. Given his yearlong war of words with the newly anointed CEO, Monahan, it's hard to imagine that he will have a role in golf's new firmament. But Norman didn't give an inch when he finally spoke to his colleagues.

By way of an opening, he said, "Congratulations, you changed golf, and you did it in less than a year." The folks on the call had taken huge professional risks to join LIV and were understandably nervous. He radiated confidence, saying that the 2024 LIV schedule was nearly finalized. "There will be no operational changes in 2023, 2024, 2025, and into the future," he said. Then came the mic drop: "LIV is a stand-alone entity and will continue to be that moving forward. And that comes right from the top."

The man at the top is not Monahan or McIlroy or Tiger Woods. Or the European Tour's Keith Pelley or the lords of the Seminole grillroom. No, Norman was referring to Al-Rumayyan, who, when he is not called "H.E." around LIV is sometimes referred to simply as "the Investor." In trying to make sense of how the ground has shifted beneath their feet, Tour loyalists were quick to point out that the majority of the seats on NewCo's board of directors will be held by the Tour, with Dunne and Ed Herlihy already pledged to serve. On paper, that gives the Tour control over NewCo, but things work differently in the real world: the PGA Tour has a Player Advisory Council, a board of directors, and a well-defined governance structure, but the Investor had circumvented all of that over cigars with Dunne. The overarching lesson in this war between the tours is that money always wins. Al-Rumayyan controls the money, so he controls the future of professional golf, even if he is graciously allowing the appointed CEO to be in charge of the day-to-day bureaucracy. Al-Rumayyan has courtly manners and a gentle voice, but beneath the polished exterior is an utter ruthlessness: when the PGA Tour top brass proposed a secret side deal to oust Norman upon the execution of the framework agreement, Al-Rumayyan assented to moving Norman into an "advisory role," sacrificing at the altar LIV's highest-profile cheerleader. This pragmatic move would not come to light until a Senate hearing five weeks after the NewCo announcement. But if and when Norman loses out in another power struggle, this time he can declare a larger victory and ride off into the sunset, knowing that after three decades he finally helped bring about the sweeping change to the sport he first tried to sell at the 1994 Shark Shootout. Someone close to him says, "He has a huge golden parachute. Greg will be fine."

What lies ahead for Monahan also became muddled when, a week after the NewCo news broke, the Tour announced that he would be relinquishing oversight of day-to-day operations while dealing with an unspecified "medical situation." It was easy to imagine that the relentless stress had finally caught up with him. Even before Monahan was felled in the war of attrition, Max Homa said, "I definitely worry about Jay. Have you seen him on TV? He looks exhausted. I always tell him to get more sleep—I don't think he ever sleeps. People don't understand how hard his job is. He went from covid right into this, which have been unprecedented challenges." Monahan returned to work after a month away, his stature in the game diminished and many key players expressing something less than sympathy. "I'd say he has a lot of tough questions to answer," said Xander Schauffele. "I don't trust easily. He had my trust. And he has a lot less of it now. I don't stand alone when I say that." Indeed, Hall of Famer Ernie Els had a more brutal analysis: "If this happened in my day, in my prime, there's no way [Monahan] is around. No way. And the board has to change. You do shit like this, I'm sorry, it's not right. Talk to us, tell us what you're going to do, plan on negotiating. Don't just go rogue as a member of the board and come back with a deal and think we're all going to say yes? You're affecting people's lives. You're affecting the professional game. It's just so bad."

Whether or not Norman and Monahan become cannon fodder, what is the larger future of LIV Golf? In the initial players' meeting in Toronto, Monahan said archly that a full review of LIV's commercial viability would be conducted at season's end. Those in the room took that as an obituary, given that LIV has only trickles for revenue streams. But Monahan or his successor will not decide LIV's future. Al-Rumayyan will. The publicly released drafts of the framework agreement showed the PIF and the Tour repeatedly going back and forth on the language as to which side will determine LIV's fate. As part of that process, PGA Tour chief operating officer Ron Price sent a memo to Monahan noting that "LIV Golf is important to PIF . . ." and that its destiny would ultimately be determined by the NewCo executive board, " . . .where PIF has a strong influence." In the final framework agreement, the wording was left vague as to the exact mechanics of how the LIV question would be settled, though the heading for that section offers a clue: "PGA Tour/DP World Tour and LIV to Co-Exist."

In the wake of the announcement, Al-Rumayyan was reassuring in phone calls to the dozen LIV team captains. When business folks connected to the team franchises sought direction on whether to continue pursuing corporate deals, Jed Moore, who runs LIV day to day, unequivocally said yes. In the weeks after the NewCo announce-

ment, the Majesticks announced three new corporate deals, and LIV
unveiled a strategic partnership with Simplebet to create live betting
on its tournaments. That Al-Rumayyan flew into LIV's first event
after the NewCo announcement to press flesh at Valderrama Golf
Club in Sotogrande, Spain, was a significant development—H.E.'s
first time attending a tournament in 2023 after he had been omnipresent in the previous season. He radiated bonhomie in his pro-am
round with Mickelson and then held a meeting with LIV's four alphas:
Phil, Bryson DeChambeau, Dustin Johnson, and Brooks Koepka.
After the gathering, DeChambeau said, "We were trying to figure
out, obviously, if [LIV] was going to continue and [Al-Rumayyan's]
wholehearted belief is if he's alive, it's still moving forward in the
right direction." Johnson declared, "LIV is full steam ahead." Then,
as a further showing of solidarity, Al-Rumayyan buzzed into the following week's LIV tournament in London. (The circuit got a further boost at LIV Greenbrier in August, when DeChambeau shot
a final round 58 to surge to victory, overshadowing Lucas Glover's
low-wattage win on the PGA Tour on the same day.)

"What people fail to understand is that LIV is H.E.'s baby," says
a LIV executive. "He has poured his heart into its creation." That
included numerous meetings in which Al-Rumayyan fussed over
every little detail, down to the look of the LIV logo. H.E. now has
access to the PGA and European Tours, but their leadership will
fight hard for the status quo. LIV remains Al-Rumayyan's fiefdom.
Over the objections of almost everyone, he moved 2023's splashy
season-ending tournament from Miami to Jeddah . . . and then, a
month after the NewCo announcement, restored Trump Doral as
the concluding venue, underscoring Al-Rumayyan's absolute power.
If the Investor wants to keep LIV going and add a second or even
third event in other corners of Saudi Arabia, it shall be so. Crown
Prince Mohammed bin Salman has staked his reign on Vision 2030,
and turning the kingdom into a tourist destination is a key pillar in
diversifying the economy. Golf helped put Dubai on the map with

the international business community, but it's a crowded city with little memorable terrain; Saudi Arabia has soaring mountains and 1,500 miles of coastline that offer vast potential for epic golf destinations. If LIV can help grow an entire new sector of the economy, keeping it operational becomes a very worthwhile investment even if the tour struggles to break even. Leveraging LIV's star power offers numerous possibilities—how about a resort on the Red Sea featuring a Phil Mickelson–designed golf course and a sleek hotel with interiors curated by Paulina Gretzky? In a scenic valley outside of the capital city, a sprawling new development is already being marketed as "Riyadh's own Beverly Hills," and one of the selling points is a golf course designed by Greg Norman.

"One factor that argues for LIV's long-term survival is the fierce battle for prestige among the Gulf states and how sports has become an integral part of that," says Gerald Feierstein, a former U.S. ambassador to Yemen and now the director of the Arabian Peninsula Affairs program at the Middle East Institute. The indignation within the kingdom that Qatar—Saudi Arabia's much smaller and less powerful rival—had been awarded the 2022 World Cup had helped spur MBS's lust for hosting big-time sporting events. The PIF's purchase of Newcastle United was part of a soccer arms race that has seen storied clubs including Manchester City, Aston Villa, and Paris–Saint Germain snapped up by buyers from Saudi Arabia's rivals in the Gulf. But owning a soccer team loses a little luster when all your neighbors own one, too. Only one Middle Eastern country can crow about owning its very own worldwide golf circuit, and for Saudi Arabia that's LIV Golf, not the PGA Tour.

To get its investment back or even turn a profit, the PIF has always counted on selling the twelve LIV team franchises, in which the PIF has a 75 percent equity stake in each. (The team captains own the other 25 percent.) Internally, LIV has thrown around $500 million valuations, which seemed like science fiction—until the PIF's alliance with the PGA Tour. As part of Norman's all-call, LIV's global head of partnerships, Monica Fee, said that her phone had been "ringing off the hook," citing Marriott, Anheuser-Busch, Fox, and ESPN as having already made inquiries. For Saudi money to get the stamp of approval from the Tour allows LIV to be openly embraced by corporate America, at last. (That had always been part of Al-Rumayyan's vision for monetizing golf; how many blockbuster deals will the PIF now be able to do by leveraging relationships with the multinational corporations that sponsor Tour events?) If LIV can tap into the Tour's existing distribution channels, that will bring another level of visibility—and value—to the franchises. The framework agreement seeks to resolve a simmering issue that has, from the beginning, hurt LIV's credibility: "The Parties will cooperate in good faith and use best efforts to secure [world ranking] recognition for LIV events and players under OWGR's criteria for considering LIV's pending application."

There are clearly a number of *if*s built into any notion of LIV's sustainability and utility. Whatever the Investor's emotional attachment to LIV and the players who first supported his vision, he is a ferocious businessman with a mandate from his unforgiving boss to grow the PIF's assets to $3 trillion by 2030. After years of trying, Al-Rumayyan is finally in bed with the PGA and European Tours, so it is entirely possible that he will come to view LIV as an expendable means to an end. The Jeddah Tower attests to the Saudis' willingness to ditch a splashy project and never look back; it was supposed to be the tallest skyscraper in the world, but construction was abruptly halted in 2018, about a third of the way through, leaving the structure's carcass to loom over downtown Jeddah to this day. "The general assumption is that Saudi Arabia needs oil prices at $80 a barrel to cover their budget requirements," says Ambassador Feierstein. "The price of oil has been below that threshold for some time now. As long as the global economy is not growing, as long as China's economy is flat and there is a continued shift to less fossil fuel consumption, the Saudis will be hard pressed to make ends meet. In that climate, vanity projects and nonessential spending look a lot less attractive. They can be extremely cold blooded when it comes down to it. If it looks to them like LIV Golf is becoming an albatross, they won't have any qualms about walking away from it."

LIV and NewCo are small pieces on a vast chessboard, which was made plain when, two days before Al-Rumayyan and Monahan dropped their bombshell on CNBC, Saudi Arabia announced that it was cutting oil production by a million barrels a day, immediately spiking global prices by more than 2 percent, to $78 a barrel. Given golf's unexpected geopolitical importance, the new alliance between the PIF and the PGA Tour became a flash point on Capitol Hill. Senator Chris Murphy said, "I think it's a really serious thing to have a foreign dictatorship in charge of a major U.S. sports league. This is a watershed moment and I think we need to treat it as such." Monahan helped stoke anger with a defiant letter to lawmakers in which he blamed them for the Tour's predicament: "During this intense battle, we met with several Members of Congress and policy experts to discuss the PIF's attempt to take over the game of golf in the United States, and suggested ways that Congress could support us in these efforts. While we are grateful for the written declarations of support we received from certain members, we were largely left on our own to fend off the attacks, ostensibly due to the United States' complex geopolitical alliance with the Kingdom of Saudi Arabia."

Congressman John Garamendi, a California Democrat, responded by introducing the No Corporate Tax Exemption for Professional Sports Act, which seeks to end the tax loophole the PGA Tour (and other professional sports leagues) exploits to avoid paying federal corporate income tax. Senator Ron Wyden, a Democrat from Oregon who is the chairman of the powerful Senate Finance Committee, said that he would launch an investigation of the Tour-PIF alliance and urged the Department of Justice to explore whether the deal could give "the Saudi regime inappropriate control or access to U.S. real estate" through the PGA Tour's network of more than thirty TPC golf courses.

The Saudi question lends itself to political grandstanding, but antitrust issues present a real threat to consummating the creation of NewCo. Senators Elizabeth Warren, a Democrat from Massachusetts, and Richard Blumenthal, a Democrat from Connecticut, fired off a joint letter to Attorney General Merrick Garland and the assistant attorney general for the DOJ's Antitrust Division, demanding an investigation on the grounds that the Tour-PIF deal "appears to have a substantial adverse impact on competition, violating several provisions of U.S. antitrust law, regardless of whether the deal is structured as a merger or some sort of joint venture." (Blumenthal, in an interview, also called for Monahan's resignation: "I think the commissioner has been so discredited that he can hardly present a credible voice for [the PGA Tour].")

The end of the LIV v. Tour lawsuits does not extinguish the Department of Justice's ongoing antitrust investigation, and now there is plenty of new fodder. Monahan made a serious blunder when he said the quiet part out loud: the motivation for the PIF-Tour deal was partially "to take a competitor off the board."

"I thought it sounded brazen and sounded illegal because merger to monopoly is illegal under antitrust laws," said Tim Wu, a professor at Columbia Law School and former special assistant to President Joe Biden for technology and competition policy. "The two entities were in competition, and if [they] . . . become one, that's basically a straightforward violation of the antitrust laws."

Keeping LIV Golf going would alleviate those concerns. If LIV is shuttered, the forces behind NewCo can still argue that a unified global schedule reuniting the world's best players is a marked upgrade for golf fans and will provide vast new commercial opportunities for the players. "If the deal will be able to show it supports the growing purses for the golfers, and lead to more engagement and innovation to golf, which adds value to viewers, I don't see much of a fight coming from the U.S. government," says Tim Derdenger, associate professor of marketing and strategy at Carnegie Mellon's Tepper School of Business.

In the wake of the NewCo announcement, Al-Rumayyan, Norman, and Monahan were called to testify in front of the Senate Permanent Subcommittee on Investigations. All three men begged off, with H.E. and the Shark citing nebulous scheduling conflicts, while Monahan used his still unspecified health concerns as cover. (He conveniently returned to work the week after the hearing.) In their stead, NewCo offered up Jimmy Dunne and Ron Price, the PGA Tour's COO. Price's newly public role does not necessarily clarify the Tour's line of succession; he has long had direct oversight of board governance and government relations, as well as the Tour's communications department. At the Senate hearing, in mid-July, the biggest bombshell was that Norman's fate had already been decided. Noting that, should the deal go through, LIV Golf's assets would be moving into a new subsidiary controlled (on paper) by the PGA Tour, Price said of Norman, "It would make no sense to bring in that type of executive to manage what is now a fourteen series of events."

Said Senator Blumenthal, "So just to be clear, he's out of a job?"

"If we reach a definitive agreement, we would not have a requirement for that type of position," Price said, clinically.

As part of the Senate investigation, 276 pages of documents were released to the public, including a softcore fantasy prepared by PIF advisers PCP Capital under the title "The Best of Both Worlds." It proposed that Tiger Woods and Rory McIlroy would own LIV teams and play in at least ten LIV tournaments, which was a howler—Woods may not play ten more tournaments for the rest of his career, and McIlroy later said he'd rather retire than go all-in with LIV. Elsewhere in the proposal was the request that Al-Rumayyan be made a member of the R&A and Augusta National. At last, buried in the small print of a Senate appendix, we had come to the essential truth of what LIV Golf is all about. If H.E. were to be granted such memberships, he would penetrate the most elite strata of Western society in a way no Saudi king or ambassador before him ever has. It would give the Investor access to friendships and relationships that MBS could only dream about. Of course, the surest way *not* to become a member of Augusta National is to publicly advocate to become a member of Augusta National. But Al-Rumayyan did attend the Open Championship two weeks after the Senate hearing, and his presence was felt by Martin Slumbers, the CEO of the R & A, who suddenly signaled a willingness to take on the Saudis as corporate partners. Said Slumbers, "The world of sport has changed dramatically in the last twelve months and it is not feasible for the R & A or golf to just ignore what is a societal change on a global basis." Not long after Slumbers found religion, word leaked out that Saudi Arabian soccer club Al Hilal had offered French star Kylian Mbappe a one-year contract for $776 million. Who could have ever imagined that LIV golfers would seem so underpaid?

If professional golf is to be reunified, a crucial first step will be making whole those who stayed loyal to the PGA Tour. In a media blitz to sell the deal after it was announced, Dunne said that the plan was to grant certain players equity in NewCo. That could become quite valuable over time but does not have the immediate gratification of cold, hard cash. The for-profit NewCo will have the power to dispense spot bonuses or stipends or even put players on seven-figure salaries, all the way down to the grumpy proletariat who crowded the players meeting in Toronto. Everyone agrees that the Rory McIlroys and Jon Rahms should get paid, but the sense of entitlement on the PGA Tour runs deep. Chesson Hadley, a onetime winner and not exactly a coveted commodity for LIV, said, "I would like to be rewarded for some loyalty. Those guys didn't do the wrong thing, who went to LIV. They made a business decision. I don't hold that against anybody. But I would like to be rewarded for my decision to stay loyal." Already in 2023, the PGA Tour has given each of its members a $500,000 stipend, committed to a future of no-cut signature events with bloated purses, and gifted $100 million through its fishy Player Impact Program. There are no rules anymore, and the notion that a golfer's compensation should be tied to his scores is suddenly as antiquated as a persimmon driver.

Whether LIV continues to play a full schedule or blows away in the wind, its players, and especially its stars, will need to be reintegrated into the PGA and European Tours. (The Asian Tour, suddenly flush with PIF money, will remain a catchall for lesser players cut adrift by LIV.) Among PGA and European Tour loyalists, this is a very touchy subject. "There still has to be consequences to actions," says McIlroy. "The people that left the PGA Tour irreparably harmed this tour, started litigation against it. Like, we can't just welcome them back in. Like, that's not going to happen. And I think that was the one thing that Jay was trying to get across [in the players' meeting], like, 'Guys, we're not just going to bring these guys back in and pretend like nothing's happened.'"

Dunne laid out how the process is envisioned: "Players on the LIV [tour] that wanted to reinstate into the PGA Tour would go through a process [and] suspension. Whatever the penalty was, they'd have to decide whether they wanted to do that or not and then they could play."

If the purpose of NewCo is to reunify the game, vengeance and retribution are not ideal starting points. As long as LIV is a going concern, the PGA Tour will have to tread carefully on doling out penalties, because it will need Johnson, Mickelson, DeChambeau, Brooks Koepka, and Cam Smith more than they will need the Tour. After meeting with Al-Rumayyan in Spain, LIV's key players—who have been empowered, coddled, and remunerated in ways they never could have imagined—expressed little interest in returning to the increasingly fractured and politicized PGA Tour. "I know that from a player experience, all of the difficulties and challenges and things that take a lot of excessive energy and output throughout the week have been fixed at LIV," said Mickelson. "So the player experience here is incredible. I just can't envision a better scenario for me as a player than playing out here on LIV."

One idea that immediately gained traction in PGA Tour circles is that as long as LIV is conducting tournaments, its players would be precluded from regaining PGA Tour membership but could accept sponsor's exemptions into Tour events; the limit for nonmembers is seven per season. That way the LIV players could cherry-pick their favorite events, bringing buzz and eyeballs to the PGA Tour and keeping corporate sponsors happy but not taking any full-time jobs or qualifying for the big-money FedEx Cup playoffs or the Tour's lucrative retirement plan. A few cosanctioned LIV events could become must-see TV—imagine the delicious frisson of a tournament that brings together the six strongest LIV teams versus six teams of Tour members. Joel Dahmen had some fun with the notion of such synergy, tweeting, "I've grown up being a fan of the 4 Aces. Maybe one day I get to play for them on the PGA Tour!" Max Homa tweeted, "Now that we're all friends, is it too late for us to workshop some of these team names?" He included a screenshot of a cheeky Google search: "wtf is a Cleek?" On the subject of friendship, McIlroy and Sergio García had a conciliatory chat in the days after the NewCo announcement, and, even though García finished 27th at the U.S. Open, he said, "It was a great event for me . . . more than anything, because I gained a friend back, a friend that I kind of felt like I lost in the last year or so."

One possible outcome in professional golf's shakeup is that the LIV tour will be cannibalized into a handful of team events under the NewCo umbrella. The framework agreement stated that the powers that be "will make a good faith assessment of the benefits of team golf in general, and PIF, the PGA Tour and the DP World Tour will work together in an effort to determine how best to integrate team golf into PGA Tour and DP World Tour events going forward."

Even with this new spirit of cooperation, it will be hard for the golf establishment to break its old way of thinking. In the wake of the NewCo announcement, Keith Pelley slammed the door on any LIV players representing Europe at the 2023 Ryder Cup, saying that they would have to pay their outstanding fines and serve their suspensions, and even then, "There would have to be an exceptional circumstance to allow them to reinstate their membership based on the rules and regulations. The deadline was May 1."

At LIV, the détente was taken as a chance to plot the fortification of the roster. One team captain, upon hearing the news, said, "It's time to start recruiting." A LIV executive went further, saying "Now we can finally get Hideki [Matsuyama] and Jon Rahm. I would say every big name on the PGA Tour will get an offer. Except Rory. Nobody wants that little bitch on their team." The framework agreement had explicitly forbidden any players from switching tours before December 31, 2023, or until a final agreement is reached— whichever comes first. But after input from the Department of Justice that such language constituted a potential violation of antitrust laws, the provision was excised and the plot thickened.

There is a third-rail possibility in which the NewCo deal falls apart. One of the key takeaways from Dunne's testimony in the Senate was the fragility of the truce. He called the initial messaging that the Tour and PIF had a done deal to unify the game "very misleading and inaccurate." Said Dunne, "There is no merger. There is no deal. There is simply an agreement to try to get to an agreement and settle lawsuits."

What happens if the two sides disagree on how to agree on an agreement? The framework deal states that if a definitive contract cannot be finalized "the parties can revert to operating their respective businesses in the state that existed pre-agreement in their discretion." Even if the deal is not consummated, this messy process would still have been a win for LIV, as its quest for world ranking points has been expedited and its financial backers have been embraced by the golf establishment for all the world to see. For the PGA Tour leadership, walking away from the Saudis would restore some goodwill with the players and many golf fans, and the legal morass will have gone away forever; the lawsuits were dismissed "with prejudice," meaning that they cannot be refiled. The whole exercise would still have been useful in making it clear that a for-profit model is the key to the Tour's future. The would-be PIF money could be replaced by private equity/

venture capital firms like Raine Capital and Silver Lake, which have already been sniffing around the pro game. There are plenty of Wall Street billionaires who would love to fill PIF's vacated seat at the table.

"None of us are mad that the Tour is changing its business model," says a member of the Player Advisory Council. "It was long overdue, and the for-profit model makes a ton of sense. Of course, everyone is pissed off that we were lied to and kept in the dark, but to me the biggest frustration comes from: Why are we taking the Saudi money when there is so much other money out there? Billions of dollars of institutional investor money is being poured into the NBA. Even more is being poured into [European Premier League teams]. We could have that money without selling our souls."

Eighteen days after the framework agreement was announced, Eamon Lynch wrote for *Golfweek*, "Patrick Cantlay, who carries himself with the assurance of a man convinced he'd be a partner at Goldman Sachs if he wasn't merely sporting its logo on his cap, has been trying to rally players against the deal with the Saudis, and against members of the Tour's policy board who architected or support it." Cantlay is a member of the board, which must ratify any final agreement with the PIF. He is known for driving hard bargains; a fellow player who has worked with Cantlay on governance issues calls him "a terrific penis." Translation: He's a dick. (Of course, if Cantlay is salty perhaps it is because he turned down a $75 million offer from LIV.) The discord among Tour leadership spilled out into the open when Randall Stephenson, the former CEO of AT&T, resigned as a PGA Tour board member three days before the Senate hearings, explicitly citing Jamal Khashoggi in a letter to fellow board members that was subsequently leaked to the *Washington Post*. As his twelve-year tenure ended, Stephenson wrote, "I hope, as this board moves forward, it will comprehensively rethink its governance model and keep its options open to evaluate alternative sources of capital beyond the current framework agreement." That's business; the resignation of Stephenson, an Augusta National member, was also personal. "He's used to being in the room, not being excluded and deceived," says an associate of Stephenson's. "He feels like Jay Monahan and Jimmy Dunne screwed him over. He doesn't want to be anywhere near this deal." Cantlay put himself in charge of the subcommittee responsible for choosing Stephenson's successor.

As contentious as the battle between LIV Golf and the PGA Tour has been, winning the peace was never going to be easy. The stakes are particularly high for the Tour. Should the deal collapse, LIV can aggressively recruit the top players it previously missed out on, and this time around it will be a much easier sell. If Monahan and Dunne were comfortable taking the PIF's money, why would any golfer give it a second thought? The anxiety gripping the Tour was codified at the end of July, when forty-one top players sent a sternly worded letter to Monahan demanding more transparency and oversight in the ongoing negotiations with the PIF. The embattled commissioner responded the next day, creating a sixth seat for the players on the Tour policy board, though they still don't have a voting majority with six independent directors hanging on the commissioner's every word. Tiger Woods had been noticeably silent in the wake of the framework agreement but he was the key signatory of the letter and he snatched the new board seat. Woods has always preferred to exert soft power; it is a significant development that he has now put himself on the firing lines. Says the member of the Tour's Player Advisory Council, "No offense to [board members] Peter Malnati or Webb Simpson, but we need Tiger in the room. We need his presence. He's not going to take any shit from Jay or Jimmy Dunne, because he doesn't have to. What you're seeing with Cantlay, with Tiger, with Colin Neville"—Woods's and McIlroy's wingman at the Delaware 23 meeting, who has been named a special advisor to the player board members—"is the players trying to take back control of the Tour." With a rueful laugh, he added, "Before it's too late."

· · ·

The insidious thing about sportswashing is that it works. Throughout the 2023 LIV season, there were no visible protests outside the country club gates and far fewer questions put to the players about MBS, Jamal Khashoggi, and Saudi Arabia's record on human rights. When DeChambeau was queried about sportswashing at LIV Adelaide, he replied, "Well, we talked about that last year, and we already kind of kicked that to the curb." There was no follow-up question.

As a result of their being embraced by the PGA and European Tours, the Saudis have further achieved the acceptance they crave. "This was part of establishing Saudi Arabia on the global stage," said Kristian Coates Ulrichsen, a fellow for the Middle East at Rice University's Baker Institute for Public Policy. "And in this case, it shows that Saudi Arabia is welcome again at the highest kind of table in the United States, especially after what happened post-2018. That period of isolation is now definitely over." Through NewCo, the Saudis would not be getting a seat at the table—they would own the table, and the chairs, and the entire building. Ulrichsen called the deal "highly strategic" on the part of MBS, saying that it "reaches a segment of Middle America, also beyond the Beltway, and really engages with them to tell the story of a changing Saudi Arabia. This isn't the Saudi Arabia you thought you knew based on 9/11 or Khashoggi or Yemen." A former U.S. president was dazzled by the art of the deal. "Great news from LIV golf," Donald Trump wrote on social media. "A big, beautiful, and glamorous deal for the wonderful world of golf."

After Monahan cravenly abandoned his moralistic argument, all eyes were on Golf Channel's Brandel Chamblee, the most vociferous critic of MBS and Saudi Arabia in the golf media. In the aftermath of the NewCo announcement, Koepka's only public comment came in the form of one pithy tweet: "Welfare Check on Chamblee." When he went on the air later that day, Chamblee stuck to his guns, saying, "I think this is one of the saddest days in the history of professional golf." None of his critiques has been wrong on the merits, but like another idealist—McIlroy—Chamblee failed to recognize that his side had never had a chance. Money always wins.

One of the most disorienting aspects of the Tour's new partnership with the PIF was seeing Dunne as a high-profile cheerleader. The cognitive dissonance he was feeling erupted during a long Golf Channel interview when he was asked about his previous critical statements of the Saudis and how he remains haunted by all the friends and colleagues he lost on 9/11. "I am quite certain the people I'm dealing with had nothing to do with it," he said. "If someone can find someone who unequivocally was involved with it, I'll kill them myself." Of all the outrageous things said throughout this saga, that had to be the most out of pocket.

Dunne also employed the same talking points for which LIV golfers had been relentlessly belittled. "The PIF, I think, has about $100 billion invested in the United States," he said. "They're very involved in the United States economy, so maybe to the casual person, they don't understand the presence that they have. They're also very involved in sport. . . . I'm invested in a lot of private equity firms that have taken money from the PIF, and I understand that and I'm totally comfortable with that." He became emotional discussing golf as a force for good, an idea that had always led to much eye-rolling whenever Greg Norman brought it up. "Golf is very important to me," Dunne said. "It's been a very important part of my life. Anything I can do to unite the game, get some of these issues behind us, and to bring golf to every corner of the world, I think the world will be a better place. I don't mean to be that idealistic about it, but I do believe it's hard to dislike people that you play golf with. The more we can share experiences, the more we can get to know each other, the more we can improve our whole world."

Amid all the speculating and pontificating, the hand-wringing and boardroom maneuvering, the fizzy tweets and sour grapes, LIV's humble origin story is easily lost, but Gary Davidson hasn't forgotten. He was part of the Performance54 consulting group way back when it joined forces with a London lawyer, Andy Gardiner, who had been filling up notebooks with his ideas on how to reinvent professional golf through something called the Premier Golf League. With the ouster of so many top executives, Davidson has risen to become LIV's chief operating officer. At the 2023 season opener at El Camaleón Mayakoba Golf Course, he stood on the crowded driving range following the first round. The sky was turning the color of cotton candy, and reggaeton music played softly in the background. Watching the players and caddies go about their rituals, Davidson had a blissed-out look on his face. "All of this was just an idea," he said, his Scottish burr tinged with wonder.

That idea traveled all the way to the headquarters of the European Tour, and Phil Mickelson carried it furtively to various back alleys. The idea moved like a virus from the House of Saud to Ponte Vedra Beach, from the patio at the Bear's Club to the halls of Mar-a-Lago, from St. Andrews to the Seminole grillroom and all the way to a California courthouse. It traveled to a cigar lounge in London, a restaurant in Venice, a burger joint in Omaha. Lives were changed, fortunes amassed, friendships lost, legacies elevated, and reputations shattered. The inescapable pull of the idea sucked in an all-star cast of characters: Phil, Rory, Tiger, Monahan, the Shark, Trump, MBS, H.E., DJ, Brooks, Bryson, Big Jack, Pelley, Poults, Cam, Rahm, Pat (and Ashley!) Perez, Patrick (and Justine!) Reed, Gooch, Brandel, Dunne, Larry Klayman, and countless others. The idea became a mirror, an X-ray machine, a Rorschach test, revealing so much about so many. It was a simple idea, really: to make professional golf slightly different, a tad more fun. The idea corrupted those with a lust for power and a craving for gold. It was weaponized by politicians, pundits, dreamers, trolls, hucksters, and hypocrites. That little idea sparked a war—and a fragile peace—that changed golf forever.

Acknowledgments
and Source Notes

This book began with an ambush. During the 2022 U.S. Open, my longtime editor, Jofie Ferrari-Adler, and my career-long agent, David Black, persuaded me to take the train from Boston to New York City so we could have lunch and celebrate my recently published Mickelson biography, *Phil*. As the appetizers arrived, they presented a contract they had negotiated on the sly. Their passion for this project was such that I signed on the dotted line before the last bite of chocolate mousse disappeared. Thanks to Jofie and David for their advocacy and tireless support.

Starting and finishing a book in just over a year is kind of crazy, especially one with this many protagonists and subplots, all of it playing out in real time. I couldn't have done it without a small army behind me. I am indebted to my old friend Michael Bamberger for his guidance and many suggestions that helped shape the manuscript. Mark Godich is an ace copy editor who improved the prose in literally a thousand ways. (Mark hates the use of *literally*.) For the past three decades, Matt Ginella has been a great friend and colleague; his stewardship of the Fire Pit Collective allowed me to immerse myself in this book, and along the way he shared many strong ideas on how to chase the story. Thanks, pards. A tip of the cap to my FPC colleagues Jake Muldowney and Chris Petruccelli, who do so much to keep us humming along. I am indebted to Carolyn Kelly, Jonathan Evans, David Kass, and Meredith Vilarello—the awesome team at Simon & Schuster who helped bring this book to life and get it out into the world. Lastly, a huge thanks to my loved ones who never stopped cheering me on: Frances, Olivia, Abby, Michayla, Ben, Louisa, Aunt Harriet, and Myron. And Brandy, too.

This was a tricky book to report, in part because everyone was suing everyone else, or so it seemed. Government scrutiny didn't help, either: One key protagonist said that he couldn't respond to my emails because the Securities and Exchange Commission was monitoring his inbox, while another character in this book beseeched me face-to-face not to text him anymore, because the Department of Justice had access to his phone. Meanwhile, according to the wording in their contracts, LIV players are supposed to get authorization before consenting to one-on-one interviews. All of this is a long way of saying that I tried to keep anonymous sources to a minimum but at times it was unavoidable in the service of getting the story. The phrase "anonymous LIV executive" covers six current and former higher-ups, but, per my agreement with each individual, I could not provide any further identifying details. Who knew that researching a golf book could be so cloak and dagger?

Statements from press conferences, press releases, publicly available documents, and similar sources are not included.

FOREWORD

3 *"I was shell-shocked"*: Dave Seanor, "A Man and an Idea Ahead of Their Time," *Sports Illustrated*, November 14, 2019.

CHAPTER 1

This chapter owes much to Jim Gorant's excellent history of the 1968 rebellion, "War for the Tour: The Day the PGA Championship Nearly Died," Golf.com, August 8, 2018. The quotes from Goalby, Zarley, Elbin, Nicklaus, Arledge, and Mairs are drawn from Gorant's article.

10 *"I played 36 holes today"*: Dan Jenkins, "There's Never Been an Open like It," *Sports Illustrated*, June 19, 1978.

CHAPTER 2

Greg Norman looked me in the eye, shook my hand, and promised he would sit for interviews for this book—and then repeatedly begged off. In a text message he wrote, "A deal is a deal for sure . . . but the timing is not right now and I hope you respect that. Thanks for being a solid part of the golf ecosystem." Whenever he saw me at LIV tournaments, he would jump into his cart and zoom off with a panicked look in his eyes. Sigh.

For recreating Norman's early life, a strong resource was Lauren St. John's biography *Shark: The Biography of Greg Norman*, published in 1998 by Rutledge Hill Press. The quotes from Cogill, Marshall, and Thomson are drawn from there.

16 *"Before I'm thirty"*: Lauren St. John, *Shark: The Biography of Greg Norman* (City: Rutledge Hill Press, 1998).

17 *"I'll be all right"*: Ibid.

18 *"Even when I started"*: Rick Reilly, "On Top of the World," *Sports Illustrated*, April 15, 1996.

18 *"I bet you I'll marry"*: St. John, *Shark*.

20 *"I feel sorry for Greg"*: Reilly, "On Top of the World."

21 *"It was the first time"*: Rick Reilly, "Day of Glory for a Golden Oldie," *Sports Illustrated*, April 21, 1986.

23 *"He said, 'It's okay'"*: Ben Smith, "Sportswriter Tells Crazy Greg Norman Tale," GolfMagic, May 11, 2022.

24 *"Not if I have"*: Jaime Diaz, "The Graham Mutiny," *Sports Illustrated*, September 16, 1996.

24 *"It was audacious"*: Dave Seanor, "A Man and an Idea Ahead of Their Time," *Sports Illustrated*, November 14, 2019.

25 *"What world tour?"*: Ibid.

26 *"How long have you known"*: Tim Rosaforte, "Norman Chews Out Finchem for Stealing His World Tour Idea," *Sports Illustrated*, September 23, 1996.

28 *"Very few people know this"*: Alex Myers, "Greg Norman Upset Tiger Woods Didn't Respond to His Handwritten Letter: 'Maybe Tiger Just Dislikes Me,'" *Golf Digest*, November 4, 2019.

28   *"Greg Norman at one time":* Peta Hellard, "Greg Norman Betrayed Best Mate," *Daily Telegraph*, August 19, 2007.

29   *"It was tough":* Ken Fang, "Report: Greg Norman's Tenure at Fox Is Over After One Year," Awful Announcing, January 18, 2016.

CHAPTER 3

32   *"Funny enough":* No Laying Up (podcast), November 16, 2021.

34   *"We are looking":* Ibid.

34   *"I wanted the team component":* Neil Tappin, "Premier Golf League Exclusive: 'A Brilliant Model That Is Better for the Game,'" *Golf Monthly*, September 16, 2021.

37   *"It was fascinating":* Martin Dempster, "Mickelson Plays Pro-Am with PGL Chief," *Scotsman*, January 29, 2020.

37   *"As far as we're concerned":* No Laying Up (podcast), November 16, 2021.

CHAPTER 4

Jay Monahan looked me in the eye and promised to sit for an interview for this book. Then he dodged all my attempts to set up a time and place. Finally, a Tour flak called to say that the commissioner would not be doing any one-on-one interviews—which was funny because a couple days before, ESPN had published a sit-down interview with Monahan. Eventually I emailed him five pointed questions. He responded to three of them, but the stilted language had the fingerprints of so many lawyers and publicists as to be unusable. At least I was able to bird-dog him at a few press conferences.

42   *"How you play the game":* Jim McCabe, "Leader in Clubhouse," *Boston Globe*, January 15, 2017.

44   *"He's from Boston":* Ibid.

49   *"All we want":* Bob Harig, "Premier Golf League CEO Seeks Meeting with PGA Tour Commissioner to Explain Concept," ESPN, June 9, 2021.

49   *"Think about the individual's right":* Iain Carter, "Premier Golf League: Revolutionary £250M Series Scheduled to Begin in 2023," BBC, June 7, 2021.

49 *"once-in-a-lifetime windfall bonus"*: *No Laying Up* (podcast), November 16, 2021.

50 *"In my role as PAC chairman"*: *No Laying Up* (podcast), December 17, 2021.

51 *"What are they going to do"*: Tom Hanson, "Heavy Hitter," *Sports Illustrated*, October 12, 1998.

CHAPTER 5

56 *"I am convinced"*: Eric Lichtblau, "Saudi Arabia May Be Tied to 9/11, 2 Ex-Senators Say," *New York Times*, February 29, 2012.

57 *"Significant questions remain unanswered"*: Rym Momtaz and Trevor J. Ladd, "Ex-Senators Say Saudia Arabia May Be Linked to 9/11," ABC News, March 1, 2012.

58 *"Omar Albayoumi was paid a monthly stipend"*: Tim Golden, "Focus of 9/11 Families' Lawsuit Against Saudi Arabia Turns to a Saudi Student Who May Have Been a Spy," ProPublica, April 27, 2023.

60 *"We were living"*: Graeme Wood, "Absolute Power," *Atlantic*, March 3, 2022.

62 *"Now I will rest"*: Bradley Hope and Justin Scheck, *Blood and Oil: Mohammed bin Salman's Ruthless Quest for Global Power* (City: John Murray, 2020).

63 *"They pay cash"*: William Shaw, "When Do Friends In Need Become So Disposable?," *The Pilot*, November 16, 2019.

64 *"Who is secretary of state"*: Jessica Kwong, "Jared Kushner Conducted Foreign Policy Via Private, Unrecorded Conversations with Leaders, Angering Tillerson: Report," *Newsweek*, March 20, 2018.

64 *"We could not understand"*: Alex Emmons, Ryan Grim, and Clayton Swisher, "Saudi Crown Prince Boasted That Jared Kushner Was 'In His Pocket,'" The Intercept, March 21, 2018.

69 *"Has the sacrificial animal"*: David Gardner, "A Meticulous Account of the Killing of Journalist Jamal Khashoggi," *Financial Times*, December 6, 2019.

69 *"This is against"*: Hope and Scheck, *Blood and Oil*.

70 *"would clearly change"*: Richard Branson, "My Statement on the Kingdom of Saudi Arabia," Virgin, October 10, 2018.

71 *"I saved his ass"*: Bob Woodward, *Rage* (New York: Simon & Schuster, 2020).

73 *"It just didn't sit well"*: Tom Kershaw, "Paul Casey: 'I'd be a Hypocrite if I Was Paid to Be in Saudi Arabia. Anybody Who Says Sport Isn't Political, That's Rubbish,'" *Independent*, March 25, 2019.

75 *"We had a pretty testy"*: Paul Kimmage, "Paul Kimmage Meets Rory McIlroy—Part Two: Taking Golf's Torch from Tiger, LIV, and Why Money Is Not the Most Important Thing," Independent.ie, December 3, 2022.

CHAPTER 8

102 *"You're going to tell me"*: Matthew Futterman, "Arnold Palmer, IMG and the 'Handshake' That Started the Modern Sports Industry," GOLF.com, May 5, 2016.

105 *"had to do a lot"*: Jerry Greene, "'Sunday Brunch' Loves Mac and Cheese," ESPN, April 11, 2010.

CHAPTER 9

120 *"If you're a golfer"*: "Donald Trump's *New York Times* Interview: Full Transcript," *New York Times*, November 23, 2016.

121 *"I think every living moment"*: Contemporary Thinkers, contemporarythinkers.org/tom-wolfe.

122 *"I watched it"*: Michael Bamberger, "Trumped," Fire Pit Collective, May 16, 2022.

122 *"Everybody wants to make"*: Ibid.

122 *"This move is cancel culture"*: Ibid.

124 *"The revelation that a fund"*: Ewan Palmer, "Donald Trump's Saudi Arabia Payments Spark Calls for Fresh Investigation," *Newsweek*, January 16, 2023.

CHAPTER 10

142 *"Hopefully it reminds everyone"*: Paul Kimmage, "Paul Kimmage Meets Rory McIlroy—Part Two: Taking Golf's Torch from Tiger,

LIV, and Why Money Is Not the Most Important Thing," Independent.ie, December 3, 2022.

142 *"I really think golf can be"*: Ibid.

142 *"Fine. Really nice"*: Ibid.

CHAPTER 11

154 *"It's just really"*: David Dusek, "A Frustrated Bryson DeChambeau Said His Driver 'Sucks.' Cobra, His Driver Maker, Is Not Happy," *Golfweek*, July 15, 2021.

160 *"basically telling me"*: Paul Kimmage, "Paul Kimmage Meets Rory McIlroy—Part Two: Taking Golf's Torch from Tiger, LIV, and Why Money Is Not the Most Important Thing," Independent.ie, December 3, 2022.

161 *He's the right guy for this war"*: The groan-inducing talking points memo drafted for Tiger Woods was revealed in court documents first brought to light by the Twitter feed @desertdufferLLG.

163 *"This strategic expansion"*: "FedEx Express Announces $400 Million, 10-Year Investment Plan in Saudi Arabia," U.S. Saudi Business Council, October 13, 2021.

163 *"Coca-Cola is committed"*: "Coca-Cola to Build $100m Bottling Plant in Saudi Arabia," Expotrade, October 6, 2016.

CHAPTER 13

181 *"No appearance fees"*: Michael Scully, "Padraig Harrington Reveals How JP McManus Attracts Tiger Woods and More Top Golfers to Pro-Am," DublinLive, June 30, 2022.

182 *"We come together"*: Robert Hynes and Eamon Doggett, "Tiger Woods' Friendship with JP McManus as Golfing Great Plays in Adare Manor Pro-Am," Irish Mirror, July 4, 2022.

CHAPTER 14

Jeff Pearlman's *Football for a Buck*, published by Mariner Books in 2018, was indispensable for understanding Donald Trump's history with the USFL. The quotes from Donald Trump, Pete Rozelle, Jerry Argovitz, and John Bassett are drawn from the book.

CHAPTER 17

223 *"This won't change him"*: Dan Rapaport, "Players 2022: The Biggest Win of Cameron Smith's Career Came in Vintage Cameron Smith Fashion," *Golf Digest*, March 14, 2022.

CHAPTER 18

248 *"A wartime deal"*: Michael Bamberger, "The PGA Tour's New Power Broker," Fire Pit Collective, November 16, 2022.

CHAPTER 20

282 *"I said, 'If I'm willing'"*: *Full Swing*, HBO, Season 1, Episode 8.

CHAPTER 21

297 *"In my mind, I'm going"*: Matthew Rudy, "Brooks Koepka Doesn't Hold Back in Our Exclusive Poolside Interview," *Golf Digest*, September 14, 2021.
298 *"I believe in getting"*: Michael Rosenberg, "Jimmy Dunne, the Architect of the PGA Tour–LIV Golf Deal, Lays Out the Details," *Sports Illustrated*, June 8, 2023.
299 *"Let's see how"*: Alan Blinder, Lauren Hirsch, Kevin Draper, and Kate Kelly, "Secrecy, Cigars and a Venetian Wedding: How the PGA Tour Made a Deal with Saudi Arabia," *New York Times*, June 10, 2023.
300 *"We just sat down"*: *Squawk Box*, CNBC, June 6, 2023.

CHAPTER 22

306 *"We don't trust you"*: Brentley Romine, "Inside the 'Contentious' Toronto Meeting as Jay Monahan Faced Players," Golf Channel, June 6, 2023.
306 *"Just play better, Grayson"*: Ibid.
306 *"Fuck off!"*: Ibid.
310 *"If this happened"*: Bob Harig, "'The Board Has to Change': Ernie Els Slams Jay Monahan for LIV Golf Deal," *Sports Illustrated*, July 20, 2023.

311 *"We were trying"*: Alex Miceli, "'LIV Is Full Steam Ahead': Players Assured of League's Future Even with PGA Tour Alliance," *Sports Illustrated*, June 30, 2023.

311 *"LIV is full steam ahead"*: Ibid.

314 *"I think it's a really serious"*: Matt Foster, "US Senate Opens Investigation into New Partnership between PGA Tour and LIV Golf," CNN, June 13, 2023.

315 *"I think the commissioner"*: Ibid.

315 *"I thought it sounded brazen"*: Mark Schlabach; "Jimmy Dunne Outlines Plan for PGA Tour Loyalists, LIV Players Who Want Back," ESPN, June 9, 2023.

315 *"If the deal will be able"*: Lillian Rizzo, "PGA Tour Merger with LIV Golf Triggers Confusion About Sponsorships, Antitrust," CNBC, June 8, 2023.

318 *"Players on the LIV"*: Schlabach, "Jimmy Dunne Outlines Plan for PGA Tour Loyalists, LIV Players Who Want Back."

322 *"This was part of establishing"*: John Branch, "LIV Golf's al-Rumayyan and the PGA Tour's Monahan Make Strange Bedfellows," *New York Times*, June 12, 2023.

322 *"highly strategic"*: Kate Kelly and Vivian Nereim, "All About the Deep-Pocketed Saudi Wealth Fund That Rocked Golf," *New York Times,* June 7, 2023.

322 *"reaches a segment"*: Ibid.

About the Author

ALAN SHIPNUCK is the author of nine books, including the *New York Times* bestseller *Phil* and the national bestsellers *Bud, Sweat, & Tees* and *The Swinger* (with Michael Bamberger). Shipnuck has received thirteen first-place awards from the Golf Writers Association of America, breaking the record of Dan Jenkins, a member of the World Golf Hall of Fame. After a quarter-century at *Sports Illustrated* and *Golf Magazine*, Shipnuck is now a partner and executive editor at the golf media company the Fire Pit Collective, where all his writing, podcasts, and video storytelling can be found. Shipnuck lives in Carmel, California.